A Complexity Perspective on Researching Organizations

The perspective of complex responsive processes draws on analogies from the complexity sciences, bringing in the essential characteristics of human agents, understood to emerge in social processes of communicative interaction and power relating. The result is a way of thinking about life in organizations that focuses attention on how organizational members cope with the unknown as they perpetually create organizational futures together.

Providing a natural successor to the editors' earlier series *Complexity and Emergence in Organizations*, this series, *Complexity as the Experience of Organizing*, aims to develop this work further by taking very seriously the *experience* of organizational practitioners, and showing how adopting the perspective of complex responsive processes yields deeper insight into practice and so develops that practice.

In this book, all the contributors work as consultants or managers in organizations. They provide narrative accounts of their actual work, addressing questions such as:

- How does the work of the researcher actually assist managers when the uncertainty is so great that they do not know what they are doing yet?
- What does research in organizations actually achieve?
- If patterns of human interaction produce nothing but further patterns of human interaction, in the creation of which we are all participating, is there a *detached* way of understanding organizations from the position of the objective observer?

In considering such questions in terms of their daily experience, the contributors explore how the perspective of complex responsive processes assists them to make sense of their experience and so to develop their practice. *A Complexity Perspective on Researching Organizations* offers a different method for making sense of experience in a rapidly changing world by using reflective accounts of ordinary everyday life in organizations rather than idealized accounts. The editors' commentary introduces and contextualizes these experiences as well as drawing out key themes for further research.

A Complexity Perspective on Researching Organizations will be of value to readers from among those academics and business school students and practitioners who are looking for reflective accounts of real life experiences of *researching* in organizations, rather than further prescriptions of what life in organizations ought to be like.

Ralph Stacey is Director of the Complexity and Management Centre at the Business School of the University of Hertfordshire and Director of the Doctor of Management programme run by the Centre. He is one of the editors of the *Complexity and Emergence in Organizations* series, and the editor of five books in this series.

Professor **Douglas Griffin** is Associate Director of the Complexity and Management Centre at the Business School of the University of Hertfordshire and a supervisor on the Doctor of Management programme run by the Centre. He is also an independent consultant. He is one of the editors of the *Complexity and Emergence in Organizations* series, and the editor of three books in this series.

A Complexity Perspective on Researching Organizations

Taking experience seriously

Edited by
Ralph Stacey and Douglas Griffin

Routledge
Taylor & Francis Group

LONDON AND NEW YORK

First published 2005
by Routledge
2 Park Square, Milton Park, Abingdon, Oxon OX14 4RN

Simultaneously published in the USA and Canada
by Routledge
270 Madison Ave, New York, NY 10016

Routledge is an imprint of the Taylor & Francis Group

Typeset in Times by Keystroke, Jacaranda Lodge, Wolverhampton
Printed and bound in Great Britain by TJ International Ltd, Padstow,
Cornwall

British Library Cataloguing in Publication Data
A catalogue record for this book is available from the British Library

Library of Congress Cataloging in Publication Data
A complexity perspective on researching organizations: taking experience
  seriously / [edited by] Ralph Stacey and Douglas Griffin.
    p. cm.
  Includes bibliographical references and index.
  1. Complex organizations–Research–Methodology. 2. Management–
  Research–Methodology. 3. Participant observation. I. Stacey, Ralph D.
  II. Griffin, Douglas, 1946–
  HM711 .C65 2005
  302.3'5'072–dc22   2004026088

ISBN 0–415–35130–8 (hbk)
ISBN 0–415–35131–6 (pbk)

Contents

Contributors

Bjørner Christensen is an organizational consultant. He is Director of Labor Ltd, as well as Director, Researcher and Consultant at the Complexity and Management Centre, Norway. He graduated as Doctor of Management at the University of Hertfordshire in 2003.

Douglas Griffin is an independent consultant, visiting Professor at the Business School of the University of Hertfordshire, and Associate Director of the Complexity and Management Centre.

Ian Johnson is an independent consultant specializing in helping organizations undertake major change. He has worked with companies in many industries including major global firms and has a history that includes developing IT systems, managing IBM test sites, as well as process and HR work. He graduated as Doctor of Management at the University of Hertfordshire in 2003.

Mary O'Flynn is an independent consultant with organizations and groups in Ireland and the UK, facilitating the processes of organizational development and change, problem-solving, strategy and policy formation. She is a part-time lecturer in educational management at Trinity College, Dublin, and in St Patrick's College, Dublin. She graduated with an MA at the University of Hertfordshire in 2002.

Nicholas Sarra works as a consultant adult psychotherapist in the National Health Service in the UK. He specializes in organizational consultancy and development for public sector services. He is also a member of the Institute of Group Analysis. He is currently completing his thesis for the degree of Doctor of Management at the University of Hertfordshire.

Ralph Stacey is Professor of Management at the Business School of the University of Hertfordshire and Director of its Complexity and

Management Centre. He is also a member of the Institute of Group Analysis.

Richard Williams was CEO of Westminster Kingsway College, and in July 2004 he left the further education sector to take up a new role as CEO of a charity working with young people and adults across the UK. He has completed the Doctor of Management programme at the University of Hertfordshire.

Series preface
Complexity as the Experience of Organizing

Edited by Ralph Stacey, Douglas Griffin and Patricia Shaw

Complexity as the Experience of Organizing is a sequel to the highly successful series *Complexity and Emergence in Organizations* also edited by the editors of this series. The first series has attracted international attention for its development of the theory of complex responsive processes and its implications for those working in organizations. The perspective of complex responsive processes draws on analogies from the complexity sciences, bringing in the essential characteristics of human agents, namely consciousness and self-consciousness, understood to emerge in social processes of communicative interaction, power relating and evaluative choice. The result is a way of thinking about life in organizations that focuses attention on how organizational members cope with the unknown as they perpetually create organizational futures together. This second series aims to develop that work by taking seriously the experience of organizational practitioners, showing how adopting the perspective of complex responsive processes yields deeper insight into practice and so develops that practice.

Contributors to the volumes in the series work as leaders, consultants or managers in organizations. The contributors provide narrative accounts of their actual work, addressing such questions as: What does it mean, in ordinary everyday terms, to lead a large organization? How do leaders learn to lead? What does it mean, in ordinary everyday terms, to consult managers in an organization? How does the work of the consultant assist managers when the uncertainty is so great that they do not yet know what they are doing? What does executive coaching achieve? What happens in global change programs such as installing competencies, managing diversity and assuring quality? Why do organizations get stuck in repetitive patterns of behavior? What kinds of change can be facilitated? In considering such questions in terms of their daily experience, the contributors explore how the perspective of complex responsive processes assists them in making sense of their experience and so develop their practices.

The books in the series are addressed to organizational practitioners and academics who are looking for a different way of making sense of their own experience in a rapidly changing world. The books will attract readers looking for reflective accounts of ordinary everyday life in organizations rather than idealized accounts or further prescriptions.

1 Introduction: researching organizations from a complexity perspective

Ralph Stacey and Douglas Griffin

- Qualitative research methods
- The perspective of complex responsive processes
- The properties of complex responsive processes of relating
- The consequences of taking a complex responsive processes perspective
- The implications for methodology
- The chapters in this book

Over the period 2000 to 2002, a number of us at the Complexity and Management Centre at the Business School of the University of Hertfordshire published a series of books called *Complexity and Emergence in Organizations* (Stacey *et al.*, 2000; Stacey, 2001; Fonseca, 2001; Griffin, 2002; Streatfield, 2001; Shaw, 2002). These books developed a perspective according to which organizations are understood to be ongoing, iterated processes of cooperative and competitive relating between people. We argued that organizations are not systems but the ongoing patterning of interactions between people. Patterns of human interaction produce further patterns of interaction, not some *thing* outside of the interaction. We called this perspective *complex responsive processes of relating*.

Since 2000, some of the authors in the series, together with other Complexity and Management Centre colleagues in association with the Institute of Group Analysis, have been conducting a research program on organizational change leading to the degrees of Master of Arts by research or Doctor of Management. This is necessarily a part-time program because the core of the research method involves students taking their own experience seriously. If patterns of human interaction produce nothing but further patterns of human interaction, in the creation of which we are all participating, then there is no detached way of understanding organizations from the position of the objective observer. Instead, organizations have to be understood in terms of one's own personal experience of participating with others in the co-creation of the patterns of interaction that are the organization. The students' research is, therefore, their narration of current events they are involved in together with their reflections on themes of particular importance emerging in the stories of their own experience of participation with others to create the patterns of interaction that are the organization. The research stance is, then, one of detached involvement.

On a research program, it is, of course, necessary for all students to develop their own views on the methodology they are using when they explore their experience in organizations in a manner provoked by the theory of complex responsive processes. The purpose of this volume is to bring together some of their work on methodology and to provide examples of the research carried out using it. At the end of this introductory chapter, we give a brief indication of what each of these authors cover and what the central themes of the volume are. We will also be introducing each chapter with an editorial comment. Before doing this, however, we provide a short, and so necessarily compact, summary of what we mean by the theory of complex responsive processes, what it implies about leaders and leadership, and how this differs from other traditions of thought about these matters. Further details of these arguments are also set out in Chapter 2, which focuses on the implications for methodology of taking a complex responsive processes perspective.

Qualitative research methods

The move from positivist quantitative research methods to interpretive qualitative methods is no longer contested in the literature on organizations. There is a substantial literature on qualitative methods covering, among others, action research, including participative inquiry, collaborative inquiry and appreciative inquiry; ethnomethodology; narrative research; and case study methods. However, these approaches largely preserve something of the stance of the objective observer, where the researcher's emotions and fantasies are to be kept out of the research as much as possible, and the notion that the researcher should not affect what is being researched. At the same time, however, this is generally recognized as an ideal, and the fact that the observer has an impact on what is being observed is now rarely seriously questioned. The interconnection between the observer and the observed is, for example, clearly recognized in the action research approaches of second order system thinkers and in the literature on reflexivity in the research process. It is not at all unusual to equate consulting and research, as, for example, in the socio-technical systems approach, and to regard intervening in the organizational system in order to change it as the appropriate method of understanding it.

What is rarely challenged, however, is the notion that the object of organizational research is a system, that organizations are systems. It is this notion that is challenged by the perspective of complex responsive processes, and such a challenge has significant implications for appropriate research methodology. First, a very brief summary of the complex responsive processes perspective is provided (see Chapter 2 of this volume for a slightly fuller description, and the book series 'Complexity and Management in Organizations' for a detailed exposition of this perspective). Second, this chapter briefly reviews the implications of the perspective for research methods.

The perspective of complex responsive processes

From the perspective of complex responsive processes, organizations are viewed as patterns of interaction between people that are iterated as the present. Instead of abstracting from the experience of human bodily interaction, which is what we do when we posit that individuals create a system in their interaction, the perspective of complex responsive processes stays with the experience of interaction which produces nothing but further interaction. In other words, one moves from thinking in terms of a spatial metaphor, as one does when one thinks that individuals interact to produce a system outside them at a higher level, to a temporal processes way of thinking, where the temporal processes are those of human relating. Organizations are then understood as processes of human relating, because it is in the simultaneously cooperative–consensual and conflictual–competitive relating between people that everything organizational happens. It is through these ordinary, everyday processes of relating that people in organizations cope with the complexity and uncertainty of organizational life. As they do so, they perpetually construct their future together as the present.

Complex responsive processes of relating may be understood as acts of communication, relations of power, and the interplay between people's choices arising in acts of evaluation.

Acts of communication

It is because human agents are conscious and self-conscious that they are able to cooperate and reach consensus, while at the same time conflicting and competing with each other in the highly sophisticated ways in which they do. Drawing on the work of the American pragmatist George Herbert Mead (1934), one can understand consciousness (that is, mind) as arising in the communicative interaction between human bodies. Humans have evolved central nervous systems such that when one gestures to another, particularly in the form of vocal gesture or language, one evokes in one's own body responses to one's gesture that are similar to those evoked in other bodies. In other words, in their acting, humans take the attitude, the tendency to act, of the other, and it is because they have this capacity that humans can know what they are doing. It immediately follows that consciousness (knowing, mind) is a social process in which meaning emerges in the social act of gesture–response, where the gesture can never be separated from the response. Meaning does not lie in the gesture, the word, alone, but in the gesture taken together with the response to it as one social act.

Furthermore, in communicating with each other as the basis of everything they do, people do not simply take the attitude of the specific others with whom they are relating. Humans have the capacity for generalizing so that when they act they always take up the attitude of what Mead called 'the generalized other'. In other words, they always take the attitude of the group or society to their actions – they are concerned about what others might think of what they do or say. This is often unconscious and it is, of course, a powerful form of social control. According to Mead, self-consciousness is also a social process involving the capacity humans have to take themselves as an object of subjective reflection. This is a *social* process because the subject, 'I', can only ever contemplate itself as an object, 'me', which is one's perception of the attitude of society towards oneself. The 'I' is the often spontaneous and imaginative response of the socially formed individual to the 'me' as the gestures of society to oneself. Self is this emergent 'I–me' dialectic so that each self is socially formed while at the same time interacting selves are forming the social. The social may be understood as a social object. A social object is not an object in the normal sense of a thing that exists in nature but is a tendency on the part of large numbers of people to act in a similar manner in similar situations. The social object is a generalization that exists only when it is made particular in the ordinary local interaction between people. Communication, then, is not simply the sending of a signal to be received by another, but rather complex social, that is, responsive, processes of self-formation in which meaning and the society-wide pattern of the social object emerge.

Relations of power

Drawing on the work of Elias (1939), one understands how the processes of communicative interacting constitute relations of power. For Elias, power is not something which one possesses but is rather a characteristic of all human relating. In order to form, and stay in, a relationship with someone else, one cannot do whatever one wants. As soon as we enter into relationships we constrain and are constrained by others and, of course, we also enable and are enabled by others. Power is this enabling–constraining relationship where the power balance is tilted in favor of some and against others depending on the relative need they have for each other. Elias showed how such power relationships form figurations, or groupings, in which some are included and others are excluded, and where the power balance is tilted in favor of some groupings and against others. These groupings establish powerful feelings of belonging which constitute each individual's 'we' identity. These 'we' identities, derived from the groups to which we belong, are inseparable from each of our 'I' identities. As with Mead, then, we can see that processes of human relating form and are formed by individual and collective identities, which inevitably reflect complex patterns of power relating.

Choices arising in acts of evaluation

In their communicative interacting and power relating, humans are always making choices between one action and another (see Chapter 2 in this volume for a fuller development of this aspect). The choices may be made on the basis of conscious desires and intentions, or unconscious desires and choices, for example, those that are habitual, impulsive, obsessive, compulsive, compelling or inspiring. In other words, human action is always evaluative, sometimes consciously and at other times unconsciously. The criteria for evaluating these choices are values and norms, together constituting ideology. We are thus using the notion of ideology in the sense of Elias (1970), who argued that we always act on an ideology and every act of negating an ideology immediately leads to another one. Ideology is thus not abstracted from experience, understood as direct interaction between bodies, and it is not, therefore, located in some 'whole' that actually exists outside of experience, with the 'false' consciousness that this brings.

Norms (morals, the right, the 'ought') are evaluative criteria taking the form of obligatory restrictions which have emerged as generalizations and become habitual in a history of social interaction. We are all socialized to take up the norms of the particular groups and the society to which we belong, and this restricts what we can do as we particularize the generalized norms in our moment-by-moment specific action situations. Elias' work shows in detail how norms constitute major aspects of the personality structures, or identities, of interdependent people.

Values (ethics, the 'good') are individually felt voluntary compulsions to choose one desire, action or norm over another. Values arise in social processes of self-formation (Joas, 2000) – they are fundamental aspects of self, giving meaning to life, opening up opportunities for action. They arise in intense interactive experiences which are seized by the imagination and idealized as some whole to which people then feel strongly committed. Mead (1938) describes these as cult values which need to be functionalized in particular contingent situations, and this inevitably involves conflict.

Together, the voluntary compulsion of value and the obligatory restriction of norms constitute *ideology*. Ideology is the basis on which people choose desires and actions, and it unconsciously sustains power relations by making a particular figuration of power feel natural. We can see, then, that complex responsive processes of human relating form and are formed by values, norms and ideologies as integral aspects of self/identity formation in its simultaneously individual and collective form.

In describing the fundamental aspects of the complex responsive processes of human relating, we have referred on a number of occasions to *patterns* of communicative interaction, *figurations* of power relations, and *generalizations/idealizations* that are *particularized/functionalized* in specific situations. These patterns, figurations, generalizations/ idealizations and particularizations/functionalizations may all be understood as themes, taking both propositional and narrative forms, which emerge and re-emerge in the iteration in each succeeding present of the interactive processes of communication, power and evaluation. These themes organize the experience of being together, and they can be understood, in Mead's terms, as social objects and the imagined wholes of cult values which are taken up by people in their local interaction with each other in specific situations of ordinary, everyday life.

The properties of complex responsive processes of relating

By analogy with complex adaptive systems (Waldrop, 1992; Goodwin, 1994; Kauffman, 1995), the thematic patterning of interaction is understood to be:

- *Complex*. Complexity here refers to a particular dynamic or movement in time that is paradoxically stable and unstable, predictable and unpredictable, known and unknown, certain and uncertain, all at the same time. Complexity and uncertainty are both often used to refer to the situation or environment in which humans must act and this is distinguished from simple or certain environments. Prescriptions for effective action are then related to, held to be contingent upon, the type of environment. However, from the complex responsive processes perspective it is human relating itself which is complex and uncertain in the sense described above. Healthy, creative, ordinarily effective human interaction is then always complex, no matter what the situation. Patterns of human relating that lose this complexity become highly repetitive and rapidly inappropriate for dealing with the fluidity of ordinary, everyday life, taking the form of neurotic and psychotic disorders, bizarre group processes and fascist power structures.
- *Self-organizing and emergent*. Self-organizing means that agents interact with each other on the basis of their own local organizing principles, and it is in such local interaction that widespread coherence emerges without any program, plan or blueprint for that widespread pattern itself. In complex responsive processes terms, then, it is in the myriad local interactions between people that the widespread generalizations such as social objects and cult values emerge. These are particularized in the local interactions between people.
- *Evolving*. The generalizations of social object and cult value are particularized in specific situations, and this inevitably involves choices as to how to particularize them in that specific situation, which inevitably means some form of conflict. The generalizations will never be particularized in exactly the same way and the nonlinear nature of human interaction means that these small differences could be amplified into completely different generalizations. In this way, social objects and cult values evolve.

The consequences of taking a complex responsive processes perspective

We are suggesting, then, that we think about organizations in a way that is close to our ordinary, everyday life in them. We understand organizations to be the widespread patterns of interaction between people, the widespread narrative and propositional themes, which emerge in the myriad local interactions between people, both those between members of an organization and between them and other people. Thinking in this way has two important consequences.

First, no one can step outside of their interaction with others. In mainstream thinking, an organization is viewed as a system at a level above the individuals who form it. It is recognized that this organizational system is affected by patterns of power and economic relations in the wider society and these are normally thought of as forces, over and above the organization and its individual members, which shape local forms of experience. Individuals and the social are posited at different levels and causal powers are ascribed to that social level. In the kinds of process terms we are trying to use, there are no forces over and above individuals. All we have are vast numbers of continually iterated interactions between human bodies and these are local in the sense that each of us can only interact with a limited number of others. It is in the vast number of local (in this specific technical sense) interactions that widespread, global patterns of power and economic relations emerge. The widespread patterns emerge as repetition and potential transformation at the same time. We can then see highly repetitive patterns iterated over long time periods. The general comments we make about such patterns refer to what is emerging rather than to any force over and above those in whose interaction it is emerging. In their local interaction people will always be particularizing, taking up in their local interactions, these generalizations, and they may not be aware of doing so. No one can step outside of interaction to design that interaction, and from this perspective it does not make sense to think of leaders setting directions or designing widespread patterns of interaction which they can then realize. When leaders set directions or formulate organizational designs, they are in effect articulating what Mead means by social objects and cult values. What happens as a result of doing this depends upon how people take up such social objects and cult values in their local interactions with each other.

Second, then, there is no overall program, design, blueprint or plan for the organization as a 'whole'. Designs, programs, blueprints and plans exist only insofar as people are taking them up in their local interactions. Any statements that the most powerful make about organizational designs, visions and values are understood as gestures calling forth responses from many, many people in their local interactions. The most powerful can choose their own gestures but will be unable to choose the responses of others so that the outcome of their gestures will frequently produce surprising outcomes.

If one views organizations as widespread narrative patterns emerging in local interaction, what are the implications for research methodology?

The implications for methodology

If a global pattern emerges in local interactions, in a self-organizing manner, in the absence of any plan or blueprint for that global pattern, then it follows that one can only really understand an organization from within the *local interaction* in which global tendencies to act are taken up. This means that the insights/findings of the research must arise in the researcher's *reflection* on the micro detail of his or her own *experience* of interaction with others. It follows that the research method is subjective, or rather, a paradox of *detached involvement*. The term 'involvement' refers to the inevitable emotion that is aroused in the experience of interacting with others in order to accomplish some joint task. It is impossible for any of us to completely avoid every form of emotional engagement but quite possible that heightened anxiety, in conditions of not knowing, will submerge us in highly emotional, or 'involved', thinking which could take 'magico-mythical' forms. Clearly, such thinking cannot qualify as research. However, if we can never completely avoid involvement, it follows that it is impossible for any of us to achieve fully detached thinking about the action of engaging with others. By detached thinking, we mean purely rational thinking as is supposed by the classical, positivist scientific method. In relation to human action, then, the approach and thinking called for is paradoxically detached and involved at the same time.

If reflection on experience, in a detached-involved way, is central to the methodology, then it becomes important to clarify what is meant by experience. By experience, we mean the felt experience of bodily interaction between people, and this interaction is patterned primarily as narratives of relating between self and other. Reflective narrative is thus the 'raw material' from which propositional themes emerge for further reflection – together, narratives of experience and propositional themes emerging in it constitute the research. Since experience is relating between self and other, the appropriate research method is essentially reflexive in two senses. First, the individual researcher is required to reflect upon his or her own life history and how this has shaped the manner in which he or she reflects upon experience. Second, there is a social form of reflexivity requiring the researcher to locate his or her ways of making sense of experience in the wider traditions of thought that have evolved in the history of human interaction, critically distinguishing between one tradition of thought and another.

If one takes the view that knowledge emerges and evolves in a *history* of social interaction, rather than being developed by an autonomous individual, then one attaches central importance to research as a participative, social process. Research on organizations is then done by participating in a community of researchers who are together exploring the meaning they are making of their experience. This inevitably involves conflict as people explore their differences and, indeed, this conflict is essential for the movement of thought. Research proceeds by researchers engaging in argument around difference, feeling themselves compelled to justify the perspective they take in its difference from other perspectives.

Research, from this perspective, is not an activity which is separate from practice because the reflective practitioner is, on the view so far presented, inevitably also a researcher in that both are engaged in reflecting upon their own experience. It follows that research is closely linked to the iteration and possible transformation of identity. This is because identity is the answer to the questions: Who am I? Who are we? What am I doing? What are we doing? What is going on? How do we now go on together? Effective research is potentially transformative of identity, and is therefore bound to expose vulnerability and raise existential anxiety with all the emotion this brings with it.

In summary, the perspective of complex responsive process leads one to a view of methodology which is essentially exploratory and emergent. This view immediately raises a number of important issues. There is the issue to do with validity. What justification is there for saying that the methodology outlined above contributes to knowledge and the evolution of practice? Answering such a question means that one must take a position on what knowledge and truth are. Then, interacting with others and reflecting on it as methodology immediately points to the power relations involved in research and the ideologies sustaining these power relations. It becomes part of the method to identify just what these are and how they may be used rhetorically to improve one's power chances. The link to ethics is immediately obvious and the question becomes how one is to think of this. Finally, it becomes clear that a research methodology taking the form described so far is at the same time a form of personal and group development.

It is the purpose of the chapters in this book to explore the method briefly described above, as well as the issues it raises.

The chapters in this book

In Chapter 2, Ralph Stacey and Douglas Griffin develop the points made on research methodology in the previous section. They locate this in the practice of participation in a research program leading to the degree of Master of Arts or Doctor of Management at the University of Hertfordshire, delivered in association with the Institute of Group Analysis. They also distinguish this methodology from action research.

Chapter 3 is by Richard Williams who was at the time of writing Head of the Westminster Kingsway Further Education College in the UK. He asks what it means to make a contribution to knowledge and then explores how one justifies the merits of one methodology compared to another. He is also concerned with how his methodology affects his practice as Chief Executive. He emphasizes the importance of working with difference in processes of argumentation.

Chapter 4, by Bjørner Christensen, explores different ways of thinking about the relationship between consulting to organizations and researching them. Christensen, a consultant working in Norway, suggests that the method of researching complex responsive processes of relating between people is itself complex responsive processes of relating, but with the distinguishing intention of reflecting upon those processes. He suggests that such an intention amounts to a kind of second order reflexivity in that the researcher is seeking to understand how people go about making sense of what they are doing. He refers to such a second order reflexive method as 'emerging participative exploration'.

In Chapter 5, consultant Mary O'Flynn gives an account of facilitating a number of meetings of members of an organization which provides support to drug addicts. She does not explicitly discuss the methodology but instead demonstrates what it means to employ the kind of methodology discussed in previous chapters.

Chapter 6 is by Ian Johnson, until recently employed by one of the major consulting companies in the UK. His account of the sense he makes of major consulting initiatives in large organizations provides another example of what it means to use the methodology described in previous chapters.

Finally, in Chapter 7, Nicholas Sarra explores an unusual change initiative he was engaged in at a National Health Trust in the UK. He is particularly concerned with the matter of power relations.

References

Elias, N. (1939) *The Civilizing Process*, Oxford: Blackwell.

Elias, N. (1970) *What is Sociology?*, Oxford: Blackwell.

Fonseca, J. (2002) *Complexity and Innovation in Organizations*, London: Routledge.

Goodwin, B. (1994) *How the Leopard Changed its Spots*, London: Weidenfeld & Nicolson.

Griffin, D. (2002) *The Emergence of Leadership: Linking self-organization and ethics*, London: Routledge.

Joas, H. (2000) *The Genesis of Values*, Cambridge: Polity Press.

Kauffman, S. A. (1995) *At Home in the Universe*, New York: Oxford University Press.

Mead, G. H. (1934) *Mind, Self and Society*, Chicago, IL: Chicago University Press.

Mead, G. H. (1938) *The Philosophy of the Act*, Chicago, IL: Chicago University Press.

Shaw, P. (2002) *Changing Conversations in Organizations: A complexity approach to change*, London: Routledge.

Stacey, R. (2001) *Complex Responsive Processes in Organizations: Learning and knowledge creation*, London: Routledge.

Stacey, R. (2003) *Strategic Management and Organizational Dynamics: The Challenge of Complexity* (4th edn), London: Pearson Education.

Stacey, R., Griffin, D. and Shaw, P. (2000) *Complexity and Management: Fad or radical challenge to systems thinking?*, London: Routledge.

Streatfield, P. (2001) *The Paradox of Control in Organizations*, London: Routledge.

Waldrop, M. M. (1992) *Complexity: The Emerging Science at the Edge of Chaos*, Englewood Cliffs, NJ: Simon & Schuster.

2 Experience and method: a complex responsive processes perspective on research in organizations

Ralph Stacey and Douglas Griffin

- Key aspects of the complex responsive processes perspective
- Method of research: Master of Arts/Doctor of Management program
- Comparing action research and complex responsive processes approaches to research

Over the past decade, members of the Complexity and Management Centre at the Business School of the University of Hertfordshire have been developing a way of making sense of life in organizations which draws on particular insights from the natural complexity sciences (e.g. Goodwin, 1994; Kauffmann, 1995; Prigogine and Stengers, 1984; see Waldrop, 1992) to do with unpredictability, diversity, self-organization and emergence. We have been arguing that notions such as 'complex adaptive systems' cannot simply be applied to organizations or human action in general (Stacey *et al.*, 2000) because, unlike the agents in complex adaptive system simulations, human agents are conscious, self-conscious, reflexive, often spontaneous and capable of making choices. The natural complexity sciences, therefore, need to be interpreted according to some theory of human consciousness, reflexivity and choice. Concepts of self-organization and emergence had already been explored much earlier in the social sciences, particularly in the work of George Herbert Mead (1934), John Dewey (1934) and Norbert Elias (1939). The approach we have taken, therefore, is to turn to the natural complexity sciences as a source domain for analogies, to be understood, when it comes to human action, in terms of Mead's theory of mind, self and society, Dewey's theory of value, and Elias' theory of power figurations, ideology and identity formation. The perspective we have developed has come to be known as that of complex responsive processes of human relating (Fonseca, 2002; Griffin, 2002; Shaw, 2002; Stacey, 2001, 2003; Stacey *et al.*, 2000; Streatfield, 2001).

This particular way of understanding life in organizations has implications for appropriate methods of research in organizations. Initially, we referred to such appropriate methods as participative inquiry in the belief that the method of inquiry we were pursuing did not differ in major ways from recent developments in action research such as collaborative inquiry (see Reason and Bradbury, 2001). Since 2000, the Complexity and Management Centre, in association with the Institute of Group Analysis, has been engaged in a Master of Arts/Doctor of Management program whose members are organizational practitioners taking the theory of complex responsive processes as a provocation to making sense of their own organizational practice. The method of research is this making sense of one's own experience. As we have worked together, it has become increasingly clear that this method differs in major ways from action research (Christensen, 2003). Since the generic label of participative inquiry obscures such differences, it has been suggested that we call what we are doing 'emerging participative exploration' (Christensen, 2003). This is itself complex responsive processes of relating distinguished from such processes in general by its purpose, namely to research human action in groups and organizations (see Chapter 4, this volume).

The purpose of this chapter is to explore the method we are pursuing and to compare it with action research, drawing in particular upon the work of Reason and Bradbury (2001) as an example of action research. To do this, we first present a brief summary of key aspects of the theory of complex responsive processes and then describe how we are working on the Master of Arts/Doctor of Management program. The final section of the chapter seeks to draw out some differences between our method and that of action researchers.

Key aspects of the complex responsive processes perspective

Complex responsive processes of relating refer to the *actions of human bodies* as they interact with each other, so constituting the *social*, and as each interacts, *at the same time*, with himself or herself, so constituting *mind/self*. Action means the physical movements of a body constituting *gestures to and responses from others* such as the vocal gesture–response of sound, the visual gesture–response of facial expression and the felt gesture–response of changes in the bodily rhythms that are feelings/emotions. Such action is fundamentally communicative in that every gesture of one evokes responses in others. Furthermore, human beings are distinctive in that biological evolution has produced human bodies/central nervous systems which have the highly developed capacity to evoke from their own bodies similar responses to those that they evoke from other bodies. As Mead says, human beings have the capacity for communicating in significant symbols. Another way of putting this is to say that human beings have the capacity for private role play and silent conversation with themselves (mind and self) which enables them to be aware of themselves, to know what they are doing and so, through experience, to act in expectation of particular responses from others. The private role play/silent conversation, which is reflective mind, makes possible much more sophisticated forms of public role play/vocal conversation, and much more sophisticated forms of cooperation and competition, which is the social.

This is a view of human consciousness, self-consciousness and social interaction in which mind, self and society are the same processes of bodily action so that there is no notion of individuals at one level and social structures at another. Individual minds/selves paradoxically form the social while being formed by the social at the same time. Furthermore, this is a view of human self-consciousness where mind is the action of a body and so cannot be thought of as inside a person while society is outside. This is a temporal process rather than a systems theory and therefore it does not rely on concepts of society or organizations as some kind of whole or system. The theory posits that the fundamental human reality is the temporally iterated interaction between human bodies so that any concept of a whole is an imaginative construct arising in that interaction, giving a sense of unity, coherence and continuity to experience. As such it is an ideology to be deconstructed, giving rise to a new ideology in a dialectical process.

The perspective of complex responsive processes relies on a particular view of time which we have called 'the living present' (Stacey *et al.*, 2000). All action takes place in the present but this present is not a simple point separating the past from the future in a linear progression of time. Instead, the living present itself has a time structure. As we act in the living present, we do so on the basis of expectations for the future – this is because we take the attitude of the other and engage in private role play, in reflection, as we act. However, those expectations arise on the basis of our past experience which gives rise to our expectations of expectations. This past experience is not a given, however, because in each present we reconstruct, we reinterpret, the past and this reinterpretation is influenced by our expectations. The future, as expectation, is thus potentially changing the past as the account we give ourselves of what happened. The result is a circular time structure of the present in which the past influences the future and the future influences the past. The future is under perpetual construction in the living present.

It is a misunderstanding, however, to think this means that social and self-formation proceed anew in each present or that social and self-formation arise purely in the current interaction between those present to each other. Processes of social and self-formation are path-dependent – they have a history, and this history is both repeated and potentially transformed in each present. This may be understood in terms of Mead's concepts of social object and cult value.

Mead pointed to the human tendencies to generalize and idealize patterns of experience. Generalizations emerge in a history of experience and Mead referred to these as social objects. He distinguished between the physical objects to be found in nature and the social objects which are to be found only in the human experience of interaction. A social object, therefore, does not exist as a thing (physical object) but as a generalized tendency on the part of large numbers of people to act in similar ways in similar situations. For example, a restaurant is a social object in that people in a particular locality all tend to act in similar ways when they go to a restaurant. A social object is Mead's way of talking about culture or social structure. However, unlike mainstream ways of talking about the social as systems, Mead sees the social object as a generalized process which may be found only in its particularization in specific situations. It is in this particularization that social objects evolve.

Mead used the notion of cult value to refer to human processes of idealizing their generalizations. Cult values emerge in a history of interaction as highly idealized views of what is possible for the future, stripped of all obstacles to its achievement, which are ascribed to some imaginatively constructed whole. Cult values are precious aspects of collective identities that are always aspects of personal identities. However, to avoid the conformity of a cult, the cult values have to be functionalized in ordinary, everyday situations as people interact and this inevitably involves conflict. It is in this functionalization, with its conflict, that cult values evolve. Social and self-formation do not proceed anew in each present and social/self-formation do not arise purely in the current interaction between those present to each other because in all interactions, including those with themselves, people are taking up and particularizing social objects and cult values. The wider society and its history are implicated in all interactions, including those of a body with itself so that a self is always a social phenomenon.

The perspective described above presents a particular view of causality. Instead of the efficient 'if–then' causality of the classical natural sciences, or the rational causality of the autonomous individual in which individuals action is caused by their chosen goals, or the formative causality of systems thinking in which the system unfolds an already enfolded goal, this perspective is based on a transformative causality. Interaction is iterated in each present as repetition or habit and at the same time as potential transformation. Here, transformation encompasses both gradual and dramatic change. The potential for transformation arises in the capacity for spontaneous individual responses and the amplification of small differences in iterated habit from 'one' present to the 'next'. The natural complexity sciences demonstrate the possibility nonlinear interaction has for amplifying such small differences into completely different patterns which are unknowable in advance. Transformative causality therefore implies a pattern of movement, of evolution, which is paradoxically predictable and unpredictable at the same time.

What has been described so far is the communicative interaction aspect of complex responsive processes but there is another central aspect, namely power relations. Elias (1939; Elias and Scotson, 1994) argued that power is an aspect of all human relations because in relating to each other people cannot do other than both constrain and enable each other at the same time. Power is such an enabling constraint. Power relations between people form patterns that Elias called figurations, by which he meant groupings of people in which power is titled in favor of some and against others. These groupings are formed and sustained in the process of inclusion and exclusion in which groups form and sustain views of each other through processes of gossip where charisma is ascribed to one group and stigma to another. Elias refers to the identity of a group as a 'we' identity and argues that 'we' identities are inseparable aspects of each 'I' identity. Power figurations are unconsciously sustained by ideology (Dalal, 1998, 2002).

Complex responsive processes of relating are thus paradoxically enabling and constraining processes of communicative interaction and power relating between human bodies that constitute society, mind and self/identity, all at the same time. Society, mind and self are all evolving patterns of interaction that may be described as narrative themes organizing the experience of being together, as figurations, social objects or cult values. What is clear in the expositions of both Mead and Elias is that they are talking about self-organization in which widespread, global patterns emerge. In the natural complexity sciences, the term 'self-organization' refers to the interaction of agents in which each acts according to its own local organizing principles and it is in this interaction that widespread, global patterns emerge in the complete absence of any blueprint, program or plan for these global patterns. This is normally understood from a systemic perspective in which a global system emerges at one level from the interaction of other systems, agents, at a lower level. The higher level system can then act back on the lower level as a causal power.

In the human process terms we have been describing, however, there are no forces over and above individuals. All we have are vast numbers of continually iterated interactions between human bodies, and these are local in the sense that each of us can only interact with a limited number of others and also in the sense that each of us acts as an expression of our own organizing narrative themes. It is in the vast number of local (in this specific technical sense) interactions that widespread, global patterns of collective power and economic relations emerge. These widespread patterns, constituting social objects/cult values, emerge as repetition and potential transformation at the same time. We can then get highly repetitive patterns iterated over long time periods as durable social objects/cult values. The general comments we make about such patterns are articulations of social objects/cult values referring to what is being iterated or emerging rather than to any force over and above those in whose interaction it is emerging. In addition, in Elias' terms, these generalized patterns become part of the personality structures of individuals in a particular era. This is exactly what Elias means when he argues that the evolution of societies emerges in the interplay between myriad intentions and plans of individuals or groups, where no one can design or control the interplay and so no one can design or control the evolving patterns.

However, individuals do form intentions as to their next actions and they do make choices between possible actions, even possible desires. Human interaction is thus fundamentally evaluative and human desire is socially formed. Norms and values provide the criteria for choosing between desires and actions. Values may be thought of as motivating voluntary compulsions to perform one action rather than another. Values are essential aspects of self and arise in social processes of self-formation and self-transcendence (Dewey, 1934). Particularly intense experiences of interaction are seized by the imagination and idealized as imaginary wholes, or cult values. Norms may be thought of as generalized obligatory restrictions on desires and actions, and these too emerge in processes of social evolution as social objects. Together, voluntary compulsions of value and obligatory restrictions of norms constitute a paradox and the tension is transformed as ideology. Ideology is the basis for the evaluation of actions and for sustaining patterns of power relations. However, as social object, ideology may only be found in the human experience of interaction in which it is particularized and functionalized and in which it continues to evolve. This particularization involves both spontaneity and reflection at the same time. Values, norms and ideology are thus all contingent in the sense that they must be interpreted and negotiated anew in each specific situation, in each present (Griffin, 2002). This is a view of ethics and morals taking the form of 'what is good and right for me' and 'what is good and right for us'. This is not a selfish, self-interested basis for ethics because the judgment as to good and right is an honest one, to the best of our abilities, in the situation. It is not thought before action. The iterative process of interpretation and particularization of the imaginative whole of ideology amounts to the negation of the whole, and it is in this negation that further evolution arises (dialectic and Adorno's concept of the negation of negation).

We therefore reach the point where we think of an organization as an evolving pattern of interaction between people that emerges in the local interaction of those people, with its fundamental aspects of communication, power and ideology, and evaluative choices. No one, then, is designing or controlling the evolving patterns of self or society, and that includes organizations. Instead, that evolution emerges as the spontaneous choices of individuals and the amplification of small differences in the iteration of interaction from one present to another. Difference and conflict are essential to such evolution, which is patterns of movement that are predictable and unpredictable *at the same time*. This perspective is subversive of mainstream notions of control, as well as prescriptions for designing whole organizations and instigating overall change initiatives such as culture change programs, business process re-engineering and total quality management which are meant to alter the whole organization. One comes to see that even though global interventions are thought to be directed to the whole, they are simply powerful generalized gestures to an imaginative construct which will call forth many responses and counter-gestures, patterned in ways that are predictable and unpredictable at the same time. This resonates with repeated experience in which such global interventions do not achieve their promised outcome. This perspective does not, however, lead to an automatic prescription to avoid hierarchical and bureaucratic forms of organization. It is rather a way of thinking about how such forms actually function in our ordinary, everyday experience.

Ideology

The perspective of complex responsive processes does not make a claim to be value-free. It does not, therefore, take a realist epistemological position in which knowledge is unproblematically given in the reality of the object to be understood, a reality which can be discovered through the scientific method of testing hypotheses in a value-free manner. In other words, it does not make absolute truth claims. However, the perspective of complex responsive processes is also not a skeptical, postmodern one in that it does not abandon all claims to any kind of truth or to any kind of useful generalizations about human interactions that are valid for all human beings. In the tradition of Hegel, as interpreted by Mead without the theory of Absolute Spirit, the complex responsive processes perspective holds that human beings are born into an already existing society and that knowing is a social activity. Reality, then, is the experienced reality of people cooperating and conflicting with each other, so perpetually negotiating and constructing what is real 'for them'. Just as ethics and morals are 'what is good for me' and 'good for us', so truth is what is 'true for me' and 'true for us'. Truth is thus contingent and must be particularized in conflictual situations. This means that we can distinguish between 'reality congruence' and 'fantasy' in a particular contingent situation. That which is reality congruent is that which works 'for me' and 'for us' in terms of going on together in a specific situation and making sense of that experience. This is consistent with American pragmatism and its concern with practical usefulness, which is not to be confused with utilitarianism and its simple maximizing calculations of utility.

From this perspective, 'truth' becomes the useful generalizations and idealizations we find ourselves able to make across many specific situations, which must be particularized and so evolve. This is very different from a metaphysical notion of universals as given wholes, where given means transcendental in Kant's sense. Here, given/transcendental means that the universal exists in a realm that is already there before the action, outside of the interaction. Such a universal is not to be explained by the action or interaction but acts as a causal power on the action and interaction. In systems thinking, values, norms and ideology are understood in this transcendental whole sense. When it comes to complex responsive processes, the argument is that there is no causal agent outside interaction itself. Interaction is its own cause. The values and the ideology are not given outside of the interaction as a given or a transcendental whole but emerge in the interaction itself as the functionalization of cult values. Interaction explains how different forms of ideology emerge in experience as the imaginative construction of generalized and idealized 'wholes'. Thus complex responsive processes certainly implicate the emergence and evolution of values and ideology but not as something universal, given or transcendental. We are saying that ideological 'wholes' emerge as idealized creative acts of imagination in human interaction but that these are functionalized in ongoing interaction in which the idealized whole is negated, giving rise to the next ideology. This presents an evolutionary theory of values and ideologies arising in social processes of self-formation and ongoing conflictual negotiation.

So, what are the generalizations, or fundamental propositions, in the complex responsive processes perspective and what is being idealized?

The perspective makes the claim that human interdependence is a fundamental reality of human experience. In other words, fundamental to the perspective of complex responsive processes is the proposition that the human body has the capacity to take the attitude of the other, and to take itself as object to itself as subject, as the basis of communication and the enabling–constraining, or power relating, of that communicative interaction. Such communicative interaction/power relating is held to be self-organizing and to produce an emergent pattern. Processes of self-organization/emergence are also, therefore, claimed to be fundamental propositions. Further fundamental propositions have to do with the human capacity for spontaneity and reflection, as well as some capacity to choose between actions and desires, all as attributes of the capacity to take the attitude of the other. Also fundamental is the evaluative nature of human choosing. Generalizing/idealizing activities to do with norms, values and ideologies are held to be fundamental characteristic of human experience. However, the evolving patterns of communication, power and ideology are not universal but contingent on the specific interactions of specific people, negotiating the particularizations of their generalizations/idealizations with each other at specific times in specific situations.

Particular idealizations follow from these founding propositions. These are:

- Local interaction, or in other words, the experience of consciousness and self-consciousness in the interaction with others.
- Difference, diversity, conflict and negotiation in which thought moves through negation, the negation of negation, the negation of ideological 'wholes, including as alienation the issue of false consciousness, and the amplification of differences.
- Reflexivity, both as individual reflection and socially as critical location of one's reflection in traditions of thought differentiated from others.
- Discourse and the narrative patterning of experience.
- Making sense of experience, which may be knowledge for its own sake; all knowing is self-knowing.

The above propositions reflect an ideology which justifies particular approaches to researching human action – it provides the evaluative criteria for such research work. In the movement of research, negation is negated, giving rise to a new ideology, to a new imagined whole.

Method of research: Master of Arts/Doctor of Management program

The method is that of taking one's experience seriously but with a particular purpose which differentiates complex responsive processes of researching from processes of interaction in general. The purpose is to explore the complex responsive processes of human relating as a second order reflexivity. Experience is the experience of local interaction, and this immediately suggests that organizations need to be understood in terms of the experience of their members and others with whom those members interact. From the perspective of complex responsive processes, the appropriate method for understanding, for researching into, organizations is itself complex responsive processes. Research itself is also complex responsive processes and the research method becomes a reflection on ordinary everyday experience.

Experience is felt, meaningful engagement in relating to others and to oneself as we do whatever we come together to do. Experience refers to interdependence, to the social, as the fundamental human reality. Since such interaction between living bodies is patterned primarily as narrative themes, taking one's experience seriously is the activity of articulating and reflecting upon these themes. In other words, the method is that of giving an account, telling the story, of what I think and feel that I and others are doing in our interaction with each other in particular contexts over particular periods of time. Since what I and we are doing is inseparable from who I am and who we are, a meaningful narrative is also always expressing, that is, iterating or co-creating, individual and collective identities. Taking one's experience seriously, through articulating the narrative themes organizing the experience of being together, is an essentially reflexive activity and in its fullest sense this is a simultaneously individual and social process.

It is the explicitly reflexive nature of the narrative that distinguishes it as a research method from the literary story. The research narrative is explicit and ordinary, as opposed to the poetic license of the literary story which has the potential to draw attention to the epic nature of human experience or simply describing imaginative fantasy. The narrative as research method is reflexive in an individual sense insofar as the narrator is making explicit the way of thinking that he or she is reflecting in the construction of the story. In other words, the reflexive personal narrative is explaining why it has the particular focus it has and how the narrator's past experience is shaping the selection of events and their interpretation. The narrator is making explicit, as far as possible, the assumptions being made and the ideology being reflected, in explicating the particular meaning being put forward in the narrative. At the same time, the narrative as research method is no less importantly reflexive in a social sense. Social reflexivity requires the narrator to explicitly locate his or her way of thinking about the story being told in the traditions of thought of his or her society, differentiating between these traditions in a critically aware manner. In other words, the narrator as researcher engages intensively with literature relevant to his or her particular narrative accounts, and makes explicit the ideological underpinnings and power relation implications.

An example of this approach to research is provided by the Master of Arts/Doctor of Management program at the Business School of the University of Hertfordshire which is run in association with the Institute of Group Analysis. All participants are part-time and must be working in some capacity in an organizational setting. Their research is their current experience of their organizational practice. The final thesis is built up through writing a number of projects, each of which is a reflexive narrative in the sense described above – the research method is for each participant to take his or her experience seriously. In the first project, each participant provides a narrative account of the events, influences, literature and traditions of thought that are now shaping his or her practice and how he or she makes sense of it. Each of the following projects takes a particular situation in which the author is involved and presents a narrative account of what the author and others are doing in that situation. They may, for example, be involved in quality improvement initiatives or they may be trying to choose how to respond next to some action that people in another organization have taken.

The reflective narrative of some person's organizational experience is, however, only the 'raw material' of complex responsive processes of research into organizational life. It serves as the basis for discussion with others in a deepening reflection on the meaning of the narrative. The discussion may be one involving others in the narrator's organization and/or one involving members of some community of researchers. Thus, on the Master of Arts/Doctor of Management program, participants work in small learning groups of three to six members and a supervisor. They discuss each others' narratives, commenting, questioning and probing the accounts given, the literature drawn on or omitted, and the meaning being made of the experience. Each person then rewrites the narrative account and presents it once more to the group for discussion. Typically, there are five or six such iterations. The purpose of this iterative approach is to make richer sense of experience and, as the researcher goes through this process, he or she experiences movements in his or her thought. The purpose is not to solve a problem or make an improvement to the organization but to develop the practitioner's skill in paying attention to the complexity of the local, micro interactions he or she is engaged in because it is in these that wider organizational patterns emerge. However, the movement of thought is not an abstract matter because the practitioner-researchers are making sense of their own current experience of what they and others are doing in their organization and, as they do so, their practice inevitably evolves, hopefully for the better, although there can be no guarantee of this.

In this way, participants on the program build up a portfolio of projects, over a two- to three-year period, in which there emerge, usually more and more clearly, overall themes of importance to the participants in their organizational practice. The projects also chronicle movements of thought and shifts in organizational practice of the participants as they iterate through the projects to develop a thesis on organizational life. A further iteration involves discussing this movement through the projects and writing a synopsis and critical appraisal of the major themes, the movement in thought and practice, and the contribution the researcher is making to his or her community of practitioners. Instead, then, of requiring the formulation of a hypothesis which is then explored, the complex responsive processes research method offers a process in which meaningful themes about organizational life emerge. Instead of resulting in a retrospectively tidy write-up, the complex responsive processes method leads to a research account that tracks its own actual development as further reflexivity.

There is yet further reflexivity involved in the complex responsive processes research method and this involves making sense of the local, contingent process of the research itself. Thus a key aspect of the program is the time made available, and the importance attached to, reflection by supervisors and researchers on the processes of learning and researching together. This is done in a large group meeting of some thirty staff and members of the program at the start of each day of the five-day residential meetings of the whole community. The way of working together in this large group is very much influenced by the group analytic tradition (Foulkes, 1964; Kreeger, 1975) – the program is offered in association with the Institute of Group Analysis. As with group analytic large groups, all sit in a circle and talk about whatever they want to talk about, and this will inevitably include the sense they are making of the program and its research method.

The large group on the program differs in some respects from the usual group analytic one in that no one takes the role of group conductor. Although there is an acknowledged power difference between supervisory staff and participants working towards a degree, the staff members do not adopt behaviors likely to enhance that power difference. For this reason, no staff member takes on the role of conductor, leader or consultant. Instead, staff members participate fully as members of the large group and do not keep themselves separate from others on social occasions, except for daily staff meetings. The experience of the large group is an important one for a number of reasons. First, it provides group support for what is an anxiety-provoking process – the degree of critical reflection required by the complex responsive processes approach inevitably leads to some undermining of taken-for-granted aspects of ways of thinking and thus personal and collective identities. Second, the large group meetings provide a live experience of the emergence of themes organizing the experience of being together and the power relations they reflect. Early on in the program, members are invited to form themselves into small learning groups and to negotiate for a supervisor. This inevitably creates the inclusion–exclusion dynamics of power relations and the often stressful emotions that go with it. This and other experiences have close similarities to the kinds of patterns people experience in their own organizations, and the large group meetings provide opportunities for noticing and discussing these.

There are three important questions which must be addressed by any research method, and these relate to ideology, ethics and validity or legitimacy. The ideology of the complex responsive processes research method has already been addressed above. The use of narratives of personal experience of interaction with others raises important ethical questions. The first matter has to do with writing about people with whom one is interacting and the related issue of disclosing confidential material. In a more conventional approach, involving, say, interviews, the ethical approach is usually to inform those whom one is writing about of what one is doing and to show them what one has written, concealing identities as appropriate. However, a researcher writing about his or her own personal experience of his everyday work activities can hardly keep informing people that he may possibly write about what they are doing together. The best that can be done is to inform colleagues in general about what one is doing and then to write about the experience in a way that does not reveal their identities but still presents a 'reliable' account of what is going on. Other than this, there is no general ethical rule to guide the researcher in the traditional sense of thought before action. Consistent with the complex responsive processes approach, the ethics of what one does as a researcher, as with what one does in all other situations, is contingent upon the situation and the emerging and ongoing negotiation with those with whom one is interacting (Griffin, 2002).

The second ethical matter has to do with inviting people to undertake a form of research that can carry with it considerable risks. The risks are potentially hostile responses from others whom one is writing about and the threats what is written may present to existing power relations and one's own job security. Here again there can be no general ethical rule, only the contingent negotiation of how to proceed in particular situations so that the research work does not create undue risks for the researcher.

Finally, there is the matter of validity or legitimacy (see Chapter 3). Clearly, there can be no objective validity for the obvious reason that the research is an interpretation, a subjective reflection on personal experience. However, it is not any arbitrary account in that it must make sense to others, resonate with the experience of others and be persuasive to them. Furthermore, it must be justifiable in terms of a wider tradition of thought that the community being addressed finds persuasive, or at least plausible. The value of this kind of research, we would claim, is that it presents accounts of what people actually experience in their organizational practice with all its uncertainty, emotion and messiness, rather than highly rational, decontextualized accounts and their hindsight view.

In order to clarify further what is involved in the complex responsive process research method, the following section compares it with action research, particularly the collaborative inquiry strand in that tradition.

Comparing action research and complex responsive processes approaches to research

We are aware that most of the points we have been making above have been taken up in discussions on methodology from the perspectives of postmodernism, social constructionism (including action research and ethnomethodology) and Husserl's (1963) notion of the lifeworld. However, while these traditions are concerned with the same issues, they take them up in a way that is different to what we are trying to do. For example, the concept of the lifeworld was taken up by Schutz (1967), who influenced Berger and Luckman (1971), while the lifeworld concept was linked by Habermas to a Marxist tradition in his development of methodology. The concept of the lifeworld, however, reflects the Kantian (modernist) notion of the autonomous individual, which is continued by those who build a methodological position on the lifeworld concept. We, on the other hand, approach the question of methodology from the position that there is no dualism of individual and social – both are aspects of the same phenomenon, namely human interdependence. As an alternative to the lifeworld concept, we have relied on Mead's concepts of social object/cult vales and Dewey's theory of imagination (imagined wholes), which we find more compatible with analogies from the complexity sciences. This also means that we have a different perspective on the relationship between the individual and the social to that of social constructionists. Thus prominent social constructionists, such as Gergen (1999a, 1999b) and Shotter (1993) set up an either/or choice in relation to the individual and the social, and come down on the side of the social. Ethnomethodologists (Garfinkel, 1967) are also in a social constructionist tradition but come down on the side of the individual. The approach to methodology naturally reflects the wider intellectual traditions in which they are developed and action research, therefore reflects the dualism of the individual, with some coming down on the side of the individual and others granting primacy to the social. In this section we want to explore the consequences of the differences between a complex responsive response perspective, where there is no split between individual and social, and the other perspectives referred to above, where there is. The comparison we are going to make is with action research since this is so widely used in relation to organizations.

The action research and the complex responsive processes approaches have many interests in common, in that both:

- argue that positivist methods and the simple position of the objective observer are not appropriate for researching social phenomena;
- are theories of social action;
- seek to avoid splitting theory and practice;
- are concerned with emergent phenomena;
- focus on participation and relationship;
- focus on the everyday and narrative aspects of experience;
- engage with but do not move to postmodernism.

However, there are fundamental differences between the two approaches and these may not be all that immediately obvious because, although both may use the same words, they have different meanings. In particular, the words 'action', 'participation', 'relationship', 'experience' and 'emergence' have substantially different meanings in the two approaches. From the perspective that thought moves in the engagement with difference, these notes focus attention on the differences by comparing how the two perspectives deal with:

- speaking of metaphysics or a worldview;
- the individual and the social;
- ideology, power and ethics;
- learning and action.

Each of these is explored in the sections which follow.

Speaking of metaphysics or a worldview

Metaphysics (that is, 'beyond physics' or appearances) refers to all-encompassing claims about an ultimate reality. Statements about all-encompassing wholes are metaphysical statements. Kant argued that medieval metaphysics, absolutely true statements about reality, was no longer possible because we cannot know reality in itself. Instead he proposed an epistemology and ontology which focused on the conditions of the possibility of knowing reality, namely the categories of knowing. This means that we cannot make statements about knowing the absolute truth of reality itself but we can make true statements about the pre-existing categories of our own thought through which we form hypotheses about reality which we then test. On the basis of this, Kant outlined a metaphysics of morals where we form hypotheses about pre-existing, universal ethical principles which we can test in our actions. In reaction to Kant's metaphysics, Hegel attempted to create a metaphysics in his philosophy of absolute spirit but this failed. This is what postmodernist thinkers refer to as the end of the possibility of a 'grand narrative', the end of metaphysics.

For Peter Reason and colleagues, the family of approaches to action research is more than a methodology. It is an all-encompassing worldview or paradigm. In their introduction to their *Handbook of Action Research* (2001, pp. 6–7), Reason and Bradbury say:

> The emergent worldview has been described as systemic, holistic, relational, feminine, and experiential but its defining characteristic is that it is participatory: our world does not consist of separate things but of relationships which we co-author. We participate in our world, so that the 'reality' we experience is a co-creation that involves the primal givenness of the cosmos and human feeling and construing. The participative metaphor is particularly apt for action research, because as we participate in creating our world we are already embodied and breathing beings *who are necessarily acting* – and this draws us to consider how to judge the *quality* of acting.
>
> . . .
>
> We start with our intimations of the *participatory nature* of the given cosmos whose form is *relational and ecological*. Since we are part of the whole, we are already engaged in *practical being and acting*.
>
> . . .

> At the centre of a participatory worldview is a participatory understanding of the underlying nature of the cosmos which we inhabit and which we co-create . . . a seamless whole in which the parts are constantly in touch with each other.

From this perspective, action research is therefore built upon a metaphysical foundation in which the cosmos is seen as a systemic whole that is integrated, interacting, self-consistent and self-creative (although Reason argues that this is not a metaphysical construct but a radically empirical one). Humans are parts of this whole and participation means participation in this whole in a way that produces the whole. Experiential encounter with the presence of the world is the ground of our being and knowing and is prior to language and art, although it may be symbolized in language and art. Experience of our meeting with the elemental properties of the living world cannot be confused with our symbolic constructs. Those arguing in this tradition talk about a pristine acquaintance with phenomena unadulterated by preconceptions (Heron and Reason, 1997). They argue that there is a given cosmos, a primordial reality in which the mind actively participates. This is easily taken up in systemic interpretations of complexity theory and is dependent on a particular understanding of self-organization/emergence as 'systemic self-organization' where interaction creates a whole (Griffin, 2002).

Some action researchers then link this participative worldview to some notion of spiritual, ecstatic experiences in which people become aware of their own interconnectedness, and in doing so experience their true selves in the ecstatic I–Thou encounter with another (for a critique of such concepts of the individual see O'Donohue, 1993: 26–28). Rowan (in Reason and Bradbury, 2001:114–123) develops action research as a humanistic approach by linking Wilbur's (1995) notion of 'centaur consciousness' to the concept of the 'real' self.

Complex responsive processes, however, is a temporal process theory which, when it comes to understanding human action, argues against systems thinking and its spatial metaphor of 'inside' and 'outside' (see Stacey, 2003). It draws on some strands of complexity theory as a source domain for analogies and a principal analogy has to do with interaction. Computer simulations of nonlinear interaction between entities, which are different enough to impose conflicting constraints on each other, show that interaction patterns itself, from within as it were, as both continuity and potential transformation *at the same time*. We take that abstract insight and, deriving human attributes from the theories of Mead and

Elias, we argue that human interaction patterns itself in the same way. There is then no need to look for any causal agency outside of human interaction itself. We therefore do not think in terms of systems, boundaries, wholes and so on. Our way of thinking is not holistic. Wholes emerge as our own imaginative constructs taking the form of ideologies, as mentioned above and discussed further below.

As described above, the methodology is that of exploring our own experience of interaction with each other and the ways in which this patterns our experience. What we are doing is exploring interaction as complex responsive processes of relating. The theory/method is therefore not based on any 'pre-given' and it has no metaphysical or spiritual foundations. In this sense we would agree with postmodern thinkers in taking seriously the 'end' of metaphysics as expressed in the thought of Schopenhauer, Nietzsche and Heidegger. We differ from the postmodern view in arguing that the introduction of 'fragments' of metaphysics such as causality may be justified by reference to experience. We are saying, then, that experience is the experience of interacting with other people in the context of the physical world, in which metaphysical themes and spiritual understanding emerge in human interaction and are available for exploration if that is what interests the researcher. Thus, in participating in interaction with, in relating to, each other, people are not producing a whole, other than as an imaginative construct, but only further patterns of interaction. These patterns are narrative themes that organize the experience of being together. Some of these themes may be described as metaphysical or spiritual. Instead of a starting point consisting of pre-given, universal wholes, the foundation of our argument consists of a number of generalized propositions about the nature of human interaction – a claim to a general human reality which is social interaction between bodies living in a physical world. Accounts and understandings emerging in such interactions are constrained by the physical world and by social relations of power, but the patterns are always contingent and evolving. This perspective is consistent with process interpretations of complexity theory which talk of 'participative self-organization' where self-organization creates further patterns of participation rather than any system as in 'systemic' self-organization (Griffin, 2002).

In summary, the first important difference is that we do not take a participatory worldview and we are extremely skeptical of approaches giving explanations of organizational life on a spiritual or religious foundation.

The individual and the social

In the Preface to *The Handbook of Action Research* (2001: xxvi), Reason and Bradbury say:

> Structuration theory (Giddens, 1984) allows us to link the individual to social structures so that both are seen to be related as chicken and egg. As in any causal recursive loop, changes to the pattern of interaction can occur through influence either at the more micro, first- and second-person levels, or the more macro, third-person or institutional levels . . . we suggest that social and organizational realities may be understood to be sources of patterns of interaction between members: in turn, the members' dispositions and practices are shaped by social and organizational procedures. A structuration perspective therefore offers theoretical support for seeking leverage for desired change at macro levels through intervention at the individual and dyadic or small-group micro levels and vice versa. While we do not naively misunderstand the power of systems as coterminous with that of aggregates of individuals, we do believe in the power of conscious and intentional change which can result from action research work of individual and committed groups.

The action research approach is therefore one that understands the social as a system at one level constructed by individuals at another level. The social system then affects those individuals who are understood from the individual-based perspectives of humanistic and existential psychology. It is thought that individuals can leverage the social system in intended ways through action research. For some writers on action research, individuals are thought to possess a true or real self that may be actualized in what is essentially a spiritual, often pantheistic, experience. This results in a dualistic causality in which individual action is caused by individual intention, plus the effects of social systems on them, in what we have called 'rationalist causality', while the system of which they are a part operates according to what we have called 'formative causality' (see Stacey *et al.*, 2000). According to the first causality individuals are free to choose their actions, but according to the latter they are not.

Complex responsive processes theory, however, does not distinguish the individual and the social as separate levels but regards them as the same phenomenon. Human minds and human societies arise together, with the individual as the singular and the social as the plural of interdependent embodied persons. Mind is understood as social processes and the individual is thought of as social through and through (Foulkes, 1964; Stacey, 2003). Individuals are paradoxically forming and being formed by the social *at the same time*. This is a very different theory of psychology to humanistic and existential psychology, or cognitivism and psychoanalysis for that matter. Instead of thinking in terms of individuals actualizing themselves through what is ultimately a spiritual experience, the complex responsive process approach is concerned with understanding how individual and collective identities arise at the same time in the social interaction of individuals. The methodology is one in which individuals take their own experience of these social processes seriously and try to understand the nature of that experience in which their identities are under perpetual construction.

From the complex responsive processes perspective, it is not possible for committed groups of people to intentionally change the widespread patterning of their interaction. All they can change is their own interactions, and from this the widespread patterning will emerge in ways that they cannot intend or fully understand. (The issue of power differences is discussed below.) The aim of the method is, therefore, not one of changing social 'wholes' but of making sense of the 'live' experience of interaction (see another volume in this series, Shaw and Stacey, 2005). As people make sense differently they act differently, and it is in this action, in continuing interaction with others, that macro patterns change in emergent ways which cannot be predicted or controlled.

Ideology, power and ethics

In their introduction to *The Handbook of Action Research* (2001: 2), Reason and Bradbury suggest a number of interdependent characteristics of action research:

> A primary purpose of action research is to produce practical knowledge that is useful to people in the everyday conduct of their lives.
>
> . . .
>
> A wider purpose of action research is to contribute through this practical knowledge to the increased well-being . . . of human persons and communities, and to a more equitable and sustainable relationship with the wider ecology of the planet of which we are an intrinsic part.

> So action research is about working towards practical outcomes, and
> also about creating new forms of understanding . . . and more broadly,
> theories which contribute to human emancipation, to the flourishing of
> community, which help us to reflect on our place within the ecology of
> the planet and contemplate our spiritual purposes.
>
> . . .
>
> liberating ways of knowing . . . ideally involving all stakeholders.
>
> . . .
>
> Good action research emerges over time in an evolutionary and
> developmental process, as individuals develop skills of inquiry and as
> communities of inquiry develop in communities of practice. Action
> research is emancipatory.

So action research starts with a clear ideology and takes, as given, values
to do with cooperation, collaboration, democracy, emancipation,
liberation, challenge to existing power structures, human flourishing and
sustainable development. Within this holistic and systemic framework
ethics then takes the form of thought, the formulation of hypotheses about
Kantian universal categorical imperatives, before action. Action research
has a clear political agenda which is inherent in the method. It is about
empowering people. Some action researchers talk about restoring
meaning and mystery to life so that the world is experienced as a sacred
place.

The theory/method of complex responsive processes reflects a different
ideology. What it idealizes is human interaction itself with its paradoxical
cooperation and competition/conflict, difference and sameness. However,
central to the approach is the claim that the idealization cannot be taken
on its own as a given or universal because it only arises in its
particularization in contingent, local situations. The exploration concerns
how ideologies, and the power relations they sustain or change, emerge.
Ethics is ongoing negotiation as participative interaction. Truth is 'truth
for us'. Emphasis is placed on Mead's distinction between cult and
functionalized values. A cult value ascribes purpose to a whole, so giving
rise to feelings of an enlarged personality, and presents a future free of all
obstacles. Mead took such values as democracy or criminal justice to be
cult values and said that they were the most precious part of our heritage
but, at the same time, when taken simply in themselves, they are
hopelessly ideal. He pointed out how such cult values have to be
functionalized or particularized in ordinary, everyday interactions
between people. Complex responsive processes describe the methodology

for making sense of this process of functionalizing in the realization that cult values, such as democracy, deep ecology or capitalism in everyday experience, may be functionalized as crassly utilitarian. The motivation to argue that they are good or bad emerges in the local context of everyday experience.

Value orientations are unavoidable in the explanatory frameworks of the social sciences and such value orientations guide scientific inquiry, while the inquiry acts back on the value orientations. So what are the value orientations of the method of emergent exploration of experience? Joas (2000), drawing on the work of William James, draws a distinction between norms and values. Norms are social conventions that are compelling and constraining, specifying what we *ought* to do. Values, on the other hand, are criteria for judging *good* actions – they equate to the ideal. Values, as criteria for judging actions, have an attracting, motivating aspect that opens up opportunities for action. The values forming and being formed by complex responsive processes of research are the activities of creating meaning/making sense of the experience of interaction between persons and the experience of each with himself or herself. What is particularly valued is the activity of exploring and explaining the differences between alternative ways of making sense of experience. The value may be summarized as 'taking one's own experience seriously', thereby attaching particular value to the subjective. This method does not presuppose a worldview or systematic ideology but rather seeks to explore how values, including its own, emerge in experience. It is an essentially reflexive method.

Learning and action

Reason and Heron distinguish between first, second and third order research activity. First-person research activities are concerned with practices that foster the ability of individual researchers to inquire into their own lives. Second-person research activities are practices of face-to-face cooperative inquiry with others into matters of mutual concern, usually in small groups. Third-person research is practices that draw together the views of large groups of people, creating a wider community of inquiry, for example, 'whole system' conferences and dissemination of views in written form.

The process of cooperative inquiry cycles through phases of action and reflection in which different ways of knowing hold primacy. In phase 1, a group of co-researchers agree on the focus of the inquiry and develop together a set of propositions they wish to explore. They agree to undertake some action which will contribute to this exploration and they agree a set of procedures for observing and recording their own and others' experience. This is primarily propositional knowing. Phase 2 consists of co-researchers engaged in action and they record their own and others' experience. They hold lightly to the propositions with which they started. This is primarily practical knowing. In phase 3 the co-subjects become fully immersed in their experience. They develop a degree of openness in which they may see things anew. This is experiential knowing. In phase 4 after an agreed period engaged in phases 1, 2 and 3, the co-researchers reassemble to consider their original questions and propositions in the light of their experience. They may choose to amend the propositions. The group may choose to develop or amend their procedures. This is mainly propositional knowing. Ideally the inquiry is finished when the initial questions are fully answered in practice and there is a congruence of the four ways of knowing – but this is rare. Action is what is done to solve a problem.

For us, action is the ordinary experience of interaction between people in which they accomplish their living and doing together in ways that inevitably involve shame and anxiety. Action research greatly emphasizes collaboration, cooperation and appreciation. Emergent exploration seeks to understand the paradox of enabling constraints, of cooperation and conflict. The distinction between first-, second- and third-person research does not arise in our research method because, no matter whether it is one, two, or many who are involved in the research, they are always particularizing the general and the ideal which pertains to larger groups and societies.

Action research tends to take an individualist perspective on reflexivity:

> We argue that a fundamental quality of the participative worldview
> . . . is that it is self-reflexive. The participative mind . . . articulates
> reality within a paradigm, articulates the paradigm itself, and can in
> principle reach out to the wider context of that paradigm to reframe it.
> (Reason and Bradbury, 2002: 274)

From a complex responsive processes perspective individuals cannot engineer changes in their minds because their minds arise in social interaction. Reflexivity then is not an individual accomplishment but a social one that requires reflexive researchers to locate their thinking in historical traditions of thinking.

References

Berger, P. and Luckman, T. (1971) *The Social Construction of Reality*, New York: Penguin.

Christensen, B. (2003) *Reframing Consulting as Transformation from within Human Relating*, Unpublished thesis, University of Hertfordshire.

Dalal, F. (1998) *Taking the Group Seriously*, London: Jessica Kingsley.

Dalal, F. (2002) *Race, Color and Processes of Racialization*, London: Routledge.

Dewey, J. (1934) *A Common Faith*, New Haven, CT: Yale University Press.

Elias, N. (1939) *The Civilizing Process*, Oxford: Blackwell.

Elias, N. and Scotson, J. (1994) *The Established and the Outsiders*, London: Sage.

Fonseca, J. (2002) *Complexity and Innovation in Organizations*, London: Routledge.

Foulkes, S. H. (1964) *Therapeutic Group Analysis*, London: George Allen & Unwin.

Garfinkel, H. (1967) *Studies in Ethnomethodology*, Englewood Cliffs, NJ: Prentice Hall.

Gergen, M. (1999a) 'Relational Responsibility: Deconstructive Possibilities', in S. McNamee and K. J. Gergen, *Relational Responsibility: Resources for Sustainable Dialogue*, Thousand Oaks, CA: Sage.

Gergen, K. J. (1999b) *An Invitation to Social Construction*, Thousand Oaks, CA: Sage.

Goodwin, B. (1994) *How the Leopard Changed its Spots*, London: Weidenfeld & Nicolson.

Griffin, D. (2002) *The Emergence of Leadership: Linking self-organization and ethics*, London: Routledge.

Habermas, J. (1990) *Moral Consciousness and Communicative Action*, Cambridge, MA: MIT Press.

Heron, J. and Reason, P. (1997) 'A Participative Inquiry Paradigm', *Qualitative Inquiry*, 3(3): 274–294.

Husserl, L. (1963) *Cartesianische Meditationon und Pariser Vortraege*, ed. S. Strasser, The Hague: Martinus Nijoff.

Joas, H. (2000) *The Genesis of Values*, Chicago, IL: Polity Press.

Kauffman, S. A. (1995) *At Home in the Universe*, New York: Oxford University Press.

Kreeger, L. C. (ed.) (1975) *The Large Group – Dynamics and Therapy*, London: Maresfield Reprints.

Mead, G. H. (1934) *Mind, Self and Society: From the Standpoint of a Social Behaviorist*, Chicago, IL: The University of Chicago Press.

O'Donohue, J. (1993) *Person als Vermittlung: Die Dialektik von Individualität und Allgemeinheit in Hegel's 'Phänomenologie des Geistes'*, Mainz: Matthias Grünewald.

Prigogine, I. and Stengers, I. (1984) *Order out of Chaos: Man's New Dialogue with Nature*, New York: Bantam Books.

Reason, P. and Bradbury, H. (2001) *Handbook of Action Research: Participative Inquiry and Practice*, London: Sage.

Schutz, A. (1967) *The Phenomenology of the Social World*, trans. G. Walsh and F. Lehner, Evanston, IL: Northwestern University Press.

Shaw, P. (2002) *Changing Conversations in Organizations: A complexity approach to change*, London: Routledge.

Shaw, P. and Stacey, R. (eds) (2005) *Experiencing Risk, Spontaneity and Improvisation in Organizational Change: Working live*, London: Routledge.

Shotter, J. (1993) *Conversational Realities: Constructing Life Through Language*, Thousand Oaks, CA: Sage.

Stacey, R. (2001) *Complex Responsive Processes in Organizations: Learning and knowledge creation*, London: Routledge.

Stacey, R. (2003) *Complexity and Group Processes: A radically social understanding of individuals*, London: Brunner-Routledge.

Stacey, R., Griffin, D. and Shaw, P. (2000) *Complexity and Management: Fad or radical challenge to systems thinking?*, London: Routledge.

Streatfield, P. (2001) *The Paradox of Control in Organizations*, London: Routledge.

Waldrop, M. M. (1992) *Complexity: The Emerging Science at the Edge of Chaos*, Englewood Cliffs, NJ: Simon & Schuster.

Wilber, K. (1995) *Sex, Ecology and Spirituality: The Spirit of Evolution*, Boston, MA: Schambhala.

Editors' introduction to Chapter 3

In this chapter, Richard Williams, Principal and CEO of Westminster Kingsway College of Further Education in the UK, explores three questions arising for him in the methodology he follows in researching his role as leader in a major further education college in the UK.

First, he asks what it means to make a contribution to knowledge. This immediately raises questions to do with the nature of truth. In considering this matter, Williams draws on Rorty and also on Davidson. Both of these philosophers reject any notion of absolute truth and argue that claims to truth rest upon interpretation and justification; that is, on belief. What can be justified is what is true. Justification is accomplished in discourse and debate and, therefore, inevitably involves contention. As we struggle together to justify the assertions we make on the basis of belief statements, we create fuzzy narratives of experience. Justification and validity arise in complex social acts in which people refer to the sensuous experience they have in common of the real world they live in. What people are doing, as they engage in this way, is exchanging propositions, and the product of the inquiry process is a challenge to existing ways of thinking; that is, transformation and movement in the nature of the propositional beliefs held by the inquirers. As such movement occurs people find themselves fitting into the social nexus in a different way. Making a contribution to knowledge is, therefore, engaging in this social process so as to produce movement in thought and so action. This is a social perspective on research, where to research means to participate in processes of argumentation around belief statements. To participate in this way is to take up one's ethical responsibility as a member of a community of researchers.

This leads to Williams' second question, to do with how one justifies the merits of one methodology compared to another, and whether it makes any practical difference to use one methodology rather than another. What he is concerned with here is how communities of researchers justify their webs of belief in relation to other communities of researchers. This is essentially a matter of differentiating one web of beliefs from another and, in relation to this question, Williams turns to Habermas. For Habermas there are two steps involved in justification. First, there is the need to formulate established principles which amount to the universalization of the underlying argument. This attempt to ground an argument on pre-given, transcendental universals differs from the approach of Rorty and Davidson who consider argument as a socially negotiated process of justified belief, or foundational propositions, which therefore cannot be grounded in universals. The second step, for Habermas, is the process of critique where argument is essential for creativity. Critique invites development of thought by identifying differences between interlocutors. The co-existence of contradictory, contending positions is necessary for the development of thought. Making a contribution to knowledge means exploring difference and taking a position; this inevitably brings contention and conflict.

The third question Williams considers has to do with how the method of research he employs affects his own practice. He explains how, in his role as CEO, he still does what he did before so that he cannot identify dramatic changes in performance. However, as a result of thinking differently, he now relates to his work and its context in a different way. He now has a different perspective on what it is possible and impossible for him to do and he finds that this makes his difficult role more tolerable.

He draws his argument together with reference to Elias' concepts of emotional involvement and detachment. Williams understands the tension of simultaneous involvement and detachment to constitute a reflexive process of emergent self-awareness. He says:

> Although I have referred to changes in my sense of thinking and belief as a result of undertaking this research process, I believe that the major contribution of this work to my practice is that I have been able to sustain my ability to carry on in what might otherwise have been an intolerable situation. This I attribute to the fact that in the process of enquiring about myself, my role, my relationships with others, my situation in a complex figuration of interdependent relationships with others, I have experienced a movement in my emotional responses to this organizational context. Nothing much in a sense has changed other than my feelings regarding my position in relation to what is happening around me: I can explain this differently and in ways that

make sense as I observe them every day. Moreover, I can check my re-formed narrative with the narratives of others also engaged in processes of enquiry that question fundamentally many of the commonsense propositions that are supposed to account for 'how it is' in organizational life today. I have new cues, new sensitivities, and new ways of reading what is going on. This I believe to be what Elias describes in his reference to detachment. Elias' use of the idea of detachment, I believe, should not be confused with the idea of disengagement. I am now no less involved emotionally than I was when I started out on a process of research enquiry.

(p. 69)

Williams argues that research is a social process in which contending, conflictual beliefs are negotiated in the movement of thought. To contribute to knowledge is thus to engage in this movement. It becomes an ethical responsibility to negotiate one's position in argument with those taking different positions rather than excluding the alternative. This involves justifying one's beliefs to others in one's research community as well as to those in other research communities. Williams links such processes of justification to ones of differentiation, since justifying a methodology always involves differentiating it from others. The result is a methodology consisting of continual argument with its inevitable dynamics of inclusion and exclusion, reflecting patterns of power relations. He thinks this is what Rorty means when he talks about fuzziness in processes of inquiry. In differentiating argumentation there is a paradox of sustaining a position and yet remaining open to alternatives. It is this differentiation that tests true and false belief, where false means not 'reality congruent' or useful beliefs. The methodology he is arguing for is one that is able to sustain a discourse about difference, to contest contradictory claims, because sameness destroys creativity.

He then argues that the use of words is important in the debate in which knowledge is created. However, meaning is not to be found in the words alone but in the narrative in which they are used. Narrative is thus central to his methodology and, indeed, it is in accounting for and reflecting upon the narrative that the very identities of the researchers engaged in argument may shift. It is in our narrative accounts that knowledge of ourselves arises as we filter out what we pay attention to. We cannot separate out our narrative accounts from our social actions and one methodology community will differ from others but will not necessarily be right. Performative legitimacy is enabled in power relating and it is in wider power relating, argument, that some beliefs are justified while others are regarded as false. Williams follows Foucault in arguing that problematizing a view does not bring with it the obligation to proffer a solution. He argues against utopian or instrumental modes of research.

It matters what methodology one chooses because the choice affects one's sense of self and what one does.

3 Belief, truth and justification: issues of methodology, discourse and the validity of personal narratives

Richard Williams

In my professional life, I am the principal and chief executive of one of the largest post-16 educational institutions in the UK. My college is a fully incorporated entity and operates very much at the forefront of the change process that has faced all such institutions that now make up the modernized UK public sector. I have worked in senior management positions in post-16 education for eighteen years. For the past eight of these I have been a college principal working in the inner city of London with some of the most challenging social and educational agendas that have been present in education throughout this period. On reflection, I realize that my personal experience of much of this part of my career has been paradoxical in that I have found myself acting, with apparent confidence, the part of a radical modernizer while struggling more personally to make sense of the wider political, social and organizational context in which I have been active. The source of my motivation to engage at depth with a doctoral research program is, I believe, located in my inability to resolve this paradox of my lived experience.

I encountered Ralph Stacey's work seven years ago (one year after being appointed to a CEO role) while participating in a program focusing on strategic leadership issues. For me, at the time, Stacey's critical insight was that of the unpredictability of most of what happens in organizations. I was attracted too by his quite radical arguments concerning the manner in which people might behave differently towards each other if this feature of organizational life was explicitly recognized in ways that challenged the more orthodox assumptions about power and authority at work. I was attracted too by Stacey's critique of systems thinking and learning organization theories, since this enabled me to feel less bad about owning up, to myself at least, to the idea that the chaos and disorder I experienced in my own working life was far more real than I or anyone else whom I knew felt able to admit. Stacey's work also seemed to me to invite a radical challenge to conventional notions of responsibility and personal accountability. This writing and the emerging thinking of complex responsive processes helped me also to understand in a different way the resistance to change which I experienced at work.

For five years following my introduction to Stacey's work, I continued to widen the scope of my reading about the issues that had attracted my interest. Eventually I applied to join the Doctor of Management (DMan) program which Stacey and some colleagues run as the Complexity and Management Centre (CMC) at the University of Hertfordshire. I have been a member of this research group since 2002 and, as a returning part-time adult student, have become caught up once again in the rituals of assessments and examinations. There are I realize close parallels between the power relationships of academic accountability and those which I encounter daily in my life as the head of a large educational establishment. Issues of accountability, legitimacy and justification therefore abound.

My own research work focuses on management and leadership. I am trying, through a process of structured and critical reflexive narratives, to make sense of *what is really happening* when people take on leadership roles in organizations. I am doing this also by working explicitly with the ideas, and I believe methodologies, of complex responsive processes. What follows are reflections concerning the issue of methodology as they have emerged from my thinking about work on the DMan program. My reflections are at the same time general and philosophical but rooted in a reflection on my own experiences of what I think of as *doing* a leadership role at work.

In this chapter, I am seeking to make sense of the idea of methodology as it affects my work in specific roles, as a researcher, a student on a university postgraduate program of study and as the head of one of the largest and most diverse multi-ethnic inner city colleges in the post-16 sector of the UK. I am interested in issues of methodology also because I sense that my experience of being, in the more general sense of how I live my everyday life, is in transformation as a result of my extended engagement with new ways of thinking about life in organizations. I believe my response to the challenge to justify what it is that I am doing is significant for how I, and others with whom I am related, academically, professionally, socially, go on together. I think that a response to the issues that emerge from the questions I have raised requires some consideration of issues of belief, truth and justification. These issues recur in multiple and different interactions.

At some point, someone who is examining me, in my final oral examination, will ask me about my methodology. As students, we can expect to be asked to justify our approach and also to account for how the outcomes of our research add to knowledge and to practice. Examiners will judge our responses to this question against criteria prepared by university staff members and legitimated by the university's quality assurance procedures. Here there is what I think of as a gatekeeping process at work. Examiners accredited by the university and I will participate in a very specific and encoded process of power relating. At the end of this process I will be judged by them to have passed or failed the threshold set for the award of a doctoral degree. The consequences of such a process will flow from my admission to, or rejection from, a privileged community of other academic passport holders. What I can say about myself after this event will, whether as a reflection upon success or failure, be significantly different from my personal narrative prior to this examination. Yet within this transaction marked by great power inequalities, there is also something of the paradox of Hegel's master–servant relationship at work. It is evident that the academic community in general, the academic community that is interested in complex responsive processes, and the university as a corporate entity with powers under statute to design, assess and award higher degrees, all actively need to admit members in order to remain as communities and organizations of collective academic interest. The social reproduction of the process of academic enquiry of itself necessitates insider–outsider relationships, rites of passage and ceremonials. In this, all the complexities associated with the paraphernalia of such processes (as Brecht illuminated in his play about the life of Galileo) are contingent upon the admissibility, in a context of bureaucratized power relating, of beliefs concerning the legitimacy of particular sets or strings of propositions and their constitution as knowledge.

Some people at work are interested in what I am doing on this doctoral program and have engaged me in conversation about it. More often, people who know I am 'doing a doctorate' think I should justify the money being spent on my fees by being demonstrably more competent in some way. They want me to explain how this program has 'made a difference'. They think of difference in terms of competence. I have not yet been able to reconcile the work I am doing on the program with this idea. I do not know what evidence I can give them that would be meaningful in terms of the way in which this question is asked. I think of this also as a problem of justification. Sometimes I worry about what my Board members might say if they ever read anything that I had been writing and asked me to justify the value-for-money basis of my participation on the program. As I have become aware of these questions in my work context, I have noticed also that my family say that I am to some extent different now from how I was before I joined the doctoral program. I take this to be evidence of a personal process of transformation. I would say that I have a sense of this but would find it difficult to describe in detail with illustrative examples. I find it hard to recognize the changes in how I think and feel about how I am living in the micro detail of my everyday actions. The changes that I feel myself to have experienced and continue to experience seem more subtle than would be evidenced by examples that say, 'before February 2002, I used to do *A*, now I do *B*'.

I started work on this chapter in order to explore three questions.

The first of these questions arose in the context of a preliminary oral examination when I was asked how I would account for the way in which my research efforts would make a contribution to knowledge and practice. The judgment that such a contribution has been made forms a key part of the assessment process leading to the award (or not) of a doctoral degree. After the examination I started to think about this question in terms of the deconstruction of its underlying propositions. These I understand to be expressed in the words 'contribution', 'knowledge' and 'practice'. As I reflected upon the question that was asked, it seemed to me that I had not clarified in my own thinking what each of these words might be taken to *mean* in such an examination context and therefore how I would or should argue my response. As I thought about this even more, I developed a sense that the question also states unconscious assumptions about knowledge as a stock of something that by virtue of contribution goes up.

This seemed to me to be redolent of other assumptions that prevail in the national and corporate policy context with regard to education and training, and concerning the ideas of a knowledge economy and knowledge management. Here there is what I take to be a belief, now an orthodoxy of public policy, that there is a direct relationship between the economic performance of the nation or the firm and the stock of knowledge held by its citizens or employees. Universities are very much a part of the drive to knowledge growth understood in these terms. I therefore started to question whether the academic criteria that inspired the question sit within this context of assumptions; for example, the disposition of academic authority and power in the university. I also started to question how I understand the nature and utility of enquiry processes other than via this paradigm.

The second question arose to some extent from the first. This question emerged in the debate that developed recently within the CMC group concerning the distinctions between complex responsive process thinking and action research (see Chapter 2, this volume). In thinking about the issues that started to emerge in this debate I found myself struggling with how to understand or, using a word that is germane to much of the rest of this chapter, *justify* the merits of one mode of discourse relative to another. This I believe was because while I find the difference in the form of ideas, argument and 'truth claims' between the two conversations as being self-evident, what I think of as the performative implications of this difference seem less clear. Put another way, I could, and still can, see how individuals and research communities adhere, in a highly committed way, to a particular mode of discourse or debate. What I feel less certain about is the consequential effect of such differences as they manifest in the real world actions of such individuals or in the actions of others influenced by their thinking. It occurs to me, for example, that those claiming to hold to radically different views of the world are often seen to act in broadly similar ways. The relationship between what we say about our beliefs and how we act upon them, or are perceived by others to be acting, is therefore not straightforward. What is the appropriate performative measure of differences between various theoretical standpoints? As I pursued my response to this question, I realized also that I wanted to try to clarify for myself the meaning of 'contribution' and how this should be scaled (for example, negligible, acceptable or significant). I wondered too about the idea of 'practice' as it is described in the assessment criteria for the program. In the round I think of my second question as a 'so what?' question.

My third question is a more personal one. As my participation in the research process goes on, I realize that I find it quite difficult to describe how this experience is affecting my practice and that of others with whom I work. More particularly, I can see two lines of argument with regard to this question that are neither essentially inclusive nor exclusive of each other.

The first is that my behavior at work is in reality not significantly different now from how it was when I first started working on this program of research. This is because how I behaved then and how I behave now is essential to doing my job. On this basis, I do not need to think of how I was doing my job in terms of notions of worse/better, less skilled/more skilled, less competent/more competent. I might argue that how I was judged to be performing by my Board has remained unchanged after joining the doctoral research group because their performance criteria have remained unchanged. The significant differences which have occurred over this period are less tangible to third parties but nevertheless significant to me. This I understand as a transformation in my personal narrative about my work, its context and my own relations with those whom I encounter in different settings. Here, I would argue that the effect of changes to my thinking has resulted in my ability to go on or to continue to function in a context that would otherwise have been intolerable. The research process and my engagement with new thinking about life in organizations has meant that I now relate to my work and working context differently. My sense is that my attitude to what I can practically do has changed and my perspective about what I, or any other person in a CEO role, can actually be accountable for is different as a consequence. Later I will suggest how I believe these changes to be evidenced in the way in which I go about doing my job.

My second line of argument is that although I can evidence ways in which my practice has changed, these have not been meaningful in a wider organizational context such that others could point to a quantum of difference in the way things 'are around here'. So I can say that I have tried to run meetings differently, draw senior managers into a large group process, bring to the surface of my consciousness the nature of my impact on others in relational contexts at work. But in relation to all of these things, I would say too that they have been very messy, imperfect and at times dangerously misunderstood fumblings on my part to recognize with integrity my role as a participant in a process whose actions are informed by particular thoughts about conduct and being. I would therefore struggle to feel confident in mounting an argument that any of this implied something as grand as 'a contribution to practice'.

The structure of the rest of this chapter follows my attempt to grapple with these questions. In the first part I take up the arguments of Richard Rorty and Donald Davidson with respect to belief, truth and justification. I do so with the intention of exploring further the issue of meaning in relation to the ideas of 'contribution' and 'knowledge'. In the second part I review the work of Habermas in terms of his understanding of the nature of discourse and how different discourses are justified. Here I try to link my own thinking about the idea of differentiation between discourses (the complex responsive process/action research debate) to Habermas' concept of justification. In the final section I turn to Elias' work on involvement and detachment in order to theorize the nature of my own experience of the relationship between enquiry and being.

What it means to contribute to knowledge: fuzziness and solidarity

I want to begin responding to these questions by taking up Richard Rorty's position on the ideas of belief and truth and in turn of the relationship between belief, truth and justification. Rorty's position on the meaning of these ideas sits within the traditions of philosophical pragmatism. His position on the idea of truth as absolute insight is clear:

> Pragmatists – both classical and 'neo' – do not believe that there is a way things really are. So they want to replace the appearance–reality distinction by that between descriptions of the world and of ourselves which are less useful and those which are more useful. When the question 'useful for what?' is pressed, they have nothing to say except 'useful to create a better future'. When they are asked 'Better by what criterion?' they have no detailed answer, any more than the first mammals could specify in what respects they were better than the dying dinosaurs.
>
> (Rorty 1999, p. 27)

For Rorty, there is no point at which a positivistic claim to truth can be satisfied. His argument is that all claims to truth rest upon a combination of interpretation and justification. If this is the case, Rorty argues, why not simply give up on the idea that human processes of enquiry can ever gain access to ultimate or absolute truth? The key question of legitimation for Rorty therefore relates not to ways in which claims to truth can, by being grounded in the absolute, resist refutation but upon their utility as beliefs for the sense-making processes that inform ongoing human interaction. In Rorty's philosophy what can be justified is what is true. The insights of dominant intellectual traditions therefore take on the mantle of truths because it is these ideas and traditions that, in the moment that they are taken up, have survived. 'Justification is always justification from the point of view of the survivors, the victors; there is no point of view more exalted than theirs to assume' (ibid.).

Rorty's position on truth and justification draws attention both to the idea of discourse and to that of ethics. From Rorty's perspective truth emerges as a result of contention arising in the flow of debate. As such, truth is contingent equally upon the historical-cultural determinants of what is acceptable as justification and upon techniques of argumentation rather than to appeals to an absolute (Rorty 1998, pp. 32–33). This, for example, is how Rorty understands the nature of scientific enquiry. It is also the basis upon which Rorty has argued for a sense of equivalence in the status of creative modes of understanding experience relative to science. Rorty refutes the idea that science is, for all its claims to reason and empiricism, closer *per se* in its representation of reality than art: 'The image of the great scientist [should] not be of somebody who got it right but of somebody who made it new' (Rorty 1991, p. 44). Rorty's exhortation is therefore to abandon the pursuit of an absolute truth and to focus on what 'works' and what can be justified. It is clear also that Rorty's position makes sense only in the context of the practice of a participative ethical standpoint. Like Dewey and Mead before him, Rorty is optimistic about the capacity of American liberal democracy to enable (in the long run) the enrichment of the human condition in processes of fully engaged and inclusive citizenship. While I declare myself to be skeptical of Rorty's optimism in this regard, this point is important insofar as Rorty's philosophical position in relation to the possibility of (what I will call) *true belief* is contingent upon the existence of political and ideological pluralism and an understanding of this in terms of the claims of the advocates of American liberal democracy. Rorty himself actively embraces the idea of fellowship with other 'non-authoritarian' philosophies (Rorty 1999, p. 238) as essential to such flowering. Rorty says that on this basis he is content with 'fuzziness' in lieu of certainty. It is fuzziness, or *solidarity* in the face of the unknowable, rather than certainty, which provides the impulse to dialogue and an ongoing search for meaning and understanding.

In Rorty's philosophy of truth, I therefore detect also an empathy with the Gramscian concept of hegemony. Here intellectual order, the socio-politically legitimated, acceptable standpoint, emerges in processes of power relating. Such order, however, also entails vigilance and maintenance on the part of the 'victors'. Dissent, the ongoing struggle for air-time on the part of the vanquished, is however critical both to maintaining the integrity of the dominant discourse and as an ongoing process of conflict holds out the permanent possibility for a transformation in the nature of what is deemed to be right.

In terms of my preoccupations in this chapter, I take Rorty's concept of fuzziness to be significant for how a legitimate contribution to knowledge can arise in the absence of a belief in, or a commitment to, a positivist view of certainty. I believe that Rorty is arguing here that as each of us struggles to make sense of what is going on around us, we create new narratives of experience that become woven with those of others into an architecture of understanding that enables us all to go on together. Solidarity, it seems to me, signifies both that we each have the ability to recognize the sense-making struggles of others and to collaborate with each other in co-evolving new ways of understanding. These Rortian attitudes seem to me to be directly germane to the research activities that I associate with the idea of complex responsive processes and to the product of research outcomes informed by such a way of thinking. These are most often detailed and extended reflective narratives of experience that integrate (weave, in Rorty's terms) the intensely localized character of individually recalled life experiences explicitly with a critical theoretical perspective.

Rorty's abandonment of truth makes sense understood as giving up on the idea of finding a point of ultimate empirical or positivistic explanation. In substituting belief and justification for truth, Rorty is arguing for a different measure of what is to be accepted as evidence of real. I understand Rorty to be arguing that justification is a process undertaken in relation to belief, and that there is no need to go beyond belief in order to say something that is legitimate about the world and our experiences. Here it is important to appreciate that while the fundamentals of Rorty's position are grounded in Dewey and pragmatism, much of the way in which he specifies the ideas of truth, belief and justification derive from his debates with the philosopher Donald Davidson. This issue, the validity of first-person experience as authority, is what has preoccupied much of Davidson's work and what has led him, in his debates with Rorty, to develop notions of community as a basis or context within which the veracity of individual experience is tested relative to a wider claim to legitimacy. Davidson, I think, shifts the locus of concern from a preoccupation with either the absolute or the purely subjective to ways in which significant generalized meaning emerges intersubjectively. Davidson's concept of *triangulation*, to which I refer below, is therefore a metaphor to describe the occurrence of an emergent intersubjective reality. This is then a basis upon which claims to truth may be made which are neither appeals to a positivist sense of the absolute nor simply the witnessing of purely subjective experience.

Belief, community and triangulation

Davidson's philosophy, like Rorty's, is preoccupied with the issue of how it is that we can have certainty with regard to anything we might think we know about our environment and our experiences of being a part of it. Here I want to summarize what I take to be Davidson's argument because I think that he, in combination with Rorty, has much to offer that is relevant to thinking about both the mechanics and (academic) legitimation of shifts in thinking that result from enquiry processes. I also think that the way in which Davidson appears to resolve the question of how we can say that we 'know' anything is relevant to the thinking of complex responsive processes and particularly to my conviction that the idea of complex responsive processes posits simultaneously both an object of research and a process of enquiry.

Davidson proposes that each of us is always in possession of three types of knowledge: knowledge of our own minds (for which we have unique first-person authority); knowledge of 'what is going on' in other people's minds; and knowledge of the world around us. The issue for Davidson is that while each of these 'varieties of knowledge' exists relative to a single, commonly shared reality, none on its own may be said to provide a basis upon which authoritative statements about the nature of the real can be made:

> no amount of knowledge of the contents of one's own mind ensures the truth of a belief about the external world. The logical independence of the mental works equally in the other direction: no amount of knowledge of the external world entails the truth about the workings of a mind. If there is a logical or epistemic barrier between the mind and nature, it not only prevents us from seeing out; it also blocks view from outside in.
>
> (Davidson 2001a, p. 207)

From this, Davidson argues that it is only possible for us to make assertions about the nature of the real in the form of belief statements; that is, propositions as to the nature of what is true. It is this ability, namely of responding in belief statements to the experiences of sensations of being in a commonly shared real world, that enables us to exist as rational social animals. In reading Davidson and reading across from Davidson to Mead, I interpret his reference to 'making statements' as being directed both into a social world of intersubjective communication and directed to ourselves in the silent conversations we enact and experience as mind.

But if, as Davidson and Rorty both propose, statements of belief are as far as we can get in our accounts of our own and others' experiences, how are we able to discriminate between beliefs that are legitimate (in the sense of their reality congruence) from beliefs that are simply mistaken or false? Equivalently, how do we get from a purely individualized or subjective representation of real world experience to a position that is socially or objectively valid? Further, how is it that our beliefs are able to inform reliably our actions and the actions of others whom we encounter in our social relationships?

I understand Davidson's answer to these questions in the following terms.

Davidson argues that the origination of belief is in sensory experience. For Davidson, it is because we inhabit a real world in relation to which we have experiences and because this world is commonly shared by others with self-similar attributes of perception and intelligence that we make assertions through the medium of language to one another about the nature of this experience. It is in this way that we are able to have what we understand to be beliefs. Beliefs are therefore what arise for us naturally as the way in which we process sensations. It is evident here that Davidson, as do Rorty, Mead, Dewey and other more contemporary writers in the neuro-biological sciences, rejects mind–body dualism in favor of the kind of 'somatic-marker' thesis of body/mind sensation as elaborated, for example, by Damasio (1994, 1999). Thus for Davidson, the world is pre-given to our experience. As such, its relationship with the emergence of belief is causal in that our interaction with the world beyond our own bodies leads us to experience the sensations upon which our beliefs and our hypotheses concerning the beliefs of others arise. But how is it that our personal experience of being is able to be validated sufficient for it to form a basis for action for ourselves and for our interactions with others?

Here Davidson offers two explanations of how such a validation process actually occurs in the ongoing conduct of human relationships. Davidson describes the mechanics of this process as *triangulation* and represents it in the example of a situation involving a threefold interaction: 'two or more creatures simultaneously in interaction with each other and the world they share' (Davidson 2001b, p. 128):

> [*triangulation*] is the result of a threefold interaction, an interaction which is twofold from the point of view of each of the two agents: each is interacting simultaneously with the world and with the other agent.
>
> (Ibid.)

Davidson's argument here concerning the emergence of meaning in human interaction is clearly of the same kind as that of Mead's thesis of gesture and response. Like Mead, Davidson argues that the triangulation process occurs between animals as it occurs between humans. Davidson is drawing attention to the ways in which the behavior of most creatures is both fundamentally social in relation to each other and their species in relation to a pre-given environment. The distinction Davidson makes between human beings and the rest is, as Mead, in the use of symbolic forms to communicate meaning. Here Davidson draws directly upon the thinking of Wittgenstein to illuminate the enabling constraints of language as a communication medium between human beings. But it is in terms of belief and how the 'reality' of individuals' beliefs is authenticated that Davidson, I believe, offers views directly pertinent to the thinking of complex responsive processes. By taking the *triangulation* idea further and into the medium of linguistic communication Davidson situates validation in processes of complex social acts, and argues that language (as social, not private to an individual) is a context in which assumptions with regard to belief are normalized between subjects inhabiting the same primary reality. It is therefore only through the social exchange/interchange of propositions about what is going on around us that we are able to determine the true/false nature of our beliefs. It is the social process of interpretation which guarantees:

> that both a large number of our simplest perceptual beliefs are true and that the nature of these beliefs is known to others. Of course many beliefs are given content by their relations to further beliefs, or are caused by misleading sensations; any particular belief or set of beliefs about the world around us may be false. What cannot be the case is that our general picture of the world and our place in it is mistaken, for

it is this picture which informs the rest of our beliefs and makes them intelligible.

(Davidson 2001a, pp. 213–214)

Rorty and Davidson: some implications

The arguments of Rorty and Davidson seem to me to invite thinking about the product of enquiry processes in terms of challenges, transformations and movements in the nature of the propositional beliefs held by the enquirer. This I understand to be in the same conceptual terrain as that of the idea of the dialectic of negation in Hegelian philosophy. The radical difference between the position of Rorty and Davidson and that of Hegel, however, would be in the absence of any concept of the absolute as a point of destination occurring somehow at the end of the dialectical process. The idea of a contribution to knowledge and to practice is therefore to be understood qualitatively and not in terms of quantum.

Taking Rorty's argument about desirable ways of seeing scientists (as creators of new interpretations rather than solvers of problems) it seems clear that individuals who engage at depth with almost any kind of research problem will experience and be experienced by others as fitting into their social nexus differently, in the course of and after the event, from how they were before they began. In Rorty's philosophy our beliefs, as our representation to ourselves of our experience of the real and how it really is, are pretty much one and the same thing.

I regard beliefs as states attributed to organisms of a certain complexity – attributions which enable the attributor to predict or retrodict (mostly retrodict) the behavior of that organism. Thus the web of belief should be regarded not only as a self-weaving mechanism but as one which produces movements in the organism's muscles – movements which kick the organism itself into action. These actions, by shoving items in the environment around, produce new beliefs to be woven in, which in turn produce new actions, and so on for as long as the organism survives (Rorty 1991, p. 93).

In my view, Davidson draws our attention to the significance of community to research enquiry and practice. Davidson's position on meaning as emergent from *triangulation* implies that participation in processes of critical discourse with others is fundamental to securing the legitimacy of the propositional nature of research findings. However structured, research is only validated in a wider community of argumentation. To reject a positivist standpoint in relation to truth necessitates the substitution of a model of the monadic empiricist researcher as isolate for one that makes essential participation in a social process of enquiry.

The question that arises in the recognition of the essential requirement for a researcher to be affiliated with a community of practice (or discourse) is how that community, in its turn, legitimates its collective belief structure relative to that of other, possibly contending, communities.

If assumptions regarding legitimization for a process of enquiry shift from truth to justification and from an individual to a social perspective, what are the implications? What are the routines of argumentation that would be associated with the idea of justification once the idea of truth, in the evidentially verifiable sense, is abandoned? How do/can communities of enquirers establish, or seek to establish, the integrity of their own webs of belief relative to those elaborated by others? Here I want to turn to Jurgen Habermas and his arguments concerning communicative action theory and discourse ethics.

Justification and discourse

In working with Habermas' argument, I am also going to signal what for me is an essential connection between what Habermas describes as justification and what I think of also as differentiation. I think of the linkage between justification and differentiation as important for the following reasons. I situate my own current research experience and thinking within a specific context of discourse: complex responsive processes. Quite apart from the issue of how I attempt to justify my 'findings' as a result of working within this frame, there exists also the related question of how working with complex responsive process thinking differs from other modes of enquiry, such as action research. The issue of justification therefore seems to me to be also one of differentiation. Justifying a particular way of working will necessarily draw out points of differentiation. The act of justification of itself will lead to the development of an argument in which there is discrimination between different interpretations. Arguments, it seems to me, have boundaries. The integrity of a position or view of the world is sustained on the basis of its difference relative to that of others. In terms of simple set theory this means that all processes of argument are at the same time inclusive and exclusive. The dynamic character of a line of argument is therefore to a large extent in the degree to which it sustains the paradox of being at the same time permeable and malleable in the face of alternatives, yet able to sustain its inherent integrity. This, I think, is what Rorty is referring to in his idea of fuzziness and what I think of as implied by the idea of discourse. This, in terms of the arguments of Rorty and Davidson, is because while the great majority of our beliefs are true beliefs, we all adhere to many that are not. Argument between participants in a shared discipline of enquiry and between adherents to different views therefore has the effect of testing and moving the boundaries of true as against false belief (Davidson 2001a, pp. 199–202).

In the context of arguing for the validity of his theory of discourse ethics, Habermas has suggested that there are two steps necessary for any process of philosophical justification. Here, as suggested above, I take the idea of justification to signify also the idea of differentiation. Habermas argues that the first step in this process is one of establishing some principles that amount to the universalization of an underlying argument (Habermas 1990, p. 116). I think that Habermas' principles of universalization seek to retain something of Kantian universals and in so doing differ from the arguments of Rorty and Davidson who abandon universals and truth, taking up instead the concept of belief. The latter approach is closer to the notion of fundamental proposition related to a complex responsive processes view of method (see Chapter 2, this volume) where this way of looking at the world is itself contingent upon an acceptance of fundamental general propositions relating to consciousness, emergence, teleology and power which are always in the process of evolution. Habermas' second step relates to the idea that validity claims emerge in processes of critique (Habermas 1990). Habermas' work on communicative action theory highlights also the importance of seeing argument as being essential for creativity. New possibilities for thinking, understanding, relating, are conditional upon both the identification and representation of differences between 'interlocutors' and their capacity to sustain a process of discourse concerning these differences. This second step is much the same as the complex responsive processes approach.

The process of critique of the work of others therefore has two effects. The first is that critique enables a demonstration of difference and so has the potential also to illuminate underlying validity claims. The second is that critique is a process that invites development. The action of developing a critique of the work of others has, except in instances that are purely ideological in character, a reflexive dimension which takes the forms of both silent conversation with oneself and public debate. Both processes give rise to change in the form of new insights, thoughts and critical expositions which are transformative and unpredictable. For these reasons, processes of critique are paradoxically at the same time efforts to generalize a claim to truth and a means of establishing new truths; truths not yet captured by, or available to, the original line of argument.

By extension, creative possibilities cease to exist at a point when all the parties to a debate find themselves in agreement or where some are excluded by the action of others who refuse, for whatever reason, to engage with them. This argument introduces important issues of ethics in relation to the conduct of claims to truth as evidenced by what Habermas thinks happens when dialogue is felt to be no longer possible. In relation to his more general action theory, Habermas therefore sees social conduct in terms of actions emerging either from a context of active discourse in which norms of purposive relating are recognized by the participants, though not necessarily also on a basis of consensus, or from what he describes as strategic behavior on the part of one, the most powerful, acting alone against the other:

> Strategic action can be considered as a limiting case of communicative action; it occurs when ordinary language communication between interlocutors breaks down as a means of maintaining consensus, and each assumes an objectifying attitude toward the other.
>
> (Habermas 2001, pp. 12–13)

For the purposes of what I am trying to explore here in relation to methodologies, I want to draw attention to what I see as three of the significant implications of Habermas' theoretical position. The first is that the coexistence of contradictory or contending positions is essential to the process of substantiating the validity of any one claim to truth. This is for the reason that without difference no one claim to truth has criteria against which its relative attractiveness may be evaluated. The second is that sameness neutralizes creativity and is more likely to be evidence of totalitarianism than of consensual agreement. The third links Habermas back to Rorty and Davidson. Where Davidson refers to triangulation, Habermas refers to values and normalization. Both are referring to a social context as the basis of legitimation of what constitute *true beliefs*. It is therefore in the social context of what is generally held to be true that the appearance–reality issue is resolved. It is resolved in the first instance relative to the membership of a particular community of enquiry (they understand their own boundaries of agreement and disagreement), and in the second instance in a general social context which will or will not tolerate the group's existence. This, I think, links back also to Rorty's point about the historical-cultural determinants of the grounds that establish the bases for justification: beyond the margin of this tolerance there is censorship, heresy and book-burning.

Habermas is helpful too in terms of situating the thinking of complex responsive processes within a broader epistemology. In developing his own communicative action theory Habermas has created 'a framework to differentiate between different construction theories of society'. Four models are identified:

First model: *The knowing subject*. Habermas contrasts the ideas of Kant and Husserl with those of Hegel and Marx but sees similarities in their focus on a knowing or judging subject. 'Constitutive theories attribute the process of [social] generation to an acting subject. The subject can be either an intelligible ego modeled after the empirical individual subject or . . . a species subject constituting itself in history.'

Second and third models: *Structuralism and systems theories*. In these models, Habermas argues, the generative social process is understood in terms of deep structures that are without subject. 'Structuralism models these on grammar, whereas systems theory thinks of them as self-regulating.'

Fourth model: *Speech and interaction*. 'Here we are dealing with the generation of interpersonal situations of speaking and acting together – that is, with the form of the intersubjectivity of possible understanding.' Habermas cites G. H. Mead and Wittgenstein within this category (Habermas 2001, pp. 15–16).

My argument is that complex responsive process thinking is situated within the fourth of Habermas' generative social models. Much of the writing that is now associated with complex responsive processes is also in the form of a critique of writers whose work would be associated with Habermas' first, second and third models. From the perspective of complex responsive process thinking, other discourses (e.g. complex adaptive systems theory, psychoanalysis, learning organization theory, autopoietic theories) are felt to offer analogies or insights that are helpful. At the same time, they are held to offer only partial or inaccurate explanations. Systems thinking, it is argued, cannot explain the nature of human interaction. It leads to a false prospectus. Systems thinkers, notwithstanding their power dominance in our current cultural context, are simply wrong. Complex responsive process thinking therefore asserts the necessity of process thinking, an understanding of concepts of emergence, transformative teleology and power relations for a valid reality-congruent mode of enquiry.

Habermas' framework of generative theories of society is therefore helpful at a high level in differentiating complex responsive process thinking from other dominant traditions of Western thought. This approach also illuminates something of the nature of the generalized validity claims that differentiate complex responsive process thinking from other generative models which presuppose intersubjective or symbolic interchange between social agents. The limitation of Habermas' framework in this particular context is that it does not assist particularly with the process of differentiating complex responsive process thinking from other modes of discourse that can also be situated within his fourth model of generative theories.

Complex responsive processes and action research

In Chapter 2 of this volume, Stacey and Griffin took up this same issue in their critique of action research. At the outset, they draw attention to the apparent similarities between complex responsive process thinking and action research but go on to say:

> there are fundamental differences between the two approaches and these may not be all that immediately obvious because, although both use the same words, they have different meanings. In particular, the words 'action', 'participation', 'relationship', 'experience' and 'emergence' have substantially different meanings in the two approaches.
>
> (Stacey and Griffin, p. 28)

Stacey and Griffin then go on to argue that there are significant differences between the two approaches. Action research, it is argued, takes a metaphysical and systemic view of the world: this is not the case with complex responsive processes. Some action researchers adopt a participative view of human relationships that is linked to an idea of spiritual or ecstatic ways of establishing interconnectedness between individuals. Further, action research sets a systemic view of social phenomena apart from the notion of the individual: complex responsive process thinking sees the individual and the social as different aspects of the same phenomenon. Stacey and Griffin also point to differences between the approaches with respect to learning, action theories and ethics.

By focusing in this way on language and the use and meaning of words, Stacey and Griffin seem to me to be pointing to an idea that is very important to a sense of wider debate. This is that it is the underlying narratives linking these words together, rather than the words themselves, that are significant of radically different action consequences. This I take to be consistent with Rorty's view that each of us is no more than a web of beliefs that is formed and reforming at the same time in ways which both enable and constrain our abilities as actors (Rorty 1991, p. 93). Thus in this sense, it is the narrative account which makes use of a particular set of words that is significant in action terms: it is not the semantics of word meanings and definitions *per se*. To the extent that it is in our ongoing reflexive narratives that we have a knowledge of ourselves, our personal narrative structures are also those which form our principal filtering devices both in terms of what we notice about what is going on around us and how we frame our individual action responses. Rorty too makes this connection in a series of propositions in which he argues that we can 'treat our desires as if they were beliefs' and that 'beliefs are habits of action' (ibid.).

To some extent, this view also assists with providing an answer to what I think of as the 'so what' question: So what if one group of researchers believe in a connectedness with ecstatic ways of knowing, other than that another group believes them to be fantasists or to be acting in the grip of a false consciousness? What is it that makes the belief statements of action researchers objectionable other than another underlying belief about the consequences of the beliefs of action researchers as a basis for social action? I would argue that strictly speaking, there is no directly performative response to these questions. Once it is clear that there is no distinction to be made between the narratives of those whose minds are preoccupied with the thinking of action research and their social action, then the issue of value and legitimacy becomes one tested in a wider social process involving argument and counter-argument. Equivalently, those engaged with the thinking of complex responsive processes will in their ongoing social interactions with others experience these with a particular and qualitative difference. Their actions, too, will be different but not necessarily imbued with a greater degree of 'rightness' other than that which is accepted in the community as right for the occasion. The performative legitimacy of these knowledge narratives is then established in contexts of power relating. These too are essentially social in that life in organizations is an instance of wider social power-relating processes that enable some belief structures to be justified as knowledge with performative utility rather than fantasy or false consciousness.

I see these issues of the indeterminacy of 'right' and 'value' as being situated within the overall problematic of justification. It is a question also with significant implications for government policies with regard to education and training and upon what such policies place value. It has implications too for how organizations prioritize resources to enable personal and professional development. How, at either national policy or local policy levels, is the payback from postgraduate organizational research to be evaluated if not in terms of bottom-line performative outcomes such as enhanced occupational competence, greater value generation and improved effectiveness and efficiency in the attainment of core business and operational objectives? It seems to me to be very difficult to respond to these questions in the positive without recourse to layers of abstraction about organizational learning, motivation theory and mental acuity. In terms of a more general ethical standpoint, I am also unconvinced that in return for 'sponsorship', researchers have a contractual obligation to deliver a return on the investment that has been made in them in terms of the conventional assumed methods of appraising the organizational benefits of individual learning experiences.

Research of the kind with which my peers and I are engaged in the Doctoral program is undertaken in a context of academic freedom. This I think creates an entitlement to do two things differently. The first is to think of oneself as an enquirer reflecting upon aspects of the nature of human experience, for example, life in organizations generally. Such processes may or may not result in a directly beneficial performative outcome in the workplace. The second is to think about particular organizational settings, modes of relating and purposes differently. This too may not result in a directly performative outcome for a sponsor, but it may sharpen or refocus the action orientation of the enquirer in contexts that are organizationally specific or more generally referenced in their ongoing behaviors as citizens. This is without prejudice to whether or not their behaviors in either context are more or less conforming. Here I find myself drawn back to Rorty's ideas of 'fuzziness' and 'hope' as legitimate bases from which to justify the validity of a discourse. The orientation of a line of research enquiry can legitimately engage with issues of human capacity for what Rorty describes as 'betterment', without being utopian and without collapsing those questions into an instrumentalism that implies the researcher being or becoming possessed of answers. The researcher may become simply a participant in ongoing processes of interaction that are qualitatively different but this is not of itself indicative of a power weight understood in terms of new or additional expertise. Research and solutionism in the performative sense do not necessarily go hand in hand. Foucault once argued that to problematize something does not necessarily entail a responsibility for proposing a solution. I find myself in agreement with Foucault's point here and find acceptable too his idea that problematization, occurring as it does in dialogue, is of itself an appropriate and ethical standpoint to adopt in processes of enquiry (Foucault 1997).

Issues of practice: problems of involvement and detachment

When I try to draw together the foregoing themes and to understand them in terms of my own experiences of work, of living outside of work, of research and its impact upon me in terms of the changes that I am aware of in my attitudes, feelings and emotional responses, I am drawn to Norbert Elias' thesis regarding the ideas of involvement and detachment.

I reflect upon the past three years of life at work as being among the most demanding of my career. I understand these demands in terms of the physicality of sustaining a heavy workload while experiencing great personal stress. I have also been exposed in new ways to my experience to the effects on large numbers of colleagues of the application of arbitrary power, mass shaming and the sustained use of orchestrated threats to identity as a vehicle for assuring compliance and conformity. I have been deeply challenged in this experience in terms of sustaining and reworking my own narrative of myself as a senior manager, and have lived through many occasions in the past thirty-six months where I have found it difficult to maintain my confidence in my abilities. In addition, as the head of an organization employing 1,000 individuals and working within a complex web of interdependent other relationships, I have had to take account of this context in my personal dealings at work, since it has affected large numbers of people in a wide range of positions of authority or non-authority relative to the organization. For these reasons, I have come to identify my felt personal experience of this period of my professional life with Elias' reworking of Poe's narrative concerning 'The Fishermen in the Maelstrom'. Thus when I write about Elias in my reflections on methodology it is with a sense of personal identification with the themes he is exploring.

After reading the essay 'The Fishermen in the Maelstrom' I was intrigued to understand what it was about Poe's original story that had captured Elias' imagination so profoundly. What had Elias noticed in his reading of Poe?

The title of Poe's short story is 'Descent into the Maelstrom'. The story is set in a fictional location within sight of the coast of Norway. It is also the narrative of a survivor whose life has been transformed by the experiences he is retelling. Poe's literary device is to locate the voice of the story with a narrator to whom the fisherman in his turn told his own story. This has the effect of drawing the reader into the piece as a witness to the events. The background descriptions of the landscape and seascape also draw the reader into the locale of the story from which, close to the horizon, the terrible events of the maelstrom are retold. Poe's literary devices are, I would argue, intended to arouse in the reader the kind of affectual intensity of response, to be as one in the situation, as that later described by the fisherman in his own account. I think therefore that Elias viewed this story in his own creative imagination as an experience of high emotivity sufficient to trigger his reflections about involvement and detachment.

More specifically, my hypothesis is that Elias' imagination was excited by a particular passage in the story in which the fisherman recounts his direct experience of being in the maelstrom. The point here is about the observation of detail. I think Elias was attracted to the way in which Poe describes the fisherman's emerging sense of awareness. At first, we encounter the fisherman overwhelmed by the scale and intensity of his situation. However, as he looks out from his position in the boat he notices, against the vastness of the background of the raging ocean (the 'wide waste of liquid ebony'), increasing points of detail. The fisherman becomes preoccupied in his thinking with the flotsam that he observes riding the sides of the whirlpool into which he is being sucked. He progressively itemizes and then differentiates this material.

> Both above and below us were visible fragments of vessels, large masses of building timber and trunks of trees, with many smaller articles, such as pieces of house furniture, broken boxes, barrels and staves. I have already described the unnatural curiosity which had taken the place of my original terrors. It appeared to grow on me as I drew nearer and nearer to my dreadful doom. I now began to watch

with a strange interest, the numerous things that floated in our
company. I must have been delirious for I even sought amusement in
speculating upon the relative velocities of the several descents toward
the foam below.

(Poe 2003, p. 102)

Later, towards the end of this passage, the fisherman reflects:

how what I observed was, in fact the natural consequence of the forms
of floating fragments . . . and how it happened that a cylinder,
swimming in a vortex, offered more resistance to its suction, and was
drawn in with greater difficulty than an equally bulky body of any
form whatever.

(Ibid., p. 104)

At this point in the story Poe cites Archimedes' *De Incidentibus in
Fluido, lib 2* as a reference source to substantiate the scientific integrity of
the observations of his fictional character.

What Elias is noticing in Poe's story is the portrayal of a subtle but
significant movement in the relationship between the fisherman, his
physical (or situational context) and his emotional response to this
context. The fisherman never ceases to be fully immersed in this context.
Poe does not depict him as in any way rising above it, or being in control
of it. The narrative point is that the fisherman is able to use insight into
his situation, to hold himself back from his fear, in order to act in a way
that alters his position relative to the prevailing flow of events.
Significantly, the fisherman's insight is not the function on his part of the
direct application of scientific knowledge or equivalently that of a
scientific method. He recounts to the narrator how later on, after his
survival, he asked a school teacher whom he knew to explain the science
behind his observation about the buoyancy of large cylindrical objects.
The key point about the fisherman is really that in the situation of crisis,
he is able to intuit a course of action by arresting, taking command of, his
affectual responses. I believe Elias was drawn to this example because in
so much of his writing about language, power, social formations and
individualization he attempts to understand antecedent conditions of what
he describes as 'not knowing' in order to explicate the processual changes
necessary for 'knowing' to come about. In Elias' general thesis about
change there are no absolute beginnings. This is a recurrent theme
throughout all of his writing and one to which he refers explicitly in his
Two Fragments: Reflections on the Great Evolution; that is, his narrative

about the emergence and subsequent cultural dominance of scientific method. For Elias, the human capacity to intuit new ways of understanding reality contexts interdependently with adjustments to the physical and affectual relationship occurring between people and their environment (social, physical) is part of the explanation for breaks or leaps between epochs characterized by movements in knowledge and understanding.

As I have become drawn further into Elias' thinking about involvement and detachment I have been interested too in the connections between Poe's story, Elias' use of this story as a metaphor for wider human processes and Freud's writing about anxiety. In his introductory lecture on anxiety Freud distinguished two categories of anxiety state: neurotic anxiety and realistic anxiety. He devoted a considerable part of the lecture to explaining why anxiety states can lead to paralysis in the form of an inability to act. He also linked anxiety to the flight response. In his analysis of what anxiety is for, Freud attempted to understand its significance by describing an optimal response to a perception of danger in terms recognizably the same as those associated with the procedures of scientific method:

> the only expedient behavior when a danger threatens would be a cool estimate of one's own strength in comparison with the magnitude of the threat and, on the basis of that, a decision as to whether flight or defense, or possibly even attack, offers the best prospect of a successful issue. But in this situation there is no place at all for anxiety.
>
> (Freud 2001, p. 394)

How then to understand the utility of anxiety? Freud associated anxiety with 'preparedness' for action and described the affectual state of anxiety as one which provides a 'signal' (what Rorty might call a 'raw feel') leading to action. In Freud's terms, anxiety is a stage in a more complex social act. Freud argued that for anxiety to have this 'expedient benefit' its generation had to be 'limited to a mere abortive beginning'. Beyond this point, anxiety has the dysfunctional effect of immobilizing the capacity for action.

To summarize, my argument is that Elias used Poe's story as a metaphor for the situations that arise in human experience where individuals take on the feeling of being overwhelmed by the strength of the forces which they feel to be arraigned against them. The degree of anxiety that they feel in relation to such situations shifts from being a stimulus for effective action to being the cause of paralysis. Reading Elias' essay it is clear that he intended, and indeed used, this metaphor to apply variously to what he argued was the relationship between pre-scientific communities and nature, double-bind situations in contemporary international relations in this essay (Elias is preoccupied with the arms race and the cold war of the mid-twentieth century) and the more micro-level experience of individuals. What Elias was able to characterize in the use of Poe's story as metaphor, therefore, was the common aspects of the human condition in which the character of action is formed in the interdependent relationship existing between individuals' emotional responses and their sensed experience of their wider environment.

Throughout his essay, Elias moves between references to the environment that are physical and social in nature. It is in the development of Poe's story as metaphor that Elias develops also his key concept of *emotivity*. Elias uses the idea of emotivity to scale what he depicts as degrees of involvement and detachment experienced in the feeling states of individuals in response to their environmental conditions. I therefore interpret the way in which Elias juxtaposes involvement and detachment as polarities in a range of potential emotional responses also in terms of an extension of this story as a metaphorical device. What I think Elias is attempting to illustrate here is that *emotivity* takes the form of an enabling constraint in relation to all human action.

Elias' argument is that involvement and detachment cannot in reality be thought of as polarities. No one can be detached (emotionally) from his or her own experience. Yet Elias also observes from multiple narratives drawn from science, art, tribal cultures, narratives of experience and fiction that in different socio-cultural contexts and over different spans of time, people have demonstrated varied abilities to constrain their affectual responses to their surroundings. The human ability to pacify nature via the application of technologies of control, he argues, has been the result of a long-run process in which human beings have constrained their 'momentary impulses' in order to evolve technologies that have given them 'mastery' (short of catastrophic natural disasters) of the natural environment. This he describes as a *process* of detachment. In the example of 'The Fishermen in the Maelstrom' this theme recurs in another form:

> The fisherman found himself involved in a critical process which at
> first appeared wholly beyond his control. For a time, he may have

clutched at some imaginary hopes. Fantasies of a miracle, of help from some unseen persons, may have crossed his mind. After a while, however, he calmed down. He began to think more coolly; and by standing back, by controlling his fear, by seeing himself, as it were, from a distance like a figure on a chess-board forming a pattern with others, he managed to turn his thoughts away from himself to the situation in which he was caught up.

(Elias 1987, p. 46)

Later and more theoretically he goes on:

The parable of the fisherman underlines the functional interdependence of a person's emotional balance and the wider process to which it is geared. It brings into fuller relief the possible circularity of this relationship. . . . High exposure to the dangers of a process tends to heighten the emotivity of human responses. High emotivity of response lessens the chance of a realistic assessment of the critical process and hence, of a realistic practice in relation to it; relatively unrealistic practice under the pressure of strong affects lessens the chance of bringing the critical process under control.

(Ibid., p. 48)

What I find significant in these passages from Elias are the following:

- He is specifically not proposing a simple dichotomy between involvement and detachment as polarities in a binary model of feeling or awareness states.
- He is however describing (what I am going to call) a *reflexive process of emergent self-awareness* in which the interdependence of all relationships is at the same time fully recognized.
- He is also describing processes in which an adjustment to the character of self-awareness (new knowledge) changes the character of agent action responses.
- He highlights too the possibilities for 'fantasy'-oriented responses and 'realistic practices' to be present at the same time in an action response, subject to the 'emotivity' surrounding the felt experience at hand.

First-person authority

Elias' analysis of *emotivity* as constraining the emergence of both reality-congruent knowledge and reality-oriented action is, I believe, fundamental to any argument that I would make about what is distinctive in what we are doing when we are working explicitly with the thinking of complex responsive processes.

Although I have referred to changes in my sense of thinking and belief as a result of undertaking this research process, I believe that the major contribution of this work to my practice is that I have been able to sustain my ability to carry on in what might otherwise have been an intolerable situation. This I attribute to the fact that in the process of enquiring about myself, my role, my relationships with others, my situation in a complex figuration of interdependent relationships with others, I have experienced a movement in my emotional responses to this organizational context. In a sense, nothing much has changed other than my feelings regarding my position in relation to what is happening around me: I can explain this differently and in ways that make sense as I observe them every day. Moreover, I can check my re-formed narrative with the narratives of others also engaged in processes of enquiry that question fundamentally many of the commonsense propositions that are supposed to account for 'how it is' in organizational life today. I have new cues, new sensitivities and new ways of reading what is going on. I believe this to be what Elias describes in his reference to detachment. Elias' use of the idea of detachment, I believe, should not be confused with the idea of disengagement. I am now no less involved emotionally than I was when I started out on a process of research enquiry. In referring to personal experiences, I am drawing attention to being and reflecting about being, and also to a dialectical process of negation that is a movement in the nature of experience itself.

From time to time, when participating in large group processes during residential meetings of the whole research group, I have found myself feeling disconnected from much of the conversation going on in the group when the talk was about the pressures of the course. Many of those in the group said that they found the program quite onerous and demanding: the reading, writing, the anxiety of examination, the pressure of deadlines. For me, the experience has been quite the reverse. I would say that I have found the time I have spent engaged with these activities as the reason why I have been able to carry on with my job over the past two years. Being engaged with this work has transformed, literally, my ability to make sense of what it is that is going on around me and how I understand my role as an agent acting in relation to others. In saying this, I am not claiming to feel more right than anyone else in how I account for what I believe to be going on. What I am referring to is my own sense of a new/different coherence in my narrative account as it occurs in my silent conversations with myself and in conversation with others.

The emotional intensity of my experiences at work feels not to have changed. My emotional responses to the present context of my institution and how this affects the people with whom I am working are no less intense: feelings of shame, anxiety, anger, paranoia, tiredness, and highs and lows, remain daily present. At the same time, however, I am aware that the emotivity of these feelings, my sense of being taken over by them and the relationship therefore between how I feel and how I act has changed. Now, I would say, I catch myself (shaving in the morning, on train journeys, walking between meetings, during waiting time) working reflexively with *how I feel about how I feel* in situations that have just occurred or which may be about to occur. In this process, I sense a readjustment in the balance between what I just feel and what I am starting to explain.

What I am trying to do with these personal reflections is to mirror, from my experience of working through an enquiry process, the process that aroused Elias' interest in relation to the story of the fisherman. This, I think, is in the way in which the detail of the situational context is noticed alongside intense reflection concerning the nature of the interaction occurring between the individual and his or her environment. It is this reflexivity that I believe to lie both at the heart of Elias' thesis about involvement and detachment and the research methodology that I associate with complex responsive process thinking. I would argue that it is in the multiple iterations of reflection that movement in the character of personal narratives occurs. This is for the reason that the narrative is woven repeatedly in the light of new stimuli in the form of conversations with peers and supervisors, changed patterns of reading, the disciplines of writing and, most importantly, the act of working and reworking a personal narrative in the silent conversation that occurs with one's self. The process I am describing here seems to me to be very different from that described by action researchers. In working reflexively with my own experience I am not seeking to understand this in terms that are either ecstatic or metaphysical. I do not attach to my inquiry a *telos* that infers a notion of the Good. I do not have the expectation that the results of my research will translate into outcomes that are recognizable in organizational terms as a radical break with the past or with the status quo: I do not see myself as having the power to achieve such an outcome.

What I do see being different, however, is my relationship with those around me as we all go on at work, trying to provide leadership and to make sense of our experiences. In this way, I think that the changes I have experienced in the course of my work on the doctoral program have enabled me to be much more responsive, as a characteristic of how I enact my leadership role, to others as they struggle for identity, authority, personal meaning and engagement. To this extent, I am confident that the character of my participation has changed. If I return to the questions of knowledge and practice that I raised at the start of this chapter, I believe I could offer a response about my contributions to both of these that is in the affirmative. But I would do so on the basis of Rorty's argument about doing things in a way, however imperfectly, that is *new* rather than on the basis of uncovering some yet to be discovered truth about life in organizations. I think, too, that I could argue for the validity, as a basis of research, of personal narratives of experience. The case for these being a particularization of social processes in general is, I believe, overwhelming, but this, of course, is because I adhere to a particular way of arguing about the construction of true beliefs. And I take from Rorty and Davidson the idea that the legitimacy of any statement of true belief is always going to be contingent upon the strength of argument that one can mount to defend the propositional validity of the greater web of true beliefs of which it is a part.

Conclusion

It is, therefore, largely in these terms that I understand my participation in the work of the doctoral group at the University of Hertfordshire. First, after five years of background reading and thinking about ideas of complexity and complex responsive processes, I decided to seek to locate myself (intellectually, relationally, professionally) as a participant in an ongoing conversation conducted at depth with regards to these issues. Second, I regard myself now as a participant in the development of a discourse within which a particular set of propositions about human relating are core. I am therefore engaged with others in an activity of enquiry with the objective of understanding life in organizations as an aspect of more extensive social processes of human interaction. The view I would take here is that this engagement is directed explicitly at the pursuit of knowledge. Agent actions however flow from the interdependent relationship that always exists between their own selves and the self-creating webs of others. Changes in the character of our understanding, how we rework or re-create the web of beliefs that are essential to our sense of self, have a recursive relationship with perception, and perception, in its turn, with action. It follows, I think, that to structure a high-level process of enquiry around the pursuit of knowledge has at the same time both the consequences of being an end in itself and a stimulus to changing the character of individuals' actions in their responses to one another.

The research process, the grounds for collaboration between us, I find hard to justify on the basis of predetermined assumptions about contributions to practice. It strikes me that such expectations are fraught with uncertainty and issues of measurement. I do not therefore see the work on the doctoral program in terms of some linear notion of progression or betterment with regard to the performance of operational tasks at work. I would therefore argue against the idea that the notion of a contribution to practice can or should be equated with the idea of *training effect* as it applies to competency-driven personal development programs. This is not to say, however, that the experience of engaging with complex responsive process thinking is neither intended to change nor leads to change in how we are as participants in the life processes of organizations. It is, however, to argue that the character of such changes is likely to be inconsistent over time and space, unpredictable in relation to its marginal or significant impact, conflictual relative to prevailing organizational norms, and to entail, to some degree, a new struggle in the life of the individuals concerned for accommodation within their organizational setting.

Judging from my own experiences of all of this, where Rorty uses the idea of fuzziness in relation to issues of completeness in domains of thought, I would be inclined to suggest the idea of messiness to describe the effect of changes in one's thinking about life in organizations upon the equivalent domain of action: that is, the working live enactment of changing belief structures.

References

Damasio, A. R. (1994) *Descartes' Error: Emotion, Reason and the Human Brain*, London: Picador.

Damasio, A. R. (1999) *The Feeling of What Happens: Body and Emotion in the Making of Consciousness*, London: Heinemann.

Davidson, D. (2001a) *Subjective, Intersubjective, Objective*, Oxford: Oxford University Press.

Davidson, D. (2001b) *Inquiries into Truth and Interpretation*, Oxford: Oxford University Press.

Elias, N. (1987) *Involvement and Detachment*, Oxford: Blackwell.

Foucault, M. (1997) 'Polemics, Politics and Problematizations', in *Ethics: Essential Works 1954–1984 Volume 1*, ed. P. Rabinow, London: Penguin.

Freud, S. (2001) *Introductory Lectures on Psycho-Analysis*, London: Vintage.

Habermas, J. (1990) *Moral Consciousness and Communicative Action*, Cambridge, MA: MIT Press.

Habermas, J. (2001) *On the Pragmatics of Social Interaction*, Cambridge, MA: MIT Press.

Poe, A. (2003) *Tales of Mystery and Imagination*, London: Collectors' Library.

Rorty, R. (1991) *Objectivity, Relativism and Truth: Philosophical Papers Volume 1*, Cambridge: Cambridge University Press.

Rorty, R. (1998) *Truth and Progress: Philosophical Papers Volume 3*, Cambridge: Cambridge University Press.

Rorty, R. (1999) *Philosophy and Social Hope*, London: Penguin.

Editors' introduction to Chapter 4

Research and consultancy are often thought of as different, in many ways opposed, activities. Researchers are supposed to be objective and refrain from intervening in any system they are studying, while consultants, of course, are required to intervene and inevitably become involved in the internal politics of the organization they are consulting to. In this chapter, Bjørner Christensen, a consultant in Norway, argues that researching human interaction is inevitably a participative, subjective activity bound to affect what is being studied in much the same way as consulting. This is by no means a new contention, and Christensen explains how action researchers have always taken the view that the way to understand a human system is to intervene and try to change it. Action researchers are thus both researchers and consultants at the same time.

Christensen explores how the Tavistock tradition combines action research and systems thinking with psychoanalysis to present a combined research and consultation practice. From this perspective, an organization is thought of as a system created by the interaction of its subsystems. There is the task subsystem containing work roles, separated by a porous boundary from another subsystem containing individuals, their emotions and personal relationships. The task subsystem imports work roles from the personal subsystem, and when anxiety levels rise it may also import emotion and fantasy from the personal subsystem which disrupt work. Effective operation of the organization therefore requires keeping emotion and personal relationships outside the task system. Managers are thought of as operating at the boundary of the organization as system, formulating the primary task and establishing the clarity of roles and procedures required to keep anxiety at manageable levels so that the primary task may be carried out efficiently. Researchers-consultants are supposed to step back and observe their own positions in the system and then to rationally choose the interventions they should make to contain anxiety and establish clear tasks and roles. Although some impact of the observer on the observed is acknowledged, there is little notion of the co-creation of meaning.

Christensen identifies the strong link between action research, systems thinking and the notion of intervening in a system in order to change it. This leads to a split between observation and intervention, where the intention in intervening is to produce stability by keeping personal lives outside of the workplace, rationally defining tasks, authority, roles and procedures. Leaders then become detached observers operating at a boundary as holders of anxiety. Implicit in this thinking is the 'both . . . and' structure of causality in which the autonomous leader acts according to rationalist causality while others are parts of a system that formatively unfolds what the leader has enfolded in it.

Christensen then argues for taking a complex responsive processes perspective on the relationship between research and consulting as an alternative to the one described above. This leads to a move:

> from thinking of consultation as an outside intervention into a system to thinking in terms of participative self-organizing processes and transformation from within human relating. This approach offers an emergent understanding of research and consultation in which there is no ambition to implement anything or to control a series of steps to reach an end game. There is no ambition to implement a change as a new product or a new stable state. Having said this, there might be an intention to study what is going on and how to understand behavior when, say, a CEO wants to implement a new vision statement or a new strategy. The consequence is that I do not formulate working hypotheses or set up a research plan in advance. I do not use organizational diagnoses, models or methods for gathering data. On the contrary I use the opportunities I have in daily work, in ordinary meetings with clients, taking part in different conversations.
>
> (p. 87)

In doing this, the researcher-consultant understands what is going on through reflecting on his or her own experience, inviting others to engage in the same reflective processes. All human interaction may be understood as complex responsive processes and this includes research-consulting. However, Christensen points out that research-consulting is differentiated from other activities by the intention with which it is undertaken. The intention is to take a specifically reflexive attitude to what is going on;

that is, the intention is to study and open up possibilities for the transformation of the patterning of complex responsive processes of relating through conversation. Christensen identifies this difference of purpose by calling his research method 'emerging participative exploration'. Emerging participative exploration is the exploration of ordinary everyday processes of responsive relating, where the exploration takes the form of reflecting on narratives of experience. This formulation of intention differentiates emerging participative exploration from other methodologies. For example, in classical science the intention is to observe phenomena and identify the laws according to which they operate while the intention in the Tavistock approach is to intervene in, and so change, a system.

What Christensen is pointing to is the fuzzy distinction between research and other human activities. Many activities involve reflective/reflexive stances, such as psychotherapy, consulting, managing and leading. It follows that there are no clear boundaries around an activity called research and it cannot be taken as separate from practice.

Christensen then provides a narrative of his work with cadets at the Royal Norwegian Air Force Academy and explores what it means to use the approach of emerging participative exploration. He tells of the response of the cadet students to the attempts he and his colleague make to introduce a different way of working together. In doing so he brings out the reflexive way in which he works as consultant-researcher as he explores the everyday experience of power relations in ordinary conversations. He links this ordinary explorative experience with the iteration and emergence of identity as an answer to the questions: Who are we, and what are we doing together? His story shows just how difficult people find it to explore their own emerging experience, preferring instead to work with what are essentially highly abstract 'tools and techniques'. In encouraging people to reflect upon their own ordinary experience, he is in effect encouraging them to take up the methodology of emerging participative exploration. Emerging participative exploration is about making sense of how people make sense of their experience. He is pointing to how this methodology is itself emerging in experience.

Christensen explores what his intentions are in this work. His intention is to help the members of an organization explore their own experience of what they are doing together so as to better understand it. His intention is to hold the situation open so that a richer complexity of conversational themes may emerge. His intention is to contribute to people being able to live with the paradox of knowing and not knowing at the same time. He helps by contributing to the emergence of new meaning which in itself has the potential for, but not the guarantee of, improvement in organizational activities.

The main themes in this chapter, then, are the following key aspects of methodology from a complex responsive processes perspective:

- the centrality of ordinary, everyday experience;
- the subjective nature of that experience and therefore the requirement for a methodology that is subjective;
- the importance of exploring more and more deeply the narrative nature of this subjective experience;
- the reflective and reflexive nature of that methodology where reflexivity is not simply an individual matter but a social one requiring that one locates one's reflection in a tradition of thought clearly differentiated from other traditions;
- the participative nature of the reflective exploration of experience;
- the differentiating function of the intention of the researcher-consultant, even though the differentiation is fuzzy;
- the purpose of facilitating the deeper understanding of the experience of participation on the part of organizational members rather than any notion of intervening in a system in order to improve it;
- the strong link between processes of research-consultation and the iteration and emergence of identity.

4 Emerging participative exploration: consultation as research

Bjørner Christensen

- The organizational consultant and social researcher
- Merging consultation and research
- Systems thinking as a basis for observation and intervention
- Studying organizations as complex responsive processes of relating
- The narrative life of human experience
- The Royal Norwegian Air Force Academy
- Making sense of the living present
- Emerging participative exploration

In this chapter, I explore consultation and research from two different perspectives. I joined the Doctor of Management program at the University of Hertfordshire as an organizational consultant and action researcher working in the Tavistock 'tradition', and it is this tradition which provides my first perspective on the relationship between consulting and research. In my research for the program, I explored my work as a consultant and researcher from a very different perspective, namely the theory of complex responsive processes of human relating (Stacey *et al*. 2000). This led me to suggest a research methodology which I have called 'emerging participative exploration' (Christensen 2003). Here, the consultant as researcher takes part in and has the intention to study human interaction as complex responsive processes of human relating.

The organizational consultant and social researcher

The organizational consultant and the social researcher traditionally come from two different positions.

Popper claims that, to be worthy of scientific attention, an 'event must be an "observable" event; that is to say, basic statements must be testable, inter-subjectively, by "observation"' (Popper 1959, p. 102).

Popper suggests that it is possible to differentiate 'real' science from non-science by the methods used. If an activity is going to be called scientific, in his view, it has to be based on high-quality independent observation. The underlying intention of the scientist is to avoid influencing what is going on in the 'system' being observed. Scientists are not supposed to make an intervention in, or exercise an influence over, what they are studying. They are supposed to report to other professionals about their findings without covering up anything of importance. Researchers in the social sciences are expected to be observers, not intervening in what other people are doing. They are expected to develop hypotheses or research questions, observe, gather data and then use this to formulate conclusions. In Norway, where I come from, research is often paid for by government money and there is an expectation that researchers will not act in a political way. They are supposed to be objective and detached.

What is expected from the consultant, on the other hand, is usually very different. Consultation is traditionally understood as giving advice, challenging traditions of meaning in speaking and acting, and at the same time offering new possibilities for action. Implicit in this is the assumption that traditions have to be changed and that managers and others need consultants to think, speak and act differently. Consultants are often supposed to act as experts and to intervene by telling the client what to do, often influenced by an expectation that the client will buy his services again in the future. If consultants report in a written form, the client, very often the top management coalition, might advise them not to let other people read the report, even those who are participating in the work. Consultants may ally themselves with the most powerful in the organization, or with oppressed groups, or with labor union leaders; or they may help people to meet each other when they need to speak together. Consultants will, just by being present, influence conversational patterns and become part of the political processes of relating.

The problem with the scientific methods in the social sciences is that no one can stand outside human relating. Any activity named 'observation' may influence both the scientist and the social 'system' observed in ways no one can know of beforehand. This leads others to suggest merging research and consultation, and to argue that research is first of all about contributing to change and that professional consultation should be based on research methodology.

Merging consultation and research

Some fifty years ago, Kurt Lewin introduced the methodology of action research, combining observation, data gathering and analysis with interventions in a client system in order to change it. This had a significant impact, becoming important in the work of the Tavistock Institute (Miller 1993, p. 5) and cooperating bodies in Scandinavia and the USA. Lewin held that science should be for the benefit of human society, and this required very different philosophical and methodological ideas from those in the traditional natural sciences. According to Midgley, Lewin said that scientists have a choice: they can either conduct research for the sake of pure curiosity or help to improve the social conditions of which they are a part (Midgley 2000, p. 118). For Lewin, the action researcher is a participant in political processes in organizations and society.

Lewin argued for intervention as the main methodology for making change happen in social systems and thereby researching them. At the Tavistock Institute this influenced the way projects were carried out, where the aim was to develop a more democratic work life. Since then, new concepts of action research have been developed (McNiff *et al.* 1996) along with many variations such as action science (Argyris *et al.* 1985), participative or cooperative inquiry (Heron 1996), appreciative inquiry (Srivastva and Cooperider 1999), action learning (Revans 1984), and focus group research (Barbour and Kitzinger 1999). All these developments challenged the positivist way of understanding research as carried out by the detached objective observer. In doing so they all raised questions about the sharp distinction between the role of researcher and consultant described above. Action research is about improving practice rather than improving knowledge (Elliot 1991). Others agree with Elliot: 'action research is a way of defining and implementing relevant professional development' (Lomax 1990, p. 10). This view of action research and the role of the researcher is very close to a common understanding of consultation and the consultant as implementing new solutions to problems and adapting the company to changes in the surrounding world. All the later developments of action research suggest a participative way of doing research, 'with people not on or about people' (Heron 1996, p. 19).

Nevertheless, the idea of intervention based on observation seems to be a key concept both in action research and consultation. Consider some ideas of intervention and observation based on action research and systems theory.

Systems thinking as a basis for observation and intervention

Most traditional consultation and research is in one way or another grounded in open systems theory. General open systems theory applied to organizations is derived from von Bertalanffy (1968). This theoretical perspective was later developed into a socio-technical understanding of organizations (Emery and Trist 1960), with similar characteristics to those found in biology (Miller and Rice 1967).

> Originally formulated in studies of biological systems, it (open systems theory) offered a way of analyzing a human system, such as an enterprise, as an organism relating to its environment through a continuing cycle of taking in resources – raw materials, equipment, supplies, people – across the boundary, processing them in some way, and exporting the outputs.
>
> (Miller 2002, pp. 186–198)

This gave rise to concepts such as boundaries, primary task and roles, which are very important parts of the theoretical framework of the Tavistock tradition.

Immanuel Kant ([1790] 1987) introduced a systemic perspective to understanding nature in his critique of dogmatic empiricism and the natural scientific method developed by Bacon, Newton and others in the sixteenth century. He understood organisms in nature as consisting of parts and wholes, which evolve in a systemic self-organizing way (Griffin 2002). The self-organizing process, in which the whole and the parts evolve simultaneously, is a movement from an immature to a mature form of the organism as a whole. The purpose in this process is to unfold what is already enfolded in the organism or the system, to create a mature whole. In this movement, however, there is no intrinsic freedom. The movement is constrained by its given form and the processes which develop this already given form. These self-organizing processes are not able to produce novel forms; they can only unfold what is already enfolded in the system.

Such systemic self-organizing processes are a formative way of understanding causality in nature (Stacey *et al.* 2000, p. 27), which is very different to the participative self-organizing processes in the theory of complex responsive processes (Griffin 2002, p. 124). Kant argued that the formative way of understanding nature could not be used to explain and understand human activity because human beings are autonomous. He argued that it is possible for human beings to set goals for the future and to achieve these goals by choosing actions through reasoning. Kant's thoughts are taken up by Stacey and colleagues and described as rationalist teleology and formative teleology (Stacey *et al.* 2000). Although Kant argued that the formative way of understanding nature could not be used to explain and understand human activity, what happened was the opposite. Formative causality is the basis of systems theory.

Over the past fifty years systems theories in different versions, as well as the earlier scientific management (Taylor 1911) based on the natural sciences, have been used in the social sciences to understand life in organizations and how to make changes in such organizations. In the systems tradition, based on formative causality, the manager, action researcher or consultant enfolds rules and regulations, goals and budgets, visions and reward systems into the organization. All of these are then supposed to be unfolded as the system moves into the future. In this way of thinking, the processes within the system, such as communication, decision-making, production and quality, all aim to create the whole, the organization, which is supposed to be more than the sum of its parts. The idea is that the different subsystems, such as the social, technological and administrative, are in harmony to ensure that the organization is working as a whole. To control this drive towards 'wholeness', managers use cybernetic tools such as plans, goals, budgets, total quality control systems and balanced score card systems. Conflicts are dysfunctional processes disturbing the harmony, and if these occur there is a need for a process consultant to help the management to remove such conflicts and to establish harmony. Change is supposed to come from the outside as an adaptation to changes in the environment, in the same way that organisms in nature adapt to their environment.

The Tavistock Institute has, from the very beginning, emphasized systems thinking and open systems theory (Miller 1993, pp. 5–18). Here the concept of boundaries is essential. Boundaries are drawn between the whole system and the environment and between the different subsystems. Important is the analysis of the relationships between the different systems and subsystems: 'This made it possible to study relationships between the psychosocial and the techno-economic elements of organizations' (Miller 1993, p. 8). The notion of the socio-technical system made it possible to analyze the relationship between social and technical subsystems, and was a 'joint' theory of Taylorism and the American human relations school.

> Whereas Taylorism gave ascendancy to the technical system and the human relation school to the social, the socio-technical system was seen as a product of the joint optimization of the activities of both systems.
>
> (Emery and Trist 1960, pp. 83–97)

In spite of von Bertalanffy's awareness of the self-organizing capacity of open systems, also recognized by the Tavistock writers (Emery and Trist 1960, p. 85), the focus in the Tavistock tradition was more on the boundary and boundary regulation than on the self-organizing capacities of the system. The idea of understanding the organization as a system is a dominant perspective in understanding the structural aspects of an organization, its formal design, division of labor, levels of authority and reporting relationships. Furthermore, the nature of work tasks, processes and activities, and, not least, the organization's task and sentient boundaries and the transactions across them, are important (Miller and Rice 1967). The link between open systems such as organization, group and individual and the division of labor, with working roles linked to the primary task, are the main focus of attention. This approach focuses on managing the boundaries and the way the formal management perform this task. What was not addressed by the researchers within the Tavistock tradition was Kant's warning that this systemic way of understanding nature could not be used to understand human action. This formative way of understanding nature cannot explain how novelty emerges (Stacey *et al*. 2000).

The Tavistock tradition, of which I was a part and on which I built my work as a consultant, is based on systems thinking and ideas from scientific management. As in scientific management, the manager and the consultant are still equated with the researcher as the detached or participative observer. This observer participates as a special role, exemplified by the role of the consultant in group relations conferences. Here consultants participate by sitting with the group but in a very special way. They do not speak to the participants in an ordinary manner but use their observations and feelings as a resource for making working hypotheses about what is going on within the group as a system and between the group and the consultant, where the consultant is, above all, an authority figure. He or she is understood to be a container for the projected feelings of the members in the system. The intervention in this system takes the form of offering working hypotheses for the group members to work with or to reject.

The Tavistock tradition combines general systems thinking and psychoanalysis to understand organizations (Miller and Rice 1967). What is important from this perspective is the clarity of roles and control at the boundary of the system. To do this the consultant uses an action research approach of gathering data, making diagnoses, developing working hypotheses, giving feedback and then intervening in the system, often in collaboration with the manager and the employees or a smaller group of employees. The idea is to ensure that the interaction between the different subsystems of the organization is adequate. The manager and the consultant now understand the organization as a whole, a level outside of human relating, which acts back on the individual. Here human beings and human relating are subsystems. By using a psychoanalytic approach, the consultant is supposed to help the employees to control their personal boundaries in a way that ensures they are importing only their working capacity across the boundary into the organization and not their emotions. The action researcher works to mobilize employees in the working role and help them to keep other activities outside the workplace.

The action researcher is concerned with finding, choosing and implementing the processes and the cybernetic control mechanisms that make it possible for managers to control the behavior of the members of the organization in the future. In this way of consulting or managing, we clearly see the 'both . . . and' nature typical of Kant's thinking. First, there is the researcher, manager or consultant who exercises the freedom of autonomous choice, choosing the vision, goals, strategies, rules or interventions that the members of the organization are to follow in order to move from the present towards the designed future. The employees are then understood as rule-following individual entities. If they exercise their free choice, there is the need for consultation to help them stay within the boundaries of their working role, removing idiosyncratic behavior. It is evident that this way of thinking has an underlying intention to create stability, and this then has the effect of preventing spontaneous novelty from emerging (Stacey 2001b, pp. 91–114).

Despite not differentiating between the consultant and the researcher in the Tavistock tradition, there is a clear differentiation between observation and intervention, suggesting that a boundary may be drawn between the phenomenon studied and the action researcher. Observation is an activity performed from a position outside of the system studied and intervention is an activity where the researcher crosses its boundary.

David Campbell *et al.* argue that:

> Systemic thinking is a means by which people can step back and observe their own position in the system. . . . We aim to move people to the 'observer's position' so that they can see their own contribution to problems in the organization. Once in this position, they can make changes that create new feed-back loops and reverberate through other parts of the organization.
>
> (Campbell *et al.* 1994, p. 20)

Campbell *et al.* suggest some exercises to develop this skill but there is no explanation of how it is possible to stand back from, or stand outside of, human relating. For these writers it seems to be a problem to be a part of human relating when working as a consultant. The only way of getting in touch with human relational processes, or at least the best way to understand these processes, is by standing back from my own participation, and by doing this I will be able to understand what is going on. They do not explain why this is necessary.

Campbell comments on how he and his colleagues use second order cybernetics in their work:

> This is a notion that we are not merely observers of the process around us (first-order cybernetics), but that our presence and observation help create the very system we are observing. We cannot be independent of what we observe.
>
> (Campbell 1995, p. 18)

Here he is acknowledging that there may be some influence of observer on the observed but not as a co-creation of meaning between the client and the consultant. Campbell sees the observer and the observed in two different 'places', not taking part in the co-creation of meaning in the way

G.H. Mead suggests in his ideas of the social act consisting of gesture–response, claiming that the individual mind and society emerge simultaneously in human relating (Mead 1934; Stacey *et al.* 2000).

Campbell goes on:

> The main problem for an internal consultant is that he or she cannot normally step back and get sufficient distance to see the larger pattern that is influencing the problem. However, the active use of the concept of second-order cybernetics helps consultants step back by allowing them to observe their own participation in the creation of the system around them.
>
> (Campbell 1995, p. 18)

It is not clear to me what observing really means to these writers and why this 'move' is necessary. It seems as if they find it possible to make a mental move in space and by doing this to develop some kind of view or understanding that is impossible to achieve in 'ordinary' ways of relating, from participating in the relating itself. Campbell and colleagues do not explain how it is possible to stand back from relating to get the view of the whole pattern of relating and, on the basis of this, to understand the whole system in a better way.

The way observation is described makes it seem as if it is possible to be in two different positions at the same time. This systemic way of thinking has brought people to believe that there is an inside and an outside in human relating, that boundaries are real and not an abstract tool or an abstract way of describing what is called 'the organization'. They seem to suggest that one part of me (a subsystem) is supposed to be left inside the boundary of a system, while another part of me (another subsystem) is supposed, at the same time, to be moved or placed outside the boundary of the same system.

To me, however, it seems unreal to speak about outside or inside human relating; it is more a question of experienced quality and different ways of relating. What I can do is take part in conversations that include my own experience as a theme. I can talk about my own feelings and my own experience of what is going on, not as an observer, but as a participant in the ongoing relational processes of which I am a part and am not able to stand outside of.

Studying organizations as complex responsive processes of relating

Moving from a systemic way of working as a researcher and consultant to a way of working based on a complexity perspective on organizations has a profound impact on the understanding of research as well as consultation. It moves one from thinking of consultation as an outside intervention into a system to thinking in terms of participative self-organizing processes and transformation as a participant in human relating. This approach offers an emergent understanding of research and consultation in which there is no ambition to implement anything or to control a series of steps to reach an end game. There is no ambition to implement a change as a new product or a new stable state. Having said this, there may be an intention to study what is going on and how to understand behavior when, say, a CEO wants to implement a new vision statement or a new strategy. The consequence is that I do not formulate working hypotheses or set up a research plan in advance. I do not use organizational diagnoses, models or methods for gathering data. On the contrary, I use the opportunities I have in daily work, in ordinary meetings with clients, taking part in different conversations. During these conversations, or sometimes after them, I reflect and make notes on how I have conducted my work and how I have understood especially what I have experienced as striking moments.

As a researcher, I am studying complex responsive processes of relating and how to understand consulting from within human relating. This means that I write from within my own experiences and invite other participants to do the same. This is what John Shotter calls writing from within 'living moments' or 'witness-writing' rather than 'aboutness-writing' (Shotter 1993). I am trying to catch these moments of becoming, the aesthetic moments of new insight in which I feel that I understand something that might change my identity, who I am and what I am doing.

The narrative life of human experience

When a scientist, working within the paradigm of natural science, does research in organizations, he can only tell a very limited story. Using figures, tables and statistics he tells a story that can never be more than a part of 'reality'. In organizational life we can never communicate only by using propositional knowledge such as figures, procedures and manuals. This is because human interaction is in time and history is important:

consider the way we understand our momentary daily lives in terms of 'ups' and 'downs', progress and setbacks, fulfillment and frustration. To see life in this way is to participate in a storied world.

(Gergen 1999, p. 70)

Gergen is arguing that we need to 'recount our past, to identify where we have been and where we are going. In effect we identify ourselves through narration' (ibid.). When I get the 'simple' and ordinary question: 'Who are you?' I start to tell stories about my previous life, relationships to other people, my work, my hobbies, what I believe in and so on. My re-creation of my history and my hopes and expectations for the future, in the present, is the only 'property' I have and they can only be told in a narrative way. We all need stories and we tell stories all the time to each other. When I have experienced something in the past, and someone asks me what happened, I start to tell a story, my story, the way I experienced what happened. In coffee breaks and at the lunch table people tell stories all the time about their bosses, customers, children, their work, and what they have experienced in a seminar or at last Saturday night's party. In management team meetings and in the boardroom people tell stories all the time. Stories are a way of dealing with our experiences in relation to other people.

Emerging participative exploration is an exploration of ordinary daily complex responsive processes of relating between human beings. By using the word 'exploration' I emphasize the ordinary, the everyday life I am interested in understanding. In human discourse I see the conversational lives of organizations as story creating. Together we are creating stories all the time. These are not the stories with a prescribed ending, but the creation of history. They are not stories as in fairytales that unfold what is enfolded in the story at the beginning. They are the creation of transformative narratives, in which 'reality' is created in the ongoing relating between humans with the paradoxical capability for staying the same and changing at the same time (Stacey 2001a). These are the self-organizing patterning narratives, our communication, in which local themes of communication are organizing the patterning of meaning. These are the patterning processes in the living present in which the present has a time span, in which the near future (the response) can act back on the past (the gesture) and change the meaning of the past, my own and our common history.

In these 'narrative-like' processes of relating, emerging in the living present, history is created in the fluid ongoing interactions of gesture–response.

> The thematic patterning of experience, however, does not take only narrative forms. Another form is that of propositions, or rules, and these also pattern communicative interaction in much the same way, this time producing emergent abstract-systematic frameworks, such as the law, organizational procedures and scientific theories. These too constitute a history of interaction, or experience. This history, with its simultaneous aspects of narrative and propositional themes is what patterns peoples' relating to each other. Indeed it is in this history, narratively and propositionally patterned, that individual and collective identities emerge at the same time.
>
> (Stacey 2003, p. 78)

It is from this perspective that I, in my own exploration, use a narrative form to explore the ordinary, daily conversational life – the fluid processes of human relating – in which I am participating as a consultant and researcher. In emerging participative exploration I do not follow a rigid research method. I experience methodology itself as emerging and participative. From this perspective, I do not separate the meaning-making processes from other bodily actions in relating. I am a participant in exploring complex responsive processes of relating with the intention of exploring and trying to make sense of what is going on as a participant.

There is no need for a large-scale project to demonstrate what this methodology is all about. At the moment of writing I am working with the cadets at the Royal Norwegian Air Force Academy in collaboration with my colleague Stig. Consider now how our work together constitutes emerging participative exploration. Later, I will focus on the intention, and a different way of understanding help and improvement, while working from this perspective.

The Royal Norwegian Air Force Academy

I was contacted by one of the staff officers at the Air Force College Department of Leadership Studies. He had attended some lectures on complexity, which I had given to the cadets in the previous year and he wanted me to contribute to the final six-week module of the two-year advanced-level training for cadets. The module is a synopsis of the two years and the task given to the students is to write a strategy for the Norwegian Air Force in the year 2020. They are supposed to use all their previous learning in this work, which takes a written form as well as an oral presentation. The Academy is heavily influenced by systems thinking in different areas, such as technology, air power and leadership. I suggested that my colleague Stig and I do most of the work together.

In our first meeting, the two staff members said they wanted us to introduce complexity theory and work in a way that linked theory and practice. They were both aware that complexity theory was a different approach compared to systems theory, which the academy's leadership and management program was built upon. We agreed to start with a two-day event with all the cadets in a plenary meeting and then to meet with the cadets every Monday over the next six weeks working partly in plenary and partly in smaller groups. I realized from the beginning that this work would be a challenge but I expected these young people to be open-minded and willing to explore complexity theory and what it had to offer in their work on leadership and strategy in the Air Force.

Stig and I discussed the invitation and agreed to start with an introduction to complexity theory over the first two days. We did not want to make this into an ordinary lecture but wanted to start with some introduction to the theory and then invite the students to a conversation. The intention was to let other voices be heard and by doing so to give space for novelty to emerge in our conversations. We therefore asked for a plenary with chairs in a circle instead of their ordinary classroom where the cadets sit in rows in front of their computers ready to take notes from the teacher.

From the beginning I felt that the change we had introduced – changing the classroom, taking away the desks and the computers – had an immediate impact on the group. As we introduced complexity theory and the background in the natural sciences, they said: 'We have heard this before. When will you move on and give us the tools we need to write the strategy? We understand all this, it is basic, but what are the consequences for me as a leader? What tool will you give us on the basis of this theory and how can we implement it in our practice?' I could feel in my own body the dependency in their behavior. On the one hand they wanted us to give them new knowledge and at the same time they refused what we had to offer.

Right at the start there was little willingness to explore what this new way of thinking meant. A pattern of attack and defense emerged and some of the gestures from the cadets were quite aggressive. They kept defending the use of plans, rules and regulations, even when we tried to explain that complexity theory was not suggesting that we get rid of all the tools used in human relating but argued for an understanding that such mechanisms are tools in human relating. We experienced how their understanding of what we said was very different from what we suggested and one student said that we offered them a world without structure. This is a common experience when we start to speak about this perspective. Some people seem to believe that this is some kind of 'implementation of chaos' in the daily meaning of the expression. However, some did ask questions and tried to explore what we were introducing.

By the end of the day both Stig and I were affected by the critical attitude that had emerged and the strong resistance we had experienced throughout the day. I felt quite bad afterwards and I was thinking about my own part in this. At the same time, I was aware that the complex responsive processes way of understanding life in organizations is very different to what they had learned over the past two years. I had expected that these young people in their thirties and early forties would be able to take part in an exploration and not defend old truths. What happened was the opposite.

On the following day the room we had used on the previous day was occupied. We therefore met in their regular classroom, with the tables in rows and most of the cadets sitting with their laptops open. The cadet class commander of the week ordered the class to attention. They all stood up and he then reported to me in a military manner that they were all present. At first I did not realize what was happening. I had forgotten the old rituals I had been a part of many years ago. Stig, who had not experienced this before, could not understand what happened. The cadets then sat down and we invited them to raise any theme that was on their minds related to what happened the previous day or any other themes they wanted to focus on. Despite the refusal of more theory, they now wanted more input on how to use the theory in their work.

I found the arrangement of the room, with its tables in rows, to be an obstacle, preventing people from seeing each other and making conversation very difficult. It was a physical arrangement that reinforced the feeling of two parties confronting each other. It ended up in a situation in which I started to lecture and to repeat an earlier pattern in the group, a pattern with which they were all very familiar. This was a pattern that could end up with ourselves as scapegoats, having not been able to teach them anything that they could use for writing the Air Force Strategy. At the time however, teaching them felt the right thing to do. We had another break, and Stig, who had said nothing for a long time, came over to me and said: 'Bjørner, this is not very productive. I do not like it that you are drawn into the pattern of behavior they want and that you are now reproducing together with them. If we give in to this, it will be a waste of time. We must break this pattern or I am out of here. I think we should take a long break for an hour and then ask them to come back again. Do you really want to continue this?' I said: 'Yes, I want to continue, at least I want to finish the argument which was stopped when we took a break.' I felt that, by saying this, what he said also resonated with my own feeling, but I was not sure what to do. I felt the students were very upset and hostile, with only a few supporting what we were trying to do.

This was a crucial point in our work and it shows how power is not an individual 'thing' but relational processes including us all. This was indeed a process of inclusion and exclusion. I could feel that what happened was a threat to my identity. Colluding with the expectation from the cadets influenced me into a pattern that felt safe and secure and reduced my anxiety about not succeeding with this work. In hindsight, I can see that power struggles are processes of identity formation. In this case with the cadets it was fight–flight processes in which identity was at stake. Stig's strong gesture could, on one level, be understood as him wanting to leave or withdraw, but it was more a gesture to defend our identity and not be drawn into a reproduction of patterns that would not contribute to any change at all. I also realize that success was important to me in this case because I had other relationships with the Armed Forces which, in my fantasy, could be damaged if this work failed. I therefore felt very vulnerable and the students probably noticed this. The students said that they were used to lecturers who clarified objectives and expectations, teachers who knew what they were doing. Our way of working in a much more collaborative and open way, inviting them to participate, could in their view be understood as weakness. I think this was one of our contributions to the emergence of this power struggle. I saw both Stig's and my own behavior as a part of this relational pattern in which I became an expert teacher, colluding with their need to depend on someone, and Stig fighting for our identity as professionals working in a different way.

At this crucial point in our work it was important that the two of us worked together. It was of the utmost importance that Stig could both support me and challenge me at the same time. I felt that his powerful gesture towards himself, myself and the class was a way of confronting with love, to help us all, including himself, to continue to struggle and not fall into an old unproductive pattern which could prevent us all from learning. I did not feel that the way he challenged me was a 'hostile act' or a threat to my identity. I felt that he both challenged and supported me at the same time. In this process of inclusion and exclusion, it strikes me that the two of us had very different perspectives on what was going on. This difference was a very important resource and I felt that we were both able to use it in a productive way in our struggle to keep the future open for the possibility for novelty to occur. A new theme was then brought into the conversation with the staff officers, myself and afterwards with the students. This complicated the conversation. This episode tells me how important it is that the idea of the omnipotent individual change agent is questioned. In cases with large differences in identity where the consultant can expect power struggles, it seems to be important that there is more than one professional consultant present. For the consultants, it is not enough to work at relating to the client because the relating between the consultants is just as important. Therefore it is important that the exploration of the interaction between the consultants is not avoided.

When the group came back after the break, I told them about the conversation Stig and I had during the break in which one of the staff officers was involved. I said that the two of us probably disagreed on how to proceed and I asked Stig to tell them himself what he had said to me. He explained to them what he had said and challenged them with an ultimatum. They had to understand that they represented a powerful group who were not easily resisted. However, they now had to do something about it or there would be one teacher less. After some discussion about what to do, they agreed to take a break for half an hour and then come back again to talk about how they made sense of what had been going on so far and to raise any themes that were on their minds. While this took place, the two staff officers, Stig and I stayed behind and talked together. We decided that we would remove the desks and try once more to create a different space for conversations. We decided to invite them to move the tables and join us in a circle.

When the cadets came back we had moved the teacher's desk and there was an open space at the front of the room. Without us saying anything about the seating they started to move the chairs into a circle in the open space at the front of the room. We asked them not to report from their discussions but to continue the conversations in plenary. I immediately experienced a shift in my body. I felt more relaxed and much more present. The conversation now took a different direction. I felt that people listened in a different way; they looked friendlier and the way they commented and asked questions was in a much more exploratory mode. In the next break, I joined the students. They were very friendly and told me how frustrating our approach had been for them. They told us that they had just finished a large piece of written work and had expected that this final module would be rather easier for them. Furthermore, they spoke about how our way of working broke with their expectations and how difficult it was for them to understand what the impact of this new theory had on the given task for this module. I had no problem in understanding them, having seen for myself during my doctorate how difficult it was to experience learning that posed a threat to my 'old identity' as an organizational consultant working from a systemic perspective.

At the end of the day there were comments which brought laughter and I think we all left feeling quite relieved, having been able to work through a very difficult opening two days. Stig and I had a long conversation afterwards and we both felt that we had experienced a breakthrough, and that from now on the cadets would be more interested in exploring together with us. We decided that the following week we would once again invite them to explore together with us in a plenary meeting any theme they were interested in.

When we entered the classroom the following Monday, the students were once more in rows with their laptops open. We invited them to bring up any issues they were interested in. By doing this I realized that we too reproduced a pattern. This was a pattern in which we had the formal right to introduce our approach, one the students disagreed with. To us it was an invitation to include them in conversations but for them it was a confrontation forcing them to take responsibility to contribute. Our invitation collided with their expectation of sitting in a more passive way, making notes from our lecture and asking questions if there was anything they did not understand. At first, the students contributed little. I could feel the same resistance once more. I wondered whether it was possible to convince them that this was a genuine invitation and a space they could use. The physical arrangement of the classroom created the experience of two opposite parties and unspoken expectations. I was struck by the fact that once more we co-created a conflict-laden pattern in the plenary which no one really wanted. At the same time I was aware that what happened was a unique opportunity for all parties involved to learn.

The following Monday we invited an experienced fighter pilot to talk to the students about complexity theory. I thought that if these stubborn students got the message from one of their colleagues they would probably understand and be able to see more links to their daily work as leaders. The cadets listened to the pilot for more than an hour. After a break, we once more invited the cadets to explore with our guest speaker whatever they were interested in. We invited them to sit in a circle without tables. All accepted this except for one of the students, a pilot, who left the classroom in anger. The students said that the conversations with our guest speaker were interesting and fruitful.

After this event, Stig and I had a long conversation. Given the aggression and the reluctance of the students to explore anything within the large group, Stig suggested that we should not use the plenary any more but work mainly in the smaller groups. I disagreed and suggested that this would become part of the pattern we wanted to question. This time it was Stig who was influenced by the power struggle and who wanted to avoid another event in the plenary. I argued that working in the large group was a challenge and would give all of us new experiences. We discussed possible fantasies in larger groups and how we could work with the students to help them to deal with their own situation in such settings. We thought that what had happened in the large group was an example of what happens when you do not know the full situation. How can you develop an objective and clarify expectations when you do not know what is going to happen? Why should we take away from them the opportunity to explain how they react when they experience situations they do not know? This made enough sense for both of us to continue the struggle with our students.

The following Monday the same pattern was re-created once more. The cadets were sitting behind their desks, but I noticed that most of the laptops were closed. The same pattern was repeated but with some differences. We invited them once more to raise any theme they wanted to explore. The first response was about how little time there was before the written strategy had to be finished. After some minutes' silence I started to comment on what one of the group had written about the need for flexible officers in the future. I spoke about how easy it is to ask others to change, and how difficult it is to introduce changes in oneself and the social pattern of which one is a part. Then some students started to speak about the conflict that had been going on between us. During this morning plenary, they opened up and spoke about their own feelings. Some students in the front row turned around and started to look at each other when they spoke. Quite a few started to admit that what took place in the plenary was very interesting but they had problems to see the link to the task, namely writing a strategy for the Air Force in 2020.

Stig and I talked with them about large group dynamics, how easily fantasies emerge from large group situations and how difficult it is to get an overview and to understand what is going on. We talked about strategic work and political processes in which power was always present in the same way we had experienced with them. They brought in examples from the Armed Forces and how the Navy had managed to buy new torpedo boats despite the fact this was not a part of the new plan. We brought up the changes within the Norwegian Armed Forces and how these changes were linked to strategy and changes in both the I and we identity. They raised the theme about the seating as a pattern of reproduction and stability, and how this was linked to traditional roles in the classroom and in organizations and how changes in such patterns always had to do with changes in power relations. Some of them were able to link the conflict with us to other, similar events in their own careers. One of them got up and said: 'What I have experienced here is exactly what I have experienced in staff meetings or in groups with high-ranking officers.' After the morning plenary we worked in smaller groups and the difference in climate was striking. I encountered more friendly people with a genuine interest in important issues and a curiosity to explore the consequences of the complexity perspective.

Making sense of the living present

Sitting in the plenary meeting with the students, talking to them together with the staff in the breaks, and discussing with my colleague what is going on after the event, are all sense-making processes. I do not see sense-making as an activity separated from 'the action', as something going on in a reflection period after the 'event' is over. Sense-making is a bodily action and the feeling of making sense or losing sense is a part of my bodily experience in the living present. My way of understanding processes of reflecting is unlike the reflection described in Kolb's Learning Style Inventory in which he suggests a learning cycle with four different steps (Kolb *et al.* 1984, p. 39). First, there is the concrete experiment, followed by reflective observation, leading to abstract conceptualization, in turn leading to forming hypotheses and then active experimentation to try out new learning in new situations. In Kolb's terms, one would think of the plenary meetings as the experiment, and the discussion Stig and I had afterwards as reflection during which we formed hypotheses to be tried out with the students. However, when Stig and I talked with the students after meetings, we were doing what we had been doing in meetings with them, namely talking about our own experiences and how we made sense of them. These conversations between us were no different to conversations in the plenary sessions. Although the students were not present when Stig and I talked, I saw that some of the same feelings were being reproduced when we discussed what we had been through. Speaking about our history and our feelings gave rise to new perspectives and new ways of understanding what we had been a part of. Sense-making, in my view, does not proceed in different, distinct stages but is an ongoing process.

The cadets are trained to take up positions in a military organization and their education focuses on the importance of setting goals and planning operations. They are used to teachers who tell them what they are supposed to learn and who clarify expectations beforehand. Our failure to do this was what some of the students complained about regarding our 'teaching'. The underlying assumption, most often taken for granted, is that it is possible for an individual, the teacher, to set the objectives for the lesson beforehand and clarify the students' expectations of what they want to learn before the lesson starts, as if the learning is there even before 'it' starts. This understanding of the learning process is based on cognitive psychology, systems thinking and a linear sender–receiver communication model. The idea is that it is possible to transfer something called knowledge from one individual brain to another individual brain, in such a way that the knowledge 'package' becomes the same in the receiver's head as in the sender's.

> In mainstream thinking, knowledge is ultimately located in the metal models, the inner world, of individual minds, consisting of representations formed in past experience and stored in memory. When a new stimulus is encountered, relevant models are retrieved from memory to process the data and generate knowledge.
>
> (Stacey 2001a, p. 96)

What Stacey is commenting on here is the traditional way of understanding knowledge creation with knowledge existing in mental models that are possible to change in a very rational mechanistic way, and that are possible to define and transfer from one individual mind to another.

> In the complex responsive processes perspective, there is a move from thinking in terms of something already existing to thinking in terms of patterns that are continually reproduced and potentially transformed. The organizing themes of the individual, private role play of mind are being reproduced with variations and potentially transformed in the

living present. At the same time, the public display of habitual and traditional themes organizing experience is also being reproduced with variations and potentially transformed in the living present. This is knowledge as processes of continual reproduction and potential transformation of relational themes.

(Ibid., p. 197)

This view, based on the understanding of knowledge creation as complex responsive processes, and processes of reproduction and transformation of identity, is an understanding of the processes of interaction of which we are a part. Stig and I did not present any objectives for our work and we did not invite them to clarify their expectations. We invited them to explore together with us what the complex responsive processes perspective offered, to understand life in organizations as well as strategic work and to explore what was going on between all of us in the present working with these issues.

In the work with the cadets the paradoxes in social interaction became a bodily experience. All the time I felt very strongly about how much we both believed in what we were doing and yet there was always the underlying doubt at the same time. This was nothing we could have decided, it emerged in our relating, between ourselves and the cadets and between the two of us. I also felt that the two staff officers were very supportive, but early on in the process I also had a feeling that at least one of them doubted whether this work would be productive. It seems to me that exploring the paradoxes is more fruitful and gives all parties a different opportunity to explore and avoid unproductive conflicts which in many cases are a result of the wish, especially from the top management, to eliminate the paradoxes of life in organizations. In this case, the paradox was kept alive between Stig and myself. Believing and doubting emerges in both of us, not as a conscious choice but as an intrinsic part of the complex responsive processes of human relating we all experience.

I link these experiences with the cadets at the Air Force Academy to experiences with other clients. The first questions often asked by clients are: 'What will your contribution be? How can you help? What can we expect to get out of this?' These questions reflect the traditional understanding of the consultant as 'an expert who is called in for advice or information' or 'a person who gives expert advice'. The underlying assumption is that it is possible to predict the future. Some clients want guarantees that the consultant can tell them what will happen. What they ask for is a reproduction of old knowledge instead of novelty. Asking for novelty means keeping the paradoxes alive, and this is not the kind of consultation or organizational development the clients usually ask for. However, all clients ask for some kind of help and to many this is indeed consultation. When someone asks for consultation, there is always some kind of expectation, both from the consultant and the client, of some kind of help and improvement. Closely linked to the understanding of help is an expectation that something is going to be 'transferred' from the consultant to the client, often in the form of growth in individual knowledge or increased individual mastery, or the implementation of some new system. The underlying assumption is that the sender has something the receiver needs and that it is possible to transfer or send this through a communication channel. In this way of thinking it is important that the communication channel is of good quality so that the message passes through without disturbances such as those we had experienced with the cadets. In this traditional literature I have not found anything that combines help with keeping the paradoxes alive. On the contrary, most of the literature suggests that managers should collapse the paradoxes, with one vision and a strong corporate culture based on a common value base.

Now consider the idea of how one might understand the consultant as researcher from the perspective of complex responsive processes of relating, and hence the methodology that I have called 'emerging participative exploration'. In the next section I also argue for a different understanding of help and improvement (Christensen 2003).

Emerging participative exploration

The activities of research and consultation are themselves complex responsive processes of relating. They are, in principle, the same human processes as when I buy a shirt in a shop, drive my car in the traffic, negotiate with my bookkeeper, or have an argument with my teenage daughter. Although all of these interactions are examples of complex responsive processes of human or relating, I would not call them research. I would call them research when my main intention is to study the processes of relating themselves in such a way that my study will be accepted as research in a community of others. An important intention in emerging participative exploration is to avoid following a prescribed, detailed 'scientific method' and, instead, engage in a process of ongoing sense-making of the experience of participating in the fluid interactions with other people.

Emerging participative exploration is about making sense of how people are making sense of what they experience together as they participate in the ongoing, paradoxical iterations of interactions in the living present. In the very first conversations with a new client, I offer a difference that in itself will hopefully be experienced as a source of novelty. Speaking to clients about self-organization, control as a relational phenomenon, and emergence is in itself a difference and the response is very often 'you are speaking about my own real experiences as a manager'. Emerging participative exploration is first of all a way of taking our ordinary daily experiences as relating human beings seriously, and is grounded in a need to make sense of identity and difference and the themes that emerge in conversations in daily work. An important intention from this perspective is to focus on my own and my client's ordinary experiences in such a way that this results in an improved awareness of what is going on in our social interactions. My intention is to 'get as close' as possible to what is going on in the conversations I take part in. What I experience is exploration processes where I, the consultant as researcher, am trying to make sense of my own identity and understand what is going on. At the same time I am helping other people to make sense of their own identity and their own understanding of what is going on in the living present.

I suggest that this way of thinking about research and consultation is different to traditional action research, cooperative inquiry and the position of the participative observer as described in the process consultation literature (Christensen 2003, p. 144). I am not interested in generating objective knowledge to be implemented somewhere else, or in making a diagnosis of the context of which I am a part and then designing interventions to correct something. Furthermore, I am not going to 'align' the formal and the informal system (French and Bell 1990, p. 19) in the organizations of which I am a part. What I am interested in is ordinary daily conversations in the living present in which the future is perpetually constructed. I am interested in the complex responsive processes of relating in which a coherent pattern emerges spontaneously in the relating itself and in which novelty or new meaning emerges. I am seeking to reflect and understand my own participation as an explorer in these processes of how new meaning and hence identity and difference arise.

I do not try to separate reflection from 'action' because novel thought is in my experience, potentially emerging all the time as well as the reproduction of old thoughts. Reflection is an intrinsic part of human relating. My thought and hence my reflections are actions of my body. By sharing my thoughts and writings with my colleagues and with the people

I am working with and by comparing them to the different theories to which I am referring, I am able to make different meanings of past and current conversations. Reflection is going on all the time in my work. Emerging participative exploration cannot be described in detail as a methodology in advance. The research method emerges in the relating itself. Emerging participative exploration involves an intention but it is not possible to prescribe or describe in advance what will emerge.

The complex responsive processes perspective draws attention to how power relations are enabling constraints and to the dynamics of inclusion and exclusion in groups, which raise anxiety. Participating in making sense of and reporting from within these processes inevitably includes my own bodily experiences of taking part in human relating. I argue that emerging participative exploration must therefore include my own experiences of power relations, exclusion and inclusion. Participating in human relating is always a bodily experience and therefore feelings are a natural part of this kind of exploration. This is a different position to that of the objective detached observer, such as the scientist studying nature or the traditional action researcher observing and intervening in a system.

I try to be aware of how patterns of behavior from earlier relating are being repeated in the present. I also try to be aware of processes of inclusion and exclusion, as well as the anxiety emerging from these processes. I speak from my own experience with the intention of helping others to find out for themselves how they reproduce patterns and are participants in the co-creation of organizational patterns which are often called organizational culture. Emerging participative exploration takes the form of subjective narratives. I encourage people to make sense of their daily experiences using a narrative form. My intention is to help them to express their experiences with the possibility that their past, their history, might change and a new meaning might emerge in our conversations.

I also suggest that another intention from this perspective is to hold the situation open for any theme to emerge, and implicit in this is helping to articulate emergent themes. My intention is to participate in fluid conversations in order to contribute to a free-flowing quality of exploration in which ambiguity and uncertainty are lived with for long enough for something novel to emerge. I am not talking of 'Einsteinian' novelty but new ways of understanding ordinary daily problems, a fresh understanding of one's own part in the creation of organizational patterns. I try to encourage people to speak in a way that keeps paradoxes alive, addressing both hope and doubt about the future and by doing this they 'complexify' their conversations. This means that I try to understand linkages between what might be experienced as irrelevant emerging themes and the possible overall theme we have come together to explore.

My intention is to take part in making sense of how different people and myself understand what is going on. I do this without a specific task other than inviting others to explore what is said and experienced in their bodies. I have taken part in conversations and sometimes feel in my body their expectations and anxiety, and how this is the beginning of the emergence of my identity in our work. Despite the anxiety I feel from time to time it is important not to rush to a premature conclusion, but to give novelty an opportunity to emerge. For me, it is important to enter into these conversations with the intention of demonstrating that although I am not in control of what will emerge I am not afraid of not being in control. I want to demonstrate that this is a very normal situation in our conversational life. I might introduce the theme of control and not being in control (Streatfield 2001) of what we are trying to achieve together despite our intentions. By doing this I am recognizing complexity and I am ready to engage with what is going to emerge, suggesting that the others do the same.

In spite of my intentions, however, there is no guarantee that I can predict the outcome of my intention or control what will happen. I therefore do not have any objectives for the work in the traditional meaning of objectives. In spite of this my work is still purposeful. I am also aware that when taking part in conversations others may have a completely different understanding of what is going on. My intention, however, is to invite others to be curious, to explore and try to find in themselves where the solutions to their problems are located, why they are stuck and what to do differently. I try to enter into my work with a paradoxical 'open intention' not to solve problems for them but to participate with them in exploring whatever theme may emerge from our conversations. My intention is to participate in a way that influences and encourages ways of working that may result in the emergence of novel ways of speaking and relating, so transforming our conversations and hence our relating.

What I am suggesting is an intention that is linked to the realities of knowing and not knowing at the same time. I am talking about the continuous processes of making meaning in situations where the quality of conversation is the key to moving on when we do not know and are not in control. It is in the many daily conversations that employees and managers are involved in that they show how they are able to manage the paradoxical 'knowing and not knowing' and being in control and not being in control at the same time. It is in these conversations that new intentions potentially emerge. These are the conversations many of us experience as so ordinary that we do not pay attention to the importance of them. By participating and paying attention in a different way in these ordinary conversations, I am offering help so that what might be experienced as improvement might emerge.

I am helping by contributing to the emergence of new meaning, themes in conversations and aesthetic moments of insight that have not been there before. Perhaps the first experience of help is represented by the difference in the view of the future and what engaging me is all about. These are differences that cannot be known in advance; they are truly novel and arise in the conversations. The arrival of hope and some kind of understanding of the work is perhaps the first novelty to emerge. This in itself may be the first experience of help and improvement, the emergence of a different way of understanding changes and how changes emerge. Novelty emerges in the relating itself with the clients present. Help is then not to transfer anything from me to others; it is truly emergent as meaning-creating processes.

The improvement I offer clients is one of recognizing that novelty is happening in the moment. This may lead to a hope that what has emerged in these local conversations might escalate into a global conversational pattern, a new strategy, new actions, new conversations, new products or new formal structures. The improvement in understanding of individual and social identity is the source of changes in conversations taking place. Once people recognize the emergence of identity in conversations they then understand how they are themselves co-creating the patterns of relating they experience. This helps them to understand how they are taking part in political processes and how power relations are co-created, so helping them to reflect on their own part in the perpetual construction of power relating and of the future. By paying attention in this way, people will potentially experience a new understanding of how changes take place and the importance of conversations. The understanding of the non linearity and paradoxical properties of human relating may give rise to courage to act more competently in the future without knowing the output.

References

Argyris, C. (1973) *Organisationsudvikling på psykologisk grundlag*, vols 1 and 2, Copenhagen: Bedriftsøkonomens Forlag (original title: *Intervention – Theory and Method*).

Argyris, C., Putman, R. and Smith, D. (1985) *Action Science*, San Francisco, CA: Jossey-Bass.

Barbour, R.S. and Kitzinger, J. (1999) *Developing Focus Group Research. Politics, Theory and Practice*, London, Thousand Oaks, New Delhi. Sage.

Bateson, G. (1973) *Steps to an Ecology of Mind*, St Albans: Paladin.

Bion, W.R. (1994) *Experiences in Groups and Other Papers*, London: Routledge (reprinted).

Block, P. (1981) *Flawless Consulting: A Guide to Getting Your Expertise Used*, Austin, TX: Learning Concepts.

Campbell, D. (1995) *Learning Consultation: A Systemic Framework*, London: Karnac Books.

Campbell, D., Coldicott, T. and Kinsella, K. (1994) *Systemic Work with Organizations: A New Model For Managers And Change Agents*, London: Karnac Books.

Christensen, B.B. (2003) *Reframing Consulting as Transformation from Within Human Relating*, Unpublished Doctor of Management thesis, University of Hertfordshire.

Crotty, M. (1998) *The Foundations of Social Research: Meaning and Perspective in the Research Process*, St. Leonards, NSW: Sage.

Dalal, F. (1998) *Taking the Group Seriously: Toward a Post-Foulkesian Group Analytic Theory*, London: Jessica Kingsley.

Elias, N. (1978) *What is Sociology?*, New York: Colombia University Press.

Elliot, J. (1991) *Action Research for Educational Change*, Milton Keynes: Open University Press.

Emery, F.E. and Trist, E.L. (1960) 'Socio-technical systems', in C.W. Churchman and M. Verhulst (eds) *Management Sciences, Models and Techniques, Vol. 2*, Oxford: Pergamon Press, (pp. 83–97).

French, W.L. and Bell, C.B. (1984) *Organization Development: Behavioral Science Interventions for Organization Improvement*, Engelwood Cliffs, NJ: Prentice-Hall.

Gergen, K.J. (1999) *An Invitation to Social Construction*, Thousand Oaks, CA: Sage.

Griffin, D. (2002) *The Emergence of Leadership: Linking self-organization and ethics*, London: Routledge.

Heron, J. (1996) *Co-operative Inquiry: Research into Human Condition*, London: Sage.

Heron, J. and Reason, P. (2000) *A Lay Person's Guide to Co-operative Inquiry*, University of Bath: Centre for Action Research in Professional Practice.

Johannessen, S. (2003) *An Exploratory Study of Complexity, Strategy and Change in Logistics Organizations*, Unpublished thesis, Trondheim NTNU.

Kant, I. ([1790] 1987) *Critique of Judgment*, trans. W.S. Pluhar, Indianapolis: Hackett.

Kolb, D. A., Rubin, I. M. and McIntyre, J. M. (1984) *Organizational Psychology: An Experimental Approach to Organizational Behavior*, Engelwood Cliffs, NJ: Prentice-Hall.

Lomax, P. (1990) *Managing Staff Development in Schools*, Clevedon: Multi-lingual Matters.

McNiff, J., Lomax, P. and Whitehead, J. (1996) *You and Your Action Research Project*, London: Routledge.

Mead, G. H. (1934) *Mind, Self and Society: From the Standpoint of a Social Behaviorist*, Chicago, IL: The University of Chicago Press.

Midgley, G. (2000) *Systemic Intervention*, Dordrecht: Kluwer.

Miller, E. J. (1993) *From Dependency to Autonomy: Studies in Organizational Change*, London: Free Association Books.

Miller, E. J. (2002) 'The strengths and limitations of a psychodynamic perspective in organizational consultancy', in *Object Relations and Integrative Psychotherapy*, ed. I. S. Nolan and P. Nolan.

Miller, E. J. and Rice, A. K. (1967) *Systems of Organizations: Task and Sentenient Systems and their Boundary Control*, London: Tavistock Publications.

Popper, K. R. (1959) *The Logic of Scientific Discovery*, New York: Harper.

Revans, R. W. (1984) *Aksjonslæringens ABC* (original title: *The ABC of Action Learning*), Oslo: Bedriftsøkonomens Forlag.

Schein, E. H. (1987) *Process Consultation Vol II: Lessons for Managers and Consultants*, Reading, MA: Addison-Wesley.

Schein, E. H. (1988) *Process Consultation Vol I: Its Role in Organization Development*, Reading, MA: Addison-Wesley.

Shotter, J. (1993) *Conversational Realities*, London: Sage.

Srivastva, S. and Cooperider, D. L. (1999) *Appreciative Management and Leadership: The Power of Positive Thought and Action in Organizations*, Euclid, OH: William Custom.

Stacey, R. (2001a) *Complex Responsive Processes in Organizations: Learning and knowledge creation*, London: Routledge.

Stacey, R. (2001b) 'Complexity at the edge of the basic-assumption group', in *The Systems Psychodynamics of Organizations*, ed. L. Gould, L. F. Stapley and M. Stein, London: Karnac.

Stacey, R. (2003) *Complexity and Group Processes: A radically social understanding of individuals*, London: Brunner-Routledge.

Stacey, R., Griffin, D. and Shaw, P. (2000) *Complexity and Management: Fad or radical challenge to systems thinking?*, London: Routledge.

Streatfield, P. (2001) *The Paradox of Control in Organizations*, London: Routledge.

Taylor, F. W. (1911) *Scientific Management*, New York: Harper & Bros.

von Bertalanffy, L. (1968) *General Systems Theory: Foundations, Development, Applications*, New York: George Braziller.

Editors' introduction to Chapter 5

Previous chapters in this volume have dealt explicitly with the nature of methodology from a complex responsive processes perspective and, in Chapter 4, Bjørner Christensen explored the relationship between research and consulting, arguing that they are the same activity. This chapter, together with chapters 6 and 7, describe pieces of research consulting which take up the methodology described in previous chapters.

In Chapter 5, Mary O'Flynn, who is a consultant operating mainly in Ireland and the UK, explores her work as facilitator to a group of people working for an organization called the Phoenix Project. This Project consists of a number of services for those affected by drug abuse. One service of the Project, called Dave's Place, took the form of a drop-in center which offered a non-judgmental support service for drug addicts. It was housed in an old building and the lease was about to expire, but no alternative accommodation had yet been identified. Another service of the Project, called Lulu's Centre, provided services for the children of these drug addicts. This was housed in another building which also served as the office of the Director of the Phoenix Project. Regular staff meetings for the Phoenix staff, including the teams of both Dave's Place and Lulu's Centre, took place in the building occupied by the director and the Lulu Centre team. On those occasions, members of the Dave's Place team, most of whom smoked, were able to use one of the counseling rooms of Lulu's Centre as a smoking room. Members of the Lulu Centre team did not smoke. O'Flynn was asked to facilitate a day-long meeting of all the Phoenix staff and management at which the imminent closure of Dave's Place was expected to be a key issue. As it turned out, the question of smoking also became a key issue, and O'Flynn explores the symbolic meaning this had for the organization.

In this introduction to the chapter we will have little to say about the content of O'Flynn's story. Instead we will highlight aspects of the research-consulting methodology which she employs.

First, she makes it clear how she is taking her experience of relating to others seriously, particularly her own feelings and thoughts, as she works. Her method, then, is explicitly subjective and her own subjectivity is the principal resource she draws on to do her work. The work is to make sense of her experience in the task of assisting others to make sense of their experience as they interact with each other. She links the processes of sense-making in which they are all engaged with the iteration and emergence of individual and collective identities and differences, paying particular attention to patterns of power relations and the dynamics of inclusion and exclusion in which identity and difference emerge. In telling the story of this assignment, O'Flynn brings out the uncertainty, doubt and anxiety she feels in taking the particular subjective stance she takes.

What O'Flynn is describing is a method of research consulting which is a social process, which means that it is inevitably participative. However, she also seeks to preserve some 'objectivity'. This paradoxical subjective–objective form of participation was explored in Chapter 3 by Richard Williams, who drew on Elias' discussion of involvement and detachment. We might describe the form of participation characteristic of the methodology set out in this volume as *involved detachment.*

Another aspect of the method that O'Flynn follows is its reflexive nature. She talks about practitioner reflexivity as a form of evolving conversation in which she converses imaginatively with herself. She often questions what she is doing in a reflexive manner as she considers whether her own personal attitudes, reflecting her life history, for example, towards conflict, are affecting her actions more than the reality of the interactions with others. She also points to the basis of this conversing in the perspective of complex responsive processes and the traditions of thought in which it is located.

Then, she understands what she is doing to be self-organizing as she and others with whom she is working co-create the emerging patterns of their interaction. Thus she does not herself follow prescriptive steps in relation to what she is doing and she does not present prescriptive steps to those with whom she is working. Instead, she takes an explorative approach in which she acts into the meaning that is emerging.

The form in which she presents her research in this chapter is that of a narrative which serves as the basis of her reflection. Many propositions emerge in this reflection. So, what is it that she is conveying using this methodology?

First, she conveys clearly what it means to prepare for the work she does. She gives a realistic account of the emotional work of preparation which requires dealing with one's self-doubts and the anxiety this brings. This is in contrast to prescriptive steps to follow in order to prepare a design for what to do in advance of doing it, an approach to preparation which could be a defense against anxiety having the effect of closing down options even before the work begins. Second, she produces a piece of research which describes what it actually means to facilitate a meeting, pointing to the importance of paying attention to patterns of power relating and the dynamics of inclusion and exclusion they bring. This is important because they have a powerful effect on what people can and cannot do. Third, she makes it clear how avoiding an impulse to achieve an immediate resolution of any difficulties, solve problems, give advice and cause change, she is playing a major part in keeping the conversation fluid so that people can address important matters that are usually left to fester below the surface. Fourth, she shows how the work is about articulating themes emerging in the conversation so as to enable the group to take the next step. She keeps the exploration going by only rarely putting forward hypotheses, making interpretations, clarifying roles or identifying tasks.

The reader might well ask why the above is at all useful. The story is one of a group of people who have not found alternative accommodation in time but who spend the time at the meeting discussing whether smokers can use a room occasionally required for counseling sessions. Surely it would be more useful to discourage this kind of conversation and focus instead on solving the accommodation problem? The drawback with taking this approach is that it is all too obvious. If it were that straightforward why have a group of intelligent people not already done it? It is so obvious that it should not need the services of a consultant. The methodology O'Flynn adopts goes beyond the obvious as she seeks to promote conversation that could enable underlying issues to be brought to the surface. What her approach succeeded in doing was to enable this group of people to reflect together on the power relations between two teams, Dave's Place and Lulu's Centre, and the issues of inclusion and exclusion between them. What became clear was the issue of team identity that was at stake. What is striking is how the two teams were probably reflecting similar processes to those going on in their client groups, one dealing with drug addicts themselves and the other with the harm they caused to their children.

5 Letting go, keeping connected and change at the Phoenix Project

Mary O'Flynn

In this chapter, I explore the process of my sense-making during several days of facilitation for a project undergoing change. The story is simple and a relatively routine piece of consultancy. I wish to draw attention to my interactions with the group and how I was experiencing myself as I engaged with them. It is extraordinarily difficult to describe process and it is never possible to accurately capture the movement of our interactions, conversations and relationships. Obviously, further sense-making takes place as I reflect and write afterwards.

Exploring practice

I have always puzzled about *the how of things*: how we learn; how the way we make sense of things influences the way we interact with others; how in conversation with others the meaning we have co-created previously is elaborated, indeed sometimes changed entirely. This chapter is about my work as a consultant with a project, based in a large town in the UK, which was undergoing a major change. It is an attempt to understand how I made sense of my actions and responses as I interacted with the people in the Phoenix Project, from within the action as I participated in it. Understanding my relationships has always been central to my life and my work. Connected to this is a continuous concern to understand my actions within those relationships. Participating with the staff of Phoenix in their inquiry as they process through their change is one way of reaching a greater understanding of myself and my actions. Subsequently reflecting and writing about the process involves my action and participation in another kind of meaning-making, and brings with it an additional dimension of awareness and understanding of myself, of my working relationships and of the way I work.

Much of this chapter is an attempt to explore this kind of reflexive sense-making, the sense I make as I converse silently with my memories and with other voices of my imagination, about my work in the Phoenix Project. I examine how I made sense of some of my actions, at the time and as I write now, in the context of all the interactions as I perceived them, affected them, and was affected by them during the process of the work. In fact this is a paradoxical action I am engaged in: I am trying to capture the movement of sense-making yet, as I do so, I am contributing to further movement. This process incorporates previous movements of personal and group histories brought to the meaning-making of the situation I am recalling and reconstructing. As I write, I am changing my own understanding of the past and simultaneously creating the potential for the continuous evolution of meaning. My purpose in writing this chapter is to try to illustrate this process at work while offering a way of understanding what I am doing. I am seeking to contribute to an understanding of practitioner reflexivity as an evolving conversational process, which takes place silently and imaginatively and which is of the same kind as our public conversing with one another.

The story

As part of some work with the parent organization, I was asked to facilitate a day-long meeting with the staff and management of the Phoenix Project. During the initial conversation with Tom, the Director, I learned that the project was about to undergo a major change. They had to vacate a building that housed a drop-in centre, one of their programs called Dave's Place. The owners had given six months' notice to the

Phoenix management committee. This was now the fifth month of their notice to quit and no replacement premises had been found. The management and staff had undertaken some exploration of the issues involved in the loss of the building. They had examined various alternatives and ways of meeting and keeping contact with their client group. They wanted to hold a day-long meeting in two weeks' time to plan for the change and its implications. I was surprised at the short notice of the request. I arranged to meet with Tom, and Mary, the Chairperson of the management committee, to plan for the day.

The narrow stairs to the Phoenix main offices lies behind a dusty unobtrusive door on the street. Lulu's Centre, another of the Phoenix programs, is also housed in this building. Tom and Mary gave me a brief history of the organization and an outline of its current structure. I recall feeling a sense of *déjà vu* as I listened. The following narrative is colored by my personal experience and my memory of how the conversation evolved.

The Phoenix Project was established to offer a non-judgmental support service to drug users, many of whom were excluded from, or unable to avail themselves of, other services as a result of their drug misuse. This group were often peripheral to the normal NHS services. I was well aware that as a group of people, the Phoenix clients live a chaotic lifestyle, are in and out of prison regularly, sleep rough, and have fallen foul of most social service agencies.

Initially, the project staff worked in an outreach capacity, making contact on the streets. Eventually they found temporary premises in which they set up a drop-in centre called Dave's Place, which was staffed and open daily. Here, the clients could visit, have a cup of tea, discuss their problems, and receive some counseling and support for themselves in dealing with their problems. They were offered a listening ear and advice on health and safety issues related to their drug use. The Phoenix offers a relatively unique kind of service in that clients are accepted as 'using' drugs and the only restriction within the project is 'no dealing or violence in Dave's Place'.

Over the intervening years the Phoenix activities were expanded and developed. A second building was acquired. In addition to the outreach service and Dave's Place, the staff operate a prison visiting service where they maintain contact with their clients and continue to offer advice and safety education on drug use. They liaise with families and connect their clients to other appropriate services. A recent development, the 'family program', was set up in Lulu's Centre. It was a response to the needs of the children of these addicts and adopts a holistic approach to issues. The staff team at Lulu's Centre work intensively with the children and their parents. They liaise with statutory agencies on their behalf, often performing an advocacy role.

We explored the reason for the day's facilitation. Tom and Mary thought that the day should be spent examining issues related to the closure. They wanted to plan the change-over and to identify how the staff might support themselves through the process. I got the impression that Mary was task-focused and appeared slightly frustrated by the staff's insecurities. She wanted to spend most of the day sorting out the details of the change and planning for the future. Tom, while acknowledging the need to plan for the future, was clearly anxious to support the staff through an emotionally charged change process.

A replacement premises was mentioned. There was a possibility of acquiring a building but it was uncertain. They would know soon if they were going to gain occupancy of this building and this would mean that they could start planning, but they might not know before our planning day together. Even if they did receive confirmation, it would take six months, at least, to assume ownership and refurbish the new building. Meanwhile there was no other accommodation available. Although there was ongoing work that would be continuing, Tom and Mary had no firm idea about what they would do in the interim. How would they maintain contact with their clients or how could they be contacted by new clients? Mary assured me that there was much that could be done. Tom thought that they should be out hunting for other possible locations. This was proving difficult, as their clients were perceived as 'a serious public nuisance' and frequently caused disruption on the streets. As I listened, I was remembering my own experience in attempting to acquire a building to house women ex-offenders. I empathized with them and mentioned this. To myself, I thought it unlikely that they would acquire a suitable building, even in the longer term, and I wondered how on earth they would deal with this frustration.

Mary mentioned the notion of developing a café environment. This idea seemed to involve renting a series of coffee shops or rooms around the city center for certain periods on different days each week. Staff would be available at these places to meet their clients. Again, I thought of my own experience. I imagined that knowing their chaotic lifestyles, communicating the information of 'when and where' to their clients would be a problem. I remarked that the logistics of this might prove difficult and asked if any of these meeting points had been identified, but none had to date. Other suggestions included buying a caravan, but this raised security and siting issues. Meanwhile, the staff of Dave's Place were homeless. They would have to use the building in which we were meeting as a base. Although there was a room available at the top of the building, space was limited and an additional eight people would impact on the administrative staff and the staff and work in Lulu's Centre. Tom then referred to the impact on the staff of Dave's Place having to share the same building with the family program. I suggested that this was one of the issues we should examine together. My impression was that this would raise political issues for both groups of staff. I sensed that the staff of Lulu's Centre considered that Dave's Place staff were able to ignore, to a certain extent, some of the political issues in relation to the children of chaotic addicts. Now they would be confronted with this reality. Tom felt that this would raise difficulties for both staff groups in addition to the discomfort of sharing the limited space.

At one point during the meeting, I expressed surprise that this work had not taken place some time ago. Mary said that some work had indeed been done already. They had brainstorming sessions to identify what could be done in the absence of a building. She noted that the group had come up with many ideas, but that was as far as it went. I could empathize with this: memories flooded in of writing up lists of bullet points from meetings, with a sure feeling in my stomach that they would make little difference!

I remember noticing that I was feeling a distinct sense of confusion and having difficulty understanding what was going on in the organization. I was feeling swamped by all sorts of diverse information. I felt unable to get a clear sense of how Tom and Mary wished us to spend the time during the day. Throughout the conversation, I sensed their feeling of unreality about it all. Later I wondered to myself, if Mary was denying the reality of the impact that the change would have for the staff. Tom, understandably, appeared to be almost paralyzed with anxiety about how he would manage it all.

Eventually, I suggested that whether or not another building had been acquired or identified did not seem to be the main issue. We were going to be working together anyway, with or without a building in the offing. I remember Tom mentioned that with no premises available, Dave's Place staff were worried about a loss of contact with their clients as a consequence of the closure. I realized that this, in turn, would generate a fear that the loss of work would place their jobs at risk. Tom indicated that he had assured the staff that this would not happen, that there was sufficient funding for the immediate future, that a building would be found, that alternative ways of working are possible. I thought he appeared slightly irritated as he remarked that they did not seem to be reassured. I suggested that it might be helpful for everybody to have the opportunity to articulate their concerns about this so that we could make sense of their fears together. Mary chipped in that the staff 'are inclined to revel in misery!' However, Tom was clearly anxious about their deeply felt sense of insecurity. His aim for *the day* was 'consolidation and affirmation' as well as planning for the way forward. When I inquired what he meant by this he agreed that the team needed to voice their fears and to identify ways in which they could support themselves through the changeover, to build their confidence. He also pointed out that he wanted to review the kind of service Phoenix was offering, to examine how they would continue to operate their service and to draw up a plan for what needed to happen during the changeover period. He felt that the work of the day should involve a reassessment and reorientation for all so that everybody would realize the implications of the management decisions for their work. As I write this from my notes of the day, it seems a rather ambiguous statement to me now. Why did it not seem odd at the time? I wonder why I did not pursue it with him.

In discussing the timetable for the day, Tom remarked that there were several smokers on the staff and he warned me that we would have to have regular breaks or the smokers would get restless! Indeed, smoking turned out to be quite a powerful and symbolic issue, but more about that below.

My silent conversation: intention and identity

Working in a new situation, co-creating the future with an unknown group of people is both exciting and filled with tension. As usual I had the jitters. Why did I think I could make a difference? Yes, I was coming to the group with an understanding of their work context and situation. I have worked with offenders, many of whom were addicts. For years I have been involved in the management of a similar type of organization and with similar community organizations. I have seen through many changes over that period. I had also consulted to a sister organization. But this was not a guarantee that I would be able to contribute to the present situation in Phoenix.

Even as I write 'guarantee' and 'contribute', I become aware of catching myself thinking 'is that what I am about?' I cannot 'guarantee' anything. I watch my thoughts move backwards and forwards. Do I mean, 'participate in a way that would contribute effectively?' But every group and situation is different. There cannot be a specific 'way' to do it. Neither the group nor I can control the future. We will co-create the future during our day together. We have some notion of what is required from the day. We have a sense of purpose, some conscious intention. Of course, I know that the self-organization of our conversations will have an outcome but one which we cannot know in advance and which we will never fully know whether or not our intention is conscious. Even deliberately or forcefully imposing intention will have an outcome of some kind, which may or may not be what was intended.

I find it hard to shake the belief that I 'should' have some way of knowing how to intervene, or I 'should' know the best thing to do in order to enable this group to make sense of their concerns. I am being paid for my thinking and skill in moving the process of meaning-making along. I have difficulty relinquishing the notion that I 'should' have the answers to help the Phoenix team resolve their problems. Once again, I note in my silent conversation that I am overlooking the fact that making meaning will arise in the process of our interactions. This leads me to thinking about my participation with the group in the process of our joint meaning-making.

I grappled with the function of my role as facilitator. I wanted to focus on the movement of the conversation and our sense-making together. In paying close attention to the here and now of the interactions, in listening intently, I hoped to identify the themes emerging in our conversations. Why? In the belief that the difficulties which concerned everybody in Phoenix would arise and that by bringing them into focus we would be able to make sense of them together. Some of these were likely to be contentious. I expected that they might be the kind of issues where strong emotions are played out, patterning the conversations in the struggle of communicative interaction and in the power play in which we recognize and assert our needs and desires and continuously renegotiate identity and difference.

I knew that in this process of meaning-making, conflicts and tensions would surface. Yes, we would deal with them, but I noticed how anxious

I was about this. Griffin points to the difficulty we have in speaking of 'our conflicting interests, feelings and motives' (Griffin, 2002, p. 156). I recognized that I was fearful in case we would not be able to manage the conflict when it arose. But, I asked myself, what do I mean by 'managing' it? Smoothing things over? Suppressing it? Achieving consensus so that everybody is happy? Griffin goes on to say that 'we *can seek through conflict the active recognition* of difference and thus *at the same time* recreate and possibly transform our identity' (ibid.).

My past history and dislike of conflict flow into my silent conversation. I know that in acknowledging difference, I am creating my own identity. Without others, with whom I can perceive a difference, I cannot be aware of my identity. Indeed, the existence of others is always a necessary condition of my identity. It puts me in touch with my experience of myself, validates my existence. Identity is not a possession. Rather, it is relational and contingent, defined in terms of difference. It is both continuous with the past and created anew. The realization and continual definition of my identity emerges in my interactions with others. Dalal points out that identity is 'a phenomenon that is embedded in a network of social interactions and relations' (Dalal, 1998, p. 190). This interdependent and evolving process emphasizes individuality, my difference within the group. Awareness of both interdependence and Sartre's *nausea* of aloneness is always present. For me, it is emphasized at the moment in the paradox of being both a facilitator trying to hold an 'objective' stance and, at the same time, a participant inquirer, only able to make sense with others from within our work together. Anxiety rises as I realize my interdependence and at the same time my desire to control and to deny interdependence. The difficulty will be to hold this paradox open without collapsing it to either pole. During this work, as the Phoenix team and I engage in the movement of our conversation together, our individual and our group identities will be emerging. At the same time, in our meaning-making we will be involved in forming the individual and group identities of each other. In this same conversation, at the same time, our individual differences and group differences will be forming and being formed by us both as individuals and as group members. The co-creation of identity and difference will emerge in the interactions and responses of the day in Phoenix.

As I anticipate the work of the day with the Phoenix people, I struggle with doubts about my ability to handle conflict. Do we *always* have to seek difference through conflict? Perhaps that depends on the constraints of the particular moment we are creating together, constraints that are also enabling. In the complexity of our exchanges it is possible that there will be times when it is appropriate to highlight difference by focusing on conflict, to emphasize heterogeneity. There may be other times when it is more sensitive to emphasize coherence. My decisions about this will involve the 'aesthetic' moment of resonance and intuition. This intuitive sense will be informed by the emerging ethics of the situation and by the sense of integrity from within it. It will be my thinking in action in the movement of the living present. It involves my intention, which will be both forming the movement and being formed in the movement of the group process.

Immediately the dilemma arises again in my silent conversation: 'How will I know if I am deceiving myself or not?' Yes, I will bring my own embodied personal, historical, interpersonal patterning, personality, biases, intellectual ability and knowledge base to the gesture and response of understanding meaning in the process of its making, but psychological forces are always at play within the matrix of relationships that are a group. I cannot be sure that my informed intuition is not false judgment. I may be colluding to deny conflict or to pursue unconscious transferences, projections and fantasies – ways of making sense of interactions that I bring from my training in group analysis. Of course I cannot be sure about any of this. I can only go on participating in the negotiation of meaning as it emerges from the conversation of gestures and responses in the movement of the living present. I can authentically take responsibility for my commitment to paying attention and to my participation in the process without blame or seeking cause and effect.

Griffin calls this the 'primary human reality' of our conversations in everyday life (Griffin, 2002, p. 109). It involves the detail of our choices and actions as we relate to each other and make sense of our experience. It is the paradoxical movement of both continuity and transformation of minds and selves at the same time as they relate to each other. Stacey *et al.* define this as 'the living present' (Stacey *et al.*, 2000, pp. 35–36). In the gesture and response of interactions and sense-making each moment takes its meaning from, is influenced by, previous moments. At the same time, every gesture and response influences and has the potential to transform the next moment. Paradoxically, the future and the past are both continuously constructed in the living present. It is a moving process of meaning-making.

I catch myself wondering if I will remember the conversations so that I may be aware of patterns and themes. I recall that I have sometimes become absorbed in the content of the stories people tell, empathizing with the individuals involved! If this happens and I fail to notice other elements, will I miss aspects in the complexity of interactions? Here I am worrying about control again! Of course it is not possible to notice or to remember everything in this complex process. Participation will require intensity in listening to the movement of conversation. It will involve noticing who is engaging with whom, being alert to emerging patterns in interactions and conversations, being aware of the flow of associations arising in the patterns, paying attention to interruptions, to abrupt shifts in focus and to the emotional atmosphere in the group process. Meaning is always under perpetual construction and, as a participant, my gestures and responses will be part of the meaning-making, both my own and that of others. I know that each person in the group will bring their own particular personal history to the sense-making of their responses and interactions. I know that the interactions of the group members will bring with them the group's history of patterns of interaction, their conversational themes. I also know that paying attention to these patterns in the living present of the meaning-making is all I will be able to do. Some of these patterns will resonate with me and others will pass me by unawares. Subsequently, perhaps drawing the group's attention to some of the themes and patterns in the interactions would offer the potential for creative change in the conversation.

Thinking about all of this raises anxiety about how I will manage the day. With their approaching homelessness and the ambiguity about a replacement building, I wondered what staff morale would be like. Will I be able to contain my own anxiety in order to hold theirs? Will I be 'good enough'? Reducing anxiety to a manageable level will enable more meaningful conversations. Participating in this inquiry into their organizational life, will I be able to enable a free-flowing conversation in which the people working in Phoenix will feel safe enough to create new meaning together? It seems to me that in participating actively to create a context for others to articulate their fears I must acknowledge to myself and accept my own fragility, my own fear of what the day will bring. Making sense of experience and of the uncertainty of what is happening to us in the living present is an unpredictable process. If conflict rises and things became difficult will I be held responsible for allowing it to happen and for the discomfort of the situation? In trying to make sense together in the messiness of the situation, will I be able to accept these expectations and projections? All these thoughts occupied me, buzzing around in my head.

The precious time during this day together will be spent exploring the possibilities of the change that is being imposed on Phoenix. Constraint can also be enabling. What will enable their change in spite of the constraints? As a consultant, I want to add value to the Phoenix change process. Will I be able to work in a way that will earn my fee? I remind myself that the most important thing is to create an opportunity for conversation, for fears to be articulated and explored so that we can make sense of them together. I know that it will be important for everybody to be able to acknowledge their anxiety about the changes. Recognizing the increased loss of control will force up anxiety levels and push us to search for new patterns of meaning. In this process, I know that new conversations will emerge. As well as dealing with the practicalities of changing premises, changing the conversation will change the thinking. I hoped that the group would be able to change the conversation from one of demoralization to one of hope and courage in facing the unknown future.

As I look back on what I have written in this section, I wonder if I have managed to convey the process of my personal experience, the rise and fall of my own doubt, demoralization, hope and courage as I contemplated the work ahead. This process of anticipation, fantasy and self-questioning takes place as an ongoing, spontaneously occurring silent conversation, in which I am reshaping my own experiences and sense of myself; in other words, my history. In so doing I am giving potential shape to my future experiences with the group. In a sense this is a form of preparation for the work. In the following section I give an account of the work itself as I remember making sense of it at the time.

Day one: fear of the unknown

We started by identifying expectations for the day. Just as Tom had intimated, many of the comments were about their need for clarification of various issues, roles and plans, as well as the need for reassurance and support from the management committee. I was struck by a final comment from one of the participants: 'How do we keep the conversation open?' On inquiring how that might happen, there were familiar statements about feeling safe, trust, honesty, listening to each other, respecting each other. Based on their need to engage and listen intently, it was decided to break into smaller groups to examine the various concerns. Afterwards, as I was taking feedback from these groups, I was looking for connections between various points. The session highlighted fear of the unknown about the future changes and the need for reassurance and support both from the management and for each other. We spent some time naming their fears with the intention of moving to ways of addressing them and exploring how they could support themselves during the process of change.

I had been acutely aware that Tom's anxiety about the changes resulting from the loss of the building was probably reflecting the fears of the rest of the staff. As everybody began to express their fears and concerns some of the themes absorbing people began to emerge. They were worrying about 'being boxed off', 'excluded', 'separation and splits'. I reflected privately that the theme of inclusion/exclusion seemed to be surfacing here and that it would be useful to bring this into the conversation later. Juxtaposed came . . . 'the need to let go' and 'how to stay connected'. I noticed that there were several comments about 'the need to create a space to talk', 'the difficulty of talking', 'team dynamics and conflicts'. One of the younger members suddenly started to cry and expressed her worry about being asked to do outreach work. Sitting wondering what to say, it seemed important not to rush in but to allow everybody the time to think about how to make sense of this and how they wished to respond. After a period of silence, all I could think to say was that it seemed to be a positive sign that Lucy felt safe enough to cry. In retrospect, I wonder if this was true. However, there seemed to be a gradual easing of the tension as Tom offered reassurance that nobody would be obliged to do anything they did not feel able to manage. I sensed that the group were relieved at my response to the incident and this was confirmed to me by a couple of people later during the tea break. But I wondered if I was trying to ease my own anxiety here. Yes. Was I colluding, smoothing things over, in trying to bring a sense of ease? I don't know. This seemed to be one of those moments where sensitivity was required. On one hand, I can argue defensively that people were articulating their fears and uncertainties about the future and of course they were feeling vulnerable. On the other hand, and on reflection, I think I could have explored in more depth what people thought about the challenge of different kinds of work. However, this opportunity arose at a later stage when people formed into smaller groups to discuss ways of supporting themselves during the changeover.

Based on the conversations and experiences, I sensed a level of emotional turbulence and underlying conflict. Was this the time to raise the issues of staff conflict and team dynamics, early on my first day with the group? I can only ask the question and try to understand it afterwards. However,

I noted the body language of Kate, one of the management committee, who appeared angry. I could not make eye contact with her and she remained silent for most of the day. Before we finished she stated that it was important to have another day. There was a lot of 'stuff' that still needed to be dealt with and resolved. I had a feeling that I was being held responsible for this, but perhaps I was being oversensitive.

Pause: anxiety – the patterning of conversation

I pause here to look in more detail at how I have since made sense of some interactions that caught my attention at the time. Several times early on in the day, different people mentioned the need to talk, to keep talking, that it was necessary 'to make space to talk about the impact of the closure'. This was followed by 'yes, there is not enough support for each other'. Some one else offered, 'it is difficult to talk' which was followed by, 'it is time to move on'. Pointing out that we *were* talking did not seem to be heard. We were talking about the need for conversation but we were not engaging in conversation about what was at issue. The talk about talking seemed to be a theme organizing our experience and conversation. In the self-organizing process of the interactions as people spoke, this theme of talking about talking was patterning their conversations. How does this pattern arise? What was my part in it?

Stacey connects anxiety about change to the themes of inclusion and exclusion that pattern language. He makes the point that living with anxiety 'is very difficult, perhaps impossible, in a situation in which people's complete work situation is undergoing . . . massive and uncertain change' (Stacey, 2001, p. 158). If anxiety is very great then efforts will be made to reproduce particular patterns of communicative interaction with as little variation as possible. In the turn-taking of making-meaning together we use a language that categorizes, we use a range of 'rhetorical devices' to move and persuade both ourselves and each other. In circumstances of threatened change we revert to familiar ways of talking, of using a vocabulary that sustains a sense of inclusion and comfort to deal with the intense anxiety. This seems to be what was being reflected in the patterning of the 'talking' theme. The Phoenix staff are comfortable with this language. In role with clients they engage in and encourage talk. Conversation is their *raison d'être*, but I realize that the patterning taking place here seems to be deflecting effective communication. How can we understand this further? Analogies from a complexity perspective may be helpful.

Stacey argues that coherent patterns of talking and behavior emerge in conversation and in our self-organizing interactions. Our individual mental and social realities are being constructed in this responsive process as we gesture and respond during our conversations. The repetitiveness of the theme of talk about talking in this workshop was emerging as a reflection of their need for stability. It seemed to me that the unnecessary repetition of the 'need to talk' theme was giving a sense of stability to this group threatened by the instability of the change they were facing. In talking about talking they may have been dealing with their own anxiety about facing the difficult issues and talking about them. This theme, as I perceived it, was emerging as we were making and taking turns in the talking. Nobody was deliberately steering the conversation. The conversation was patterning itself. It seemed to me that this repetitive, self-referential conversation was sustaining a sense of stability in the group in the face of threat.

Returning to the narrative of day one

What was my part in this group so far? I had organized small group conversations around issues that arose and seemed to need further discussion. Circulating during the group work, sometimes contributing and offering comments from my own experience, I was impressed with the level of involvement in the conversations. They were generally lively and energetic. I had participated actively with the members, eliciting their expectations, recording comments, looking for clarification, making connections between points as I saw them and checking to see if the links made sense to people or if there were other ways of understanding them. There were some frustrated comments about 'how external forces dictate what we can or cannot do', followed by 'we need help from other services during the change process'. Connecting these points, I wondered if the current situation might offer the time and opportunity to network. An enthusiastic discussion ensued about strengthening relationships with other agencies. It was suggested that support could be offered to other services in relation to the Phoenix clients. Someone commented that the closure might force other agencies to become more aware of the needs of the Phoenix clients.

Thus for most of the earlier part of the day I had deliberately spent in creating a context that I hoped would enable a level of connectedness and trust so that there would be greater commitment to the sense-making process. I did this in an attempt to hold the anxiety sufficiently to allow the free-flowing self-organization of the conversation. On the other hand, I wondered if there were times when I had cushioned their anxiety, smoothed things over, to the extent that the need to struggle in their own sense-making was reduced. This is a continuous balancing process required of the reflective practitioner.

After lunch, we spent some time identifying the tasks and issues that needed to be addressed. Out of this arose a discussion about their staff meetings. There was a disgruntled comment about the length of time taken discussing reports at the meetings. I suggested that we look at how the agenda was structured. In this discussion it emerged that there were difficulties with time-keeping on the part of several of the Dave's Place team. Work starts at 9.30 a.m. and the weekly staff/whole team meetings were supposed to start at 10 a.m. but because some people came late meetings rarely started before 10.45 a.m. One or two of the Dave's Place team reacted defensively: they were often late finishing work; they sometimes stayed on after working hours to tidy up or to follow up on something with or for clients; it was not possible to just walk away if somebody was having a crisis. In some ways I could understand this defensiveness. Clearly, this group were extremely committed to and caring of their clients. On the other hand, I was puzzled knowing that the team have a debrief session every evening before finishing. I wondered how they can have the debrief all together if some are still engaged with clients. But the discussion had moved on and I made a mental note to raise it later or to ask Sally, the manager of Dave's Place. In sharp contrast, the Lulu's Centre team seemed to be more punctual. The building where staff meetings took place was also their permanent workplace. On the planning days when I arrived for 9.30 a.m., they were always at work in their offices.

I noted to myself that some of the Dave's Place team seemed to be identifying with and reflecting the lack of structure in the chaotic lifestyle of some of their clients. However, it also struck me that this pattern of poor time-keeping may have been reflecting one pole in the balance of power of their group relationships. Elias, Stacey, Dalal and many others argue that power is a structural characteristic of all relationships. The balance of power is continuously shifting and changing in the communication and dynamics of the relationships in every group. It is ubiquitous and inevitable in the highly complex and responsive process of all relating in the living present as we engage in our joint action and daily living together. Stacey connects polarization in the shifts in power relations to themes of inclusion and exclusion, and the anxiety that arises from these themes in our interactions and in the ordinary everyday conversations we engage in all the time (Stacey, 2001, p. 156).

Complaints about the agenda for the weekly staff meeting seemed to illustrate another pole in the power relations. At these meetings it appeared that discussion about Lulu's Centre issues was taking up a large portion of the meeting time. I got the feeling that these meetings were engendering low energy. It struck me that perhaps this might be the team of Lulu's Centre unconsciously attempting to assert themselves in the power relationships. Competition and cooperation are a part of all these relations, at the same time carrying the potential for transformation.

We concluded the day by negotiating a timetable and structure for the staff meeting agenda, setting a date for evaluation in two months' time. Finally, we reviewed our initial list of expectations for the day, identifying what still needed to be discussed, and recapping on what had been achieved.

Day two: a theme organizing behavior

Reflecting on our day's work together I realized that although we had done much valuable talking, we had not made any plans in relation to the closure of the building. We had not discussed any of the details about moving buildings or any of the issues that needed to be examined in relation to the changing work practice of Dave's Place staff. I sensed a resistance to addressing what needed to be done. It occurred to me that this was probably defensiveness. Defense mechanisms arise as an unconscious denial of the inevitability of reality as people protect themselves against the anxiety of unknown change and the feeling of loss of control. I recalled Mary's complaint at our first briefing meeting . . . that the group were very good at talking but now they needed to get down to doing. I felt that the team probably knew what needed to be discussed but they were finding it difficult to do it.

Bearing this in mind, I decided that planning might ground the group in the reality of the present as we moved into the future. I felt that a focus on discussion of the practical aspects of the impending change would contain some of their anxiety, offering a sense of purpose to the process of our sense-making. I knew that I could not control the outcome, but I hoped that the potential for transformation would emerge through the continuous process of meaning-making.

We began the day by drawing up a 'to do' list. There were several comments about preparing the clients for the closing! As we made the list, tension arose when someone asked about 'the availability of the smoking room'. A heated discussion ensued in which there were several reactive and defensive responses. Apparently, this room was normally used for counseling clients of Lulu's Centre. (The Dave's Place team would not be meeting their clients in this building.) I pointed out that this seemed to be a thorny issue that needed exploring so that a compromise solution could be negotiated. By chance, I asked if there was anywhere else that could be used as a smoking room. Tom pointed out, first, that there was another small counseling room. It was mostly used as a storeroom but it was supposed to be an additional counseling room. It could be cleared out and used regularly as a counseling room. The Lulu's Centre team did not seem very happy about this and several people acknowledged that it was quite a small room. Alternatively, Tom suggested that the smokers could use the other counseling room whenever it was free, provided that it was vacated immediately and without question if it was needed. One of the smokers suggested that this was unsatisfactory, since break-time was their normal time for a smoke and 'what if' the room was in use. The possibility of ensuring that the room would always be free at these times was not feasible. The staff of Lulu's Centre were very defensive. They considered this room to be part of their working space where they met their clients. They argued that they could not terminate a conversation just because it was the smoker's break-time. Also, if smokers were using the room and the Lulu's Centre staff needed it they would not feel comfortable having to ask the smokers to vacate it each time. The smokers reacted that of course they would vacate the room immediately in such instances. They were indignant that anybody would think anything else. But doubt hung in the air. I asked how often both counseling rooms would be required at the same time. Not very often – at the moment at least. Finally, a compromise proposal was agreed and I suggested that we would review the decision at the next day-long meeting which was scheduled for a couple of weeks after the changeover. It seemed to me that here was power alive and at play. My sense was that smoking was an identity issue. More about that below.

As we moved into the process of day two, I asked everybody to take a few minutes quietly to visualize exactly what they would do on the first morning after the closure of the Dave's Place building and then to talk it through with a few others. I did this for a number of reasons. First, I sensed that part of the 'talking about talking theme' of our previous day together was a defense mechanism arising from anxiety about the move. I thought a simple visualization would offer an opportunity for people to face the ordinariness and practicalities of their first day after the move. My hope was that some of the anxiety arising from their anticipation about it might be reduced. Second, I thought it might raise some issues or practical actions that had not been identified in the 'to do' list. Several people talked about 'more people around', 'less room', 'noisier', 'the structure of the building', 'the use of space'. I noted a sense of claustrophobia from some of the comments. There was agreement about this and one of the Dave's Place staff suggested that much of the anxiety was about 'how we can personalize the space'.

Once again, 'smoking' arose as an issue. Even though discussion and a decision had taken place a few minutes previously, 'procedures about the use of the counseling/smoking room' were raised again. Here was iteration. I felt somewhat disappointed by these responses to the visualization, but I don't quite know why. I knew that this group were quite familiar with role play and this kind of imaginative activity. They could understand very well the kinds of difficulties they were each going to encounter. They seemed to be finding it hard to pay attention to the activity. Were they bored? The language patterns were becoming repetitive. Stacey makes an interesting point that in situations of high understanding with minimal levels of fantasy, people produce 'the dynamics of repetition . . . with very little transformation' (Stacey, 2001, p. 205). Conversely, high levels of fantasy provoking misunderstanding can lead to disintegration and fragmentation. Perhaps I had misjudged what the exercise might achieve. I suppose I was hoping that the fantasy might evoke a new way of thinking about the change and offer the potential for transformation.

Wondering how to shift the air of gloom, I commented that we seemed only to have spoken about the difficulties of the imposed change. I asked if anybody could envisage any positive dimension to the move. 'It will allow us to be more creative and innovative', remarked Paul. I was agreeably surprised by the immediate change of atmosphere in the room that this provoked. 'Yes, we will have to develop a new relationship with our clients', and 'the clients will have more responsibility in their interaction with us' were other responses. Attempting to capitalize on this, I suggested that we would have a short brainstorming session on the positive aspects of the move. The reaction was enthusiastic and exciting. They talked about new challenges, new ways of working, extending and expanding current work in prisons, clients taking more responsibility for addressing their needs and accessing other services, re-evaluation of their work, research, networking and strengthening relationships with other services, and much more. Getting the group to prioritize and link these into themes enabled us to set up areas for planning later on.

There was much enthusiasm in the discussion but I noticed that most of it focused on the role and work of the Dave's Place staff. I mentioned this and suggested that perhaps we should examine the implications of the change for all three groupings in Phoenix, the management committee, and the teams of Lulu's Centre and Dave's Place. I asked each of these groups to form into their usual teams. The task for each group was to project themselves into the shoes of one of the other teams and to articulate how they were thinking and feeling about the changeover. They were then asked to identify and prioritize the planning tasks for that group. This was an activity I had prepared beforehand, thinking that it might be useful in moving people's focus from their own immediate concerns. Why did I decide to do it? To engage empathy? Yes, although this activity was an imaginative projection into the future, I anticipated that the communicative interaction would raise consciousness of other perspectives. I hoped it would create the opportunity to get in touch with other possible points of disturbance, disruption and conflict affecting the group into which they were simulating and projecting. I also thought it might open up other positive possibilities and potential challenges. It was an aesthetic approach that, as Strati suggests, was involving my judgment in the moment based on sensory awareness and experience yielded by my perceptive faculties (Strati, 1999, p. 3). It felt risky as I tried to sense the way forward in the conversations. I knew the fantasy of this imaginative collaboration had the potential for understanding or misunderstanding. I hoped that the struggle and search for meaning might offer the opportunity for novel thinking to emerge. Making sense of this conversation might move people to recognize the reality of others more intimately. I thought that it might stimulate them to articulate some behavior patterns within and between the different groups, and that this would highlight the relationship issues of concern. In the feedback, once again, I noticed that the smoking issue would not go away. Structure and lack of it also came up several times. It seems to me that these themes were connected. Interestingly, each of the groups voiced concern about the 'disruption of roles'. I remarked that confusion between the roles of Tom and Sally had been referred to previously and that we should talk about this. As we explored their changing roles, they linked the issue to their 'changing identity'. Several people said that they found the activity quite a powerful experience. When asked why, they suggested that it helped them to move out of their own concerns and brought home to them how others were feeling.

The power of smoking

I would like to reflect further on the smoking issue which I realize made a particular impression on me as it returned over and over again. Frequently, when we took time out I noticed that the Lulu's Centre staff went into their offices and many of the Dave's Place team adjourned to the smoking room. I suspected that these were the spaces where the shadow conversations were taking place. At different stages throughout each of the first two days we broke up into smaller groups to discuss various issues. The groups were mixed in different ways at different times. As I moved around ensuring that the groups were clear about the tasks, I was struck by the fact that the group in the smoking room always seemed to be the same people, the smokers, although I was never sure. The discussion took place through a fog of smoke. It was usually lively, at times conducted with much hilarity, and at other times argument was intense.

The smoking room is a small room at the return of the stairs on the first floor. It is beside the reception office and entrance to Lulu's Centre. The door was always open, possibly to let in some air or to allow the smoke out. Interestingly, the open door meant that much of the movement around the building could be monitored. In retrospect I realize that I had never ventured through the door, as much because there was no space for another body, but also because there always seemed to be an air of independence about the group. It felt as if I might be intruding. I wondered about this and made sense of it by thinking that it was clearly connected to the balance in power relations of the group.

Puzzling about my sense of exclusion from this room, I reflected that nowadays smokers are excluded from many public buildings and must confine their habit to very limited areas. I saw a connection between my sense of a powerfully flaunted separateness and the marginalized group who were their clients. Just like their clients, the smokers may have excluded themselves to accommodate their smoking but, with the open door and noisy exchanges, they could not be ignored. I had ensured different mixes in the groups and I think that members of the Lulu's Centre team participated in the smoking room group for at least one or two tasks. However, I cannot recall noticing any of them there. Interestingly, none of the Lulu's Centre team smoked and it seemed that all the Dave's Place team smoked. They were joined by Ann, the receptionist and administrator, whom Tom identified as 'the gatekeeper'. I note this with interest, since the reception area separates the Lulu's Centre offices and workrooms from the counseling/smoking room.

Discussing marginalization and identity, Dalal writes about 'The shrill voice from the margins' (Dalal, 1998, p. 206). Drawing on group psychoanalytic theory, the writing of Elias and Matte Blanco, Dalal suggests that power relations are a 'component of identity' (ibid., p. 204). Elias views power as 'a structural characteristic of all human relationships' (Elias, 1998, p. 116). The balance of power forms an integral element of all human relationships. It is a balance that is based on the function of the relationships we are involved in. People gather into groups around similarity. They do this to hide or deny the 'vortices' or struggle of power. This is an unconscious process, according to Dalal. I began to understand the smoking theme in terms of their loss and consequent feeling of marginalization of the Dave's Place group. I saw them as converging around their similarity. This may be viewed as an aspect of the inevitable power struggle, one which is of course always there, but which was heightened as a result of the changing work situation in Phoenix. Dalal suggests that although the manifest level (in this case the smoking) appears innocent, 'the process hides something latent and more problematic' (Dalal, 1998, p. 204). In line with Elias, he argues that marginalized groups lacking power are forced in their impotence to assert their identity. In my view, the smokers, mostly from the Dave's Place team, were cohering around this identity of smoking to assert their difference from the dominant group. I suspected they felt that the Lulu's Centre team were holding the balance of power, whether consciously or unconsciously, in this situation. According to Dalal, groups who are marginalized gather around their identity to challenge the dominant order. He suggests that they do this, paradoxically, in order to join the power centre: 'they form in order to eventually dissolve' (ibid., p. 207).

Reflecting on the smoking issue later, I sensed that an apparent lack of control in their working environment did not prepare the Dave's Place staff for the shock of homelessness. They had no control over the acquisition of a building. Their pattern of movement into the future was unstable, insecure. Their identity was threatened. Working in the other building, the Dave's Place team had been relatively autonomous and independent of Tom, the Director. Now they were transferring to the building which was the home and site of the Lulu's Place team identity and that of the Director. The site associated with the identity and power of the Dave's Place team was being withdrawn. At the same time, their identity suddenly seemed to be invested in a decrepit old building that was now being taken from them. They had imagined they were in control of 'their building', their workplace. Paradoxically, both staff and clients had frequently complained about the unsuitability of the premises with its warren of small rooms that stretched the resources of the staff to keep a watchful eye on all that was going on. The building had several disadvantages that added to the difficulty of the work. In addition, the area in which the building was situated was deemed inappropriate. Many local traders complained frequently and bitterly about the clients' antisocial behavior detracting from business.

Ironically, it seemed to me, the staff of Dave's Place had little difficulty in accepting the chaotic lifestyle of their clients. They frequently had to deal with dangerous 'acting-out' behavior, disorder and disturbance. Many people would be fearful of working in such an environment but the team were quite comfortable and adept at managing this type of unpredictable situation and chaotic client. Indeed, perhaps they relished the unstructured nature of it. To some extent this building was where they wielded power. The team saw themselves as carrying out an important social service, one that was not being performed in exactly the same fashion by any other service in the town. This was their function, their identity, their power. It was where they felt 'in control'. The team offered help, a place of support, some shelter. This was where their skills were appreciated, where they received acknowledgment of their work. Of course, the clients might also spurn their services and no doubt on some occasions this had been the case. Although they offered a vital service, the people who availed themselves of this service had the power to accept or reject their offer. There was interdependency between the staff and their clients, an interdependence which was also their challenge. The role of the members of the Dave's Place team was dependent on the clients opting to avail themselves of their service. On the other hand, they had been relatively autonomous in the Centre. Their connection to Tom, the Director, was mainly at official meetings but otherwise was quite tenuous. Sally, the manager of the team, was a powerful personality, acknowledged as extremely skillful in working with these clients, and one of the poor time keepers. No wonder there was ambiguity about a conflict of roles between Tom and Sally.

I noted previously that Elias argues that power is a structural characteristic of all human relationships (Elias, 1998, p. 16). However, rather than reifying the notion of power, he emphasizes the importance of understanding it in terms of balances. He argues that the balance of power is grounded in the functions we perform for each other. There are times when I need you, and others when you need me. The functions we have for each other are based on the interweaving of our relationships. These relationships can be one of friendship or antagonism. I quote him to illustrate the point that the relationships of the Dave's Place team and their clients 'can only be understood and explained in terms of the immanent dynamics of their interdependence' (ibid., p. 112). Ironically it also seems to me that these interdependencies reflect those of the Dave's Place team in their new situation. Now they would be working in much closer proximity to the rest of the staff. They would have less control over their work. The dynamics of the interdependencies of the two groups, the functions they perform for each other, would be emphasized. It seemed to me that this situation offered the potential for both creative and destructive transformation. To quote Elias, 'social tensions and conflicts will never be banished from society.' He continues:

> It is easy to see that tensions and conflicts between groups which are losing functions and those acquiring new or increased functions are a vital structural feature of all development. In other words, it is not just a question of personal, mainly accidental tensions and conflicts, though the people involved usually see them as such. From the viewpoint of the intermeshing groups, they can sometimes be seen as expressions of personal animosity, sometimes as consequences of the ideology of one side or the other. On the contrary, however, this is a matter of structured conflicts and tensions. In many cases they and their results form the very kernel of a process of development.
>
> (Elias, 1998, p. 173)

Another pause: intimations of conflict

Before I continue, I want to muse on another issue that has been preoccupying me. After the first day, Tom hinted at staff conflict. There were some personality clashes. He wondered if I should know about them. My immediate reaction was that I did not think it was necessary at this point but that I would think about it. The information Tom was offering might color my view. I felt I did not want to know more about these conflicts at this stage because I wanted to make sense of the balance of power for myself. I saw myself as consulting to the whole group and I asked myself why Tom mentioned these personality clashes. What were the power relations here? Identity is what is at stake in any power struggle. The social existence of the group needs such conflict. Tom's identity and sense of power was also at issue.

I wondered about my initial response to Tom's mention of personality conflicts. Trying to make sense of it I realized that I felt I wanted to form my own opinion. I did not wish to bring preconceptions to my interactions with the group. They might color how I would relate to the individuals concerned. Anxiety about them might distract me from paying attention to the group as a whole. I thought that the various relationships would become obvious anyway as I observed them in the interactions of the day. I then wondered if my own anxiety about conflict had caused this reluctance to hear Tom's story. Why had I resisted hearing this information? I knew that I could not be an objective observer, bracketing all assumptions. Already the group pervaded my consciousness. In order to work effectively with the whole group, to be able to pay attention to what was happening in the whole group, I felt that I needed to retain some distance, some objectivity. However, I was aware that I was already immersed in the interrelationships of the group by my agreement to engage with them, but still I dithered as I deliberated about whether it would be better to know or not to know. Now that I had been made aware of these conflicts this information would have filtered into my perception in any case. In fact I did ask Tom to tell me what he thought, and I must admit I promptly forgot it! I was obviously displaying great resistance to this information and I still wonder what it was all about.

I argued above that identity is relational and contingent, defined in terms of difference. We recognize ourselves in recognizing the difference of others. If we continually avoid conflict and the recognition and exploration of difference, constantly seeking to find only our sameness with others, we fool ourselves. Griffin points out that if we avoid conflict as our identity is continuously emerging we end up recognizing only the shell of identity we were before (Griffin, 2002, p. 156). Conflicts are part and parcel of most relationships and of every group's dynamic most of the time. The web of constantly changing interrelationships creates the unique and organic process that is the group. Relationship implies constraint. In the shifting dynamics of their relationships as group members interact, converse, work together and engage in their practice, each person is learning about and creating their individual identity. At the same time as identity is being created and is evolving, difference emerges, is emphasized. Difference is the corollary of identity. The existence of others becomes the condition of possibility of my identity, since, without others, I could not have an identity. Therefore, identity is always contingent. Identity is relational and defined in terms of difference. How can we defuse the possibility of exclusion that it entails?

Continuing the narrative: day three – conflict

Some weeks after the closure of the building I was asked to facilitate another day to review the change process. A number of incidents occurred during the day that raised the tension in the room. Initially I asked if people had any ideas about how they would like to work. They expressed a preference for whole-group work. We reviewed how they were getting on. A building had been identified and negotiations were ongoing, although Tom had indicated to me earlier that he envisaged difficulties because of the location. Some complained about the lack of work but Colette defensively listed all the work she was doing. They expressed concern that they were not keeping in touch with all their clients. They were not making contact with new clients but they were looking forward to the new Dave's Place center. During this exchange, Tom, *en passant* said, 'there will not be another Dave's Place!' What a bombshell. The group turned on him. Christine gasped, 'What do you mean?' Philip, one of the management committee who had not attended the other planning days, said emphatically '*That* is news to me.' Tom backtracked somewhat and said enigmatically, 'I mean the work will not be organized in the same way as in our previous Dave's Place center.' Subsequent angry comments questioned the lack of democratic policy-making. Someone protested that Tom and the management committee were dictating policy. This was an interesting comment, considering that one of the committee had just expressed ignorance of this information. I wondered what this was all about. I knew that I had had a conversation about this with Tom. Yet, although members of the group were now all working together in the same building, it seemed as if communication had broken down. And then I remembered that during one of our previous days I felt I had had to prod Tom into communicating some information that he had passed on to me.

On another occasion during the day, Jean, one of the Lulu's Centre team, rounded on Tom following some comment he made. I was taken by surprise. The comment seemed innocuous enough to me. She accused him of trying to shut her down. Tom appeared surprised but took the criticism and offered some explanation. After a few moments, Lucy stepped in to defend Tom and others agreed. Shortly after this it was break-time. As people scattered to the smoking room and coffee machine Jean, who was sitting beside me, turned and said she thought Tom had taken the criticism well. I asked her if she would like to say this to Tom during the next session, and she did so. Reparation was in the air.

Later during the day a disagreement arose between some of the staff of Lulu's Centre and the Dave's Place team. Referring to the lack of work, someone from Dave's Place remarked on how focused the Lulu's Centre team were. Another Dave's Place member then commented that because the Lulu's Centre team always kept their doors closed the Dave's Place team felt excluded. The Lulu's Centre team defended their need to do this, offering arguments about confidentiality if they were on the phone, but the Dave's Place team refused to accept that it was necessary to close doors if clients were not in the building. However, although the building was secure, it was possible that clients or strangers might come into reception while conversations were going on. A person on the phone would have to interrupt his or her conversation to go and close the door. Comments flew back and forth. I wondered: What do I do here? I stayed with it, and after some time I described what was happening and that I could see that people were very angry. I wondered out loud if this was the real issue, but we did not get much further with it. However, I learned some days later that Lulu's Centre team were very angry with the Dave's Place staff. They felt that they were not being heard and felt unsupported by Tom. I gather that the issue came to a head and was dealt with, and there was some resolution the following week at their staff meeting.

Eventually, after some time struggling with the above exchange, I said that perhaps the Dave's Place staff did not fully understand the actual work of Lulu's Centre. This seemed to strike a chord and we discussed how people might gain an understanding of each other's work. I suggested that perhaps people from the two different teams might occasionally work together in order to build up a common understanding of the different kind of work in the organization and of what each group actually does. Several said that they would welcome this kind of opportunity to work together.

Conclusion

In general, I notice that my way of working involves me in trying to influence the climate, mood or context of conversations in which I am participating. My initial intention is to engage in conversations that will bring to the surface the issues of concern to the group, which they may be having difficulty articulating to one another. As the inquiry progresses and the themes that pattern conversations become clearer, different types of activities may appear useful to me for keeping the focus on the continuous meaning-making around the emerging themes. I am interested in the use of language and pay particular attention to the metaphors being used. I am aware that I usually absorb the atmosphere created by a conversation, paying attention to body language – both my own and others – and notice who is not contributing. I sometimes check how I am feeling myself. I call this my aesthetic sense, consciously heightened awareness to the resonance of my sensory processes and intellectual processing in the living present.

Apart from this, although I am participating fully, many of my gestures are asking for clarification, emphasizing the different understandings and interpretations, or dwelling on particular comments. I draw the group's attention to the connections I notice between various points being made. My wont is often to listen intently for long periods. I realize that, occasionally, a particular insight emerges for me through the listening and then I am able to draw attention to it. There is nothing unusual in all of this and I am sure it is how many consultants work in similar roles. I engaged in the work by consciously acknowledging the anxiety that arose as I attempted to hold the paradoxical movement of the stability and instability of meaning, of the known and the unknown, at the same time. In other words, I tried to pay attention to the continuity and transformation in the movement of our meaning-making. I attempted to remain aware of how I was evoking and provoking, selecting and choosing my responses, in the back-and-forth organization of my thoughts as I was interacting with others and with my own silent conversation. I was trying to understand human action from within that action, as a participant in it.

I realize that as the nature of my reflections shift, as I struggle to incorporate new ways of making sense of myself and my work, the quality of that sense-making shifts in ways that I cannot control. My identity as a practitioner evolves in subtle ways so that I come to appreciate that even my own anxiety affects me in slightly different ways. It is exactly this process of spontaneous transformation that I have tried to illustrate in this chapter. I have tried to show how the public and private conversational processes are essentially the same, both beset with contradictions, conflicts, aspirations, trials and temporary resolutions in action. I have tried to illustrate and account for the process of reflective practice.

References

Dalal, F. (1998) *Taking the Group Seriously: Towards a Post-Foulkesian Group Analytic Theory*, London: Jessica Kingsley.

Elias, N. (1998) *On Civilization, Power, and Knowledge*, ed. S. Mennell and J. Goudsblom, Chicago, IL: University of Chicago Press.

Griffin, D. (2002) *The Emergence of Leadership: Linking self-organization and ethics*, London: Routledge.

Stacey, R. (2001) *Complex Responsive Processes in Organizations: Learning and knowledge creation*, London: Routledge.

Stacey, R., Griffin, D. and Shaw, P. (2000) *Complexity and Management: Fad or radical challenge to systems thinking?*, London: Routledge.

Strati, A. (1999) *Organization and Aesthetics*, London: Sage.

Editors' introduction to Chapter 6

Ian Johnson writes of his experience as a consultant working for a global consulting firm in the UK on major change programs in large companies. He argues that there is a particular way of thinking that is reflected in the major change projects that clients bring to his firm. This way of thinking is also reflected in the way consultants like him are supposed to work on these projects. The way of thinking is one in which an organization is taken to be a thing with an agency of its own in that it causes people to do what they do in their work, but it is also believed that the leaders of an organization can move it from one state to another through undertaking major transformation projects which follow prescribed steps. Johnson finds that this way of thinking does not resonate with his experience of the messy, unpredictable nature of organizational life. However, what strikes him is that despite such unrealistic thinking, it sometimes happens that the transformation programs he works on do actually seem to achieve change.

His central question, then, is: How do major transformation programs sometimes seem to produce an effect, even though they are based on simplistic thinking?

To explore his question, he picks out, and reflects upon, a few incidents in one of the major transformation programs on which he worked. One such incident involves him in behaving in a way that his seniors regard as deviant. As he reflects on the nature of deviance in organizations, drawing on Meyerson's work on 'tempered radicals', he comes to see such deviance as an important part of his practice rather than as a personality defect. He explores the idea that change has something to do with the accumulation of acts of deviance by tempered radicals but argues against regarding them as the cause of change.

He then moves on to events which suggest that consultants use their plans and procedures to manage the anxiety of their seniors, while actually working in a much more emergent way. He finds change emerging in many conversations, and reaches the conclusion that the formal methodology is really an ideology sustaining current patterns of power relations. In terms of doing the work it is a placebo. In reality, change comes about in the conversational exploration of difference. He links this to side effects – it is in the side effects of the formal methodology of the consultants, taking the form of conversation in which the consultants challenge taken-for-granted assumptions, that change comes about. The activities of the consultants which are linked to this emergent change are spontaneous and unpredictable in nature. In his reflection, he comes to see spontaneity and creativity as essential aspects of his practice as a consultant.

As in the previous chapters by Christensen (Chapter 4) and O'Flynn (Chapter 5), Johnson also adopts a methodology in which consulting and research are seen as the same activity. However, while Christensen and O'Flynn do not work explicitly to fulfill the purpose of major change in the organization, or to solve problems, the projects Johnson works on do have these as explicit purposes. What differences does this make to how he works? It seems to make surprisingly little difference because such purposes are aspects of the placebo nature of major transformation projects while, as side effects, the activities of consultants on these programs are much the same as those in which Christensen and O'Flynn engage.

Key to Johnson's methodology is the use of narrative in which he gives an account of what he does and who he interacts with. What he shows is that brief accounts of usually ignored interactions with others provide a surprisingly rich basis for reflection. He weaves his reflections through the narrative, drawing critically on relevant literature to aid him. What emerges in this methodology is the movement of thought and so changes in practice. He uses his own subjectivity and particularly emphasizes its embodied nature, so drawing attention to the importance of feelings in professional activity. His methodology is bodily reflexive and he shows how the activity of researching-consulting is one in which self/identity is iterated and potentially transformed. Far from being objective or detached as a researcher-consultant, and also far from being subjective in some given way, we see how the research-consulting activity is itself formative of self/identity. Johnson also brings out the ideological nature of research methodologies and how the ideology sustains patterns of power relating.

He draws attention to the way methodologies operate as social defenses against anxiety. Thus methodology is not some kind of neutral activity but is irretrievably intertwined with ideology and power relations, and also with anxiety and others' feelings, all linked to identity formation.

6 To understand a practice of consulting

Ian Johnson

- Business transformation (1)
- Organizations as things which can be changed in eight steps
- Business transformation (2)
- Change through personality defects?
- Tempered radicalism
- A lost opportunity
- Business transformation (3)
- Ideology and power – constraints to action
- Business transformation (4)
- Gestalt consulting and presence
- Business transformation (5)
- Role and spontaneity
- Business transformation (6)
- Bodies of thought
- Away from the placebo prescriptions

> You must be the change you wish to see in the world.
>
> (Mahatma Gandhi)

Business transformation (1)

The brief from the Director for Transformation for the piece of work I was about to engage in was, to say the least, quite vague. This project was for a major UK insurance company and virtually all she offered was, 'We want you to design and build a team that can operate across the organization and help us to deliver the big transformational programs of change required for us to remain competitive. We have got about eighty people doing this sort of work at the moment. We think it could be less if we centralize them all.' There was not much more than that. The eighty people to whom she referred were the project managers and process analysts so far identified as participating in these major projects. The CEO thought that was too many – he had an idea that forty people would be enough and he wanted them centralized in a business transformation department.

The beginning was difficult. The Director for Transformation, Joan, had been in the role for only a few months. She was always busy, always in meetings. She was trying to deliver some major cost savings for the organization which had been promised to the share market analysts and on which the new CEO's credibility depended. Joan was acting in an interim role, to which she had been seconded from our consulting organization. This made it only slightly easier for me to gain access to her. I also discovered in a conversation with Joan, part-way into the project, that she was not an insurance expert at all, and so had to work doubly hard to get to grips with how the business worked. Another issue was that my manager, Kevin, seemed to have a very intense working relationship with Joan. He had been coaching and supporting her through this project before I arrived and was now meeting with her for as many as nine or ten hours a week, making my access to her even harder.

For me, the project began with a series of conversations with some members of the executive group about what they would expect to see in a group leading major changes across the business. I also talked with some of the group of eighty people who had already been identified as doing transformation work. Catherine, my equivalent on the client's side, an HR person and their project manager for developing the new Business Transformation Department, was also involved in these conversations. We explored between us what the staff of eighty did, what executives found helpful in this and what they could do without. We talked about what additional work the staff of eighty could do which would help the executives run their parts of the business more effectively.

Organizations as things which can be changed in eight steps

For some time now I have been struggling to identify what it is that makes a difference in the way I practise while being both bound by the expectations and perceived rules of working in a major consulting practice and developing a new practice of my own. I have reflected upon the exhortations of some of the traditional writers on change, such as

Kotter (1996), with his 'eight steps' (establish a sense of urgency; create the guiding coalition; develop a vision and a strategy; communicate the change vision; empower broad-based action; generate short-term wins; consolidate gains and produce more change; anchor new approaches in the culture), whose thinking is used to legitimize much of my firm's practice. However, I do not think that this is a reasonable reflection of my experience in the real world. I see contradictions and truisms layered over poorly conceived theories of change where the organization is seen as a system to be manipulated at will by the 'leadership', herding the staff (who often seem to be portrayed as a largely homogeneous mass) into new behavior. At the same time the organization is given agency, the organization 'has' a culture, somehow 'the organization' makes us do things. The transformation project with which I introduced this chapter reflects this thinking, which to me is extremely unrealistic. Yet what has bothered me most is that even when working from such a perspective, some people sometimes seem able to make a real difference and change in an organization. This whole position strikes me as rather odd. I imagine wanting to make a chocolate cake but only being able to find a recipe for roast beef, yet when I follow the roast beef recipe I still end up with something similar to the chocolate cake I had originally desired. So what is it that is really happening here?

What I have been trying to do is to look more closely at the processes of change I experience in my life in organizations. As I have been reflecting upon and trying to explain my evolving practice, I have found that many of the examples have something of a theme to them, a theme that until recently I would not have taken seriously. I plan to explore this in this chapter and to reflect upon that theme's contribution to a practice that, despite appearing to be a roast beef recipe, manages to produce cake.

Business transformation (2)

Not long after I started working on the assignment the CEO effectively sacked Joan from her Transformation Director role – she had not forced the rest of the executives into delivering the cost reductions he wanted and he had apparently 'lost confidence' in her. He asked for someone else to be provided who could make the organization change.

The leaders of our firm promptly provided Andy as a replacement. The first I knew of all this was when Andy appeared and rumors started to fly around the consulting team that Joan was to leave by the end of the week.

I caught Joan by the coffee machine (the place where everyone goes to find out what is happening) and asked her about it. Her response sounded rehearsed: 'I have not been able to move the organization as far and as fast as was expected and so Andy has come in to take over what we've started. I'm looking forward to my next challenge.'

Joan had been in the position for four or five months by this time. She had survived at this client organization which had previously thrown out some of our consultants after a week because they were not happy with their performance. She negotiated her way through the early stages of the project where most of the executives just wanted to get rid of her, and she built the engagement into the most significant insurance project we have ever had in the UK. Yet now she seemed to be being cast aside as a failure. I felt quite angry at what seemed to be the injustice of it all. I remember feeling my heartbeat quicken and a building sense of uncertainty as I reacted by sending a note to everyone in the consulting team to invite them for drinks. The invitation suggested that the event was to 'say goodbye' to Joan and to celebrate the success thus far: 'Those who start a new business are not always the people who take it into the mainstream', it read.

Before I actually sent the note, I showed it to Joan and asked if there was anything factually incorrect about what I had said. My manager, Kevin, was in the room at the time and Joan turned to him and asked, 'Do all your people have a heart?' Kevin's reaction was very subdued – so subdued I failed to catch exactly what he said – but it did not seem important, just some dismissive quip. Joan's removal must have been something of a personal challenge for him given the vast amounts of time spent coaching her. I received a number of e-mails from people making their excuses, some of which seemed reasonable, but one or two were highly dismissive – 'I think I may be planning to wash my hair that night' being a good example. In the end the event was attended by only Joan and myself and two others out of a team of nearly thirty, and both of these other two arrived quite late.

Subsequently I was chastised by Kevin for putting a 'sweet spin' on what I was told was Joan's failure and that some of the senior people in my own company were deeply unimpressed by my interpretation of events, and, even more so, by my sharing this interpretation in the e-mail inviting everyone to the drinks evening. I was told that our company's values required us to be honest and direct, that we should not be afraid to give people difficult messages such as 'you've failed' and that I was actually embarrassing Joan by trying to change the way in which her 'failure' was viewed. As well as starting to wonder if I wanted to be in such an unfeeling organization I started to feel very vulnerable and threatened, as if through my actions I had jeopardized my own career. This was followed up by some meetings with some of those senior people in our firm to whom my boss had referred. I kept pointing out that the project was a hugely profitable engagement with a very difficult client where most people had 'crashed and burned'. Joan had survived, built the account, and got a series of projects running and led by people such as myself. If that was failure, I said, I would like to have lots of them.

We have since had a celebration of the progress that our insurance industry practice has made in the year. Joan, despite not being an insurance person, was invited and her contribution was formally appreciated. I would like to think that my action contributed to this change of heart.

Change through personality defects?

I find myself drawn to acting into the organization in a way such as that described above, actively questioning assumptions, though until recently I have not really seen this as a part of my practice so much as a personality defect, a tendency to rebellion, though grounded in a strong sense of justice. In the past I have seen my practice as being the things I do that are related to Kotter's view of the world and therefore the view of the organizations for which I have been working.

I have also found it hard to understand exactly what I am doing here. I know that in the past I have veered towards trying to categorize these actions as 'non-verbal' or 'action-oriented' in order to differentiate them from a day-to-day practice that is based largely in verbal interaction. Part of this has been down to the way actions, such as the one described above, resonate with the psychodrama work I have done, but in both psychodrama and in this example, talk is still an important aspect of the 'deviant' part of what I do. Moreno defines psychodrama as the science which explores the 'truth' by dramatic methods. Modern texts simply say that psychodrama is a psychotherapy approach in which people enact the relevant events in their lives instead of just talking about them. The important part is that it is not only verbal but multi-modal – like real life.

On reflection I have come to realize that the divisions I have tried to place upon my practice are false. My practice is 'what I do' in totality, what I bring to a relationship (whether or not that be in a work context) and the unique sense I make of a situation. What is more, taking a more inclusive, boundaryless view of my practice is actually helpful because it prevents me from placing some of the more unusual or unexpected actions I take into some separate 'container' to make my practice seem more rational and 'methodological'.

One writer whom I have encountered recently has been very helpful in two ways. First, she describes a group of people, whom she labels 'tempered radicals', who seem to be making change in organizations through actions similar to some of those I have described. Second, the way she tries to describe what is happening in deviant actions differs from the traditional way of making sense of these actions and so provides a contrast against which I can begin to develop an alternative formulation.

Tempered radicalism

I refer to an article by Debra Meyerson of Stanford University about people whose behavior may be similar to my own, which appeared in the *Fast Company* magazine. She has since followed it up with a book in which she describes how she was intrigued by what she describes as 'tempered radicals' (Meyerson 2001). These are people who, according to her,

> operate deep within big companies, well beneath the cultural radar, and are practically invisible to the top brass. They are a part of their organization, yet somehow apart as well, professional irritants who are tolerated more than embraced. Employing many different styles and strategies, typically waging small battles rather than epic wars, they work to slowly change the rules.
>
> (Meyerson : 162)

One of her many examples is of a Jewish man, Alan Levy, who would use some of his holiday allowance to take time off from work in order to observe Jewish holidays in a company whose calendar only recognized Christian holidays. Over time, people in his department came to expect this as the norm and, as they moved on to other parts of the business, they behaved in the same way. Eventually the company recognized the issue and gave people a certain number of personal days, in addition to their vacation, that they could use to observe these holidays (Meyerson 2001: 43). As she explores these examples collected together from her research and tries to make sense of what is going on, she observes many of the things that I have seen and experienced in organizations. Among the observations she makes are:

- organizations are always changing; change is not about change programs;
- it is difficult to pin-point a trigger of change;
- the source of change is differences among people;
- accepting paradox is the key to understanding change in organizations.

Meyerson dismisses major change efforts – the grand revolutionary – in favor of the improviser (Meyerson 2001: 166). In her view major change programs do not actually change much. She sees organizations as continually changing, with that change coming incrementally from the process of adaptation. This makes change hard to identify except retrospectively when those small adaptations have had time to accumulate (Meyerson 2001: 11–12). She uses the Alan Levy example, among others, to propose that change comes about not through some sort of large cultural awareness program, but through an individual simply acting differently and embodying a different set of values.

However, since small changes are happening all over the organization all of the time, it is, she suggests, extremely difficult to identify the source of a change. The continuous incremental process of change is so diffuse, one small increment potentially affected by and affecting many others, that it is impossible to trace cause. The result in her view is that without a clearly identifiable cause, these incremental changes begin to look like 'a series of random events rather than a rational set of cause and effect sequences' (Meyerson 2001: 12). I think she is pointing here to the mismatch between the way in which change is often written about as a rational program of events leading to a predetermined goal and the actual messy experience of change in the moment. Yet, despite pointing out that cause is tremendously difficult to identify, she still uses particular stories from the organizations she worked with and describes them as if the actions of the 'tempered radical' were the cause of change.

In trying to identify the underlying source of change, Meyerson comes to the conclusion that it lies in the differences between us all. Individuals are different and each has different things that they value. Then, in her words, these differences emerge into the 'system' of the organization where those differences may lead to behavior which challenges the norms of that organization. When people act on their convictions it 'sets in motion a powerful cycle. Even small acts can have far reaching effects, affirming an actor's sense of self, fuelling their sense of efficacy, and making a difference for others' (Meyerson 2001: 16). Her cycle is one where the action of an individual, which she sees as the starting point of change, triggers a wide range of outcomes which affect the world, changing the context for future action.

In order to make this view of the world work, to explain the differences that make some people 'tempered radicals', Meyerson sees them as operating at the margins of the organization – marginalized perhaps by their gender, race, sexual orientation, religion or ideology. This is the source of the difference that, when expressed in the organization, brings about adaptive changes through small exchanges between individuals. This is not to say that someone necessarily sets out to make changes. They simply act according to their own personal identity and beliefs, and in doing so create a new context for future action. This view of Meyerson's is a very different view to the mainstream writing about change where change is planned and brought about by the leadership, but it marginalizes change and locates it in a subgroup of people who are not operating in what may be called the 'mainstream' of the organization.

What does come through as important from her writing, though she does not seem to explore it fully herself, is the role that paradox plays in change in organizations. For example, an individual's activity in the organization is guided by his or her values and beliefs at the same time as it is shaping those values and beliefs. 'Small wins are driven by people's values, beliefs and identity. But small wins also shape people's values, beliefs and identities. By acting on them people affirm, extend and revise their "selves"' (Meyerson 2001: 119). The way in which she describes it – a simple relationship of one causing the other, which then causes the first – suggests a simple circular feedback loop, which I think misses what is in fact a simultaneous and paradoxical shaping while being shaped.

Meyerson notices something somewhat paradoxical in language too. She describes the experience of a sociologist working with a group of defense strategists at a military think-tank. To gain credibility, and to be able to communicate better within the organization, the sociologist learned to use the language of the strategist but found that the move virtually eliminated the sociologist's ability to speak and think critically about the system:

> Using insider language is like wielding a double edged sword. On the one hand it is imperative to use terms that allow us to gain credibility

and communicate effectively. On the other hand, adopting insider
language carries the danger of changing how we think and silencing
our own perspectives.

(Meyerson 2001: 150)

Her writing is a little confused about the choice someone has as to the
language they use. Earlier in the book she talks about communication
from the point of view of the individual having an autonomous choice as
to how they communicate and the language they use (Meyerson 2001:
115). She states that relying on language that is already legitimate, the
prevailing vocabulary, will not unfreeze people from their current way of
thinking and people continue to think in restricted ways – restricted by
their language. To change people's thinking, you should choose to use
different language. Yet later she is, as noted above, talking about the
sociologist losing her ability to challenge because she took up the
language of the strategists – suddenly the language is shaping the choices
of the individual rather than the other way around. I would argue that the
language we use both enables and constrains our communication at the
same time.

She also locates change in a subgroup of people rather than the process of
interaction as if only the subgroup had the 'difference' that she sees as
important, whereas I would see the potential for difference arising in any
relationship.

A lost opportunity

Despite some of my misgivings about the interpretation of the 'tempered
radicals' ideas, Meyerson seems to be noticing a similar dynamic within
organizations. She is looking at the same sorts of interactions that intrigue
me, and noticing many of the same attributes of organizations that enable
these actions to seemingly produce change, but our theories as to how
change comes about from these interactions are markedly different. To
begin with she writes from a position of what I would call the
autonomous individual, who is free to choose what they will do and how
they will do it, based purely upon their own desires, beliefs and personal
values.

However, while I believe that people are free in the sense that the future is
not predetermined, I do not believe that people are free to choose 'any'
response whatsoever, nor do I believe we are self-contained, autonomous.

People are hugely constrained in what they can do, particularly in terms of power relationships and ideology (topics we will return to below). Confronting the leadership directly in any organization can be a risky proposition. Instead, in the 'Joan's departure' narrative above, I responded in a way that fits neatly within the way we would normally behave when a valued colleague moves on, despite the undercurrent that suggested Joan was viewed differently. What we customarily think of as 'individual choice' is as much created by the others in any relationship as it is created by us.

The people whom Meyerson identifies as tempered radicals are therefore not making an entirely free and independent choice about what they are doing; their choices are socially constructed. Someone who is a tempered radical is to an extent 'created' by the relationships they have and are not free to choose to be what Meyerson is seeing in these organizations. This brings us back to earlier comments about being able to identify a cause for change, in that if our actions are not entirely our own, in the sense that they emerge in response to a web of relations, it makes identifying *the* cause even harder.

Another problem with the position Myerson takes is that she appears to contradict herself as she attempts to explain what is going on. This is perhaps an attempt not to move too far away from the language of her intended audience – language commonly accepted in business. For example, she seems to be saying, on the one hand, that change is about small adaptive changes that can occur anywhere in the organization, and whose cause is virtually unknowable, yet she manages to identify and locate cause in a subset of the people in the organization whom she calls 'tempered radicals'. Locating change in this subset, separate from people relating in general, seems to be avoiding the real complexity of the dynamic she has observed.

I find that I am ultimately disappointed by the book as it shows an awareness of some of the most interesting dynamics in an organization and yet ends up with a story that is very similar to the endless stream of business books where change is created by the few with the many taking a quite passive role. Kotter, for example, locates change in the leaders who create visions, communicate and then empower the masses (Kotter 1996). Conner again locates change in the leadership and then asks the leaders to 'cascade' leadership through the organization so that everyone is playing a part (Conner 1992). While this does suggest that everyone has a creative part to play, it still begins with a sponsor for change who is a member of the leadership team, and the 'active' role in change occurs only when people accept the cascaded change role. In this way Conner retains very clearly the split between the employees 'in the system' and the leaders 'who are outside making changes to the system'. As I reflect upon what happened when Joan left, I see what happened as coming from a complex network of interactions. While I made a move that appeared to lead to a different understanding of what happened to Joan, I am extremely aware that what I did was in part created by the, at best ambivalent, responses of those around me and my own history of relating. What we need is a way to look at change as a process in which we are all creatively participating.

Business transformation (3)

'We need to do this as quickly as we can. The CEO is under pressure to start showing results and the rest of the organization is dragging its heels. We have to lead by example.'

Back in the insurance company we were about to design a new organization structure, into which people from all over the business would be placed – the people who were managing all the major projects for the business. Bringing them all together in one place, and then weeding out the less effective ones, was seen as a good way to reduce costs. This cost reduction angle was gaining piquancy, as now the number of people in this line of work within the organization had reached 200 from the originally identified eighty mentioned earlier.

Having seen someone as apparently influential as Joan removed from the project for not making things happen at an acceptable speed, and comments from Kevin about my having to make an impact, I felt the need to try and move along quickly. The 'proper' methodology for doing this type of work can take months with distinct stages for identifying design principles, the high-level design and then the actual design based upon detailed process maps. While none of us really follow these methods slavishly, we do tend to use them for planning and managing the anxiety of our own senior management – if we have a plan that follows the methodology, the risks are lower because we are applying so-called 'best practice'. But what, I wondered, did I have to replace it if I stopped the pretense and did not hide behind our traditional method any more? There were no neat and tidy prescriptions emerging from my reflections on change, only a growing appreciation of how interaction is at the root of all I do. I decided to take a risk and then explained to my client (with some nervousness) that our methodology did not meet any of our needs in this situation. What we needed to do was talk about what we are doing and why, and from this to let our process emerge. We could design something that met our needs conversationally.

We started with Gillian and Alan, two of the people likely to be running the new function, and with Andy. We discussed the conversations Catherine and I had already had with the executive, and then tried to make some sense of what this new business transformation group would be and how it would work. Gillian and Alan had attempted a reorganization the previous year which had been stopped, but willingly shared with us the ideas they had had back then. Over the course of two weeks we explored a whole series of options and settled on one.

At this point we had to widen the scope of the conversations and consult with the unions and staff to explain our intentions, and again through these conversations the shape of the organization evolved further. Now we had staff talking about it, the employee relations people, the unions, each with a slightly different understanding of what we were doing, each raising questions and making suggestions. The result appeared to be a robust and well-thought-through structure, where we had all talked about the implications and agreed how it would work, though surprisingly little of the process was written down.

We did formally write down the design at this point. This was both so that we could attempt to communicate some of our output in writing to others in the organization, and to meet the quality management standards and engagement process created by people in my organization. We had to have written deliverables to hand over and 'demonstrate the value of our work' to the client. It was an aspect of our ideology.

Ideology and power – constraints to action

There are other ways of describing ideology rather than the passive, static definition of 'the body of ideas that reflects the beliefs and interests of a nation or political system and underlies political action' (*Collins English Dictionary* 1999). I personally see ideology as being a much more dynamic and useful concept for understanding organizations. The definition I find most meaningful is that 'ideologies are the ruling ideas of a particular society [or group] at a particular time. They are ideas that express the naturalness of any existing social order and help to maintain it' (Dalal 1998: 116, quoting Rose, Lewontin and Kanin 1984). This definition has some very interesting attributes. First, it opens up the possibility of many concurrent interacting ideologies, each expressing the naturalness of different parts of the social order. Second, it describes ideology as having the active function of maintaining those current social orders by making them seem natural and unquestionable.

There are many different descriptions of something similar to this definition of ideology. Meyerson talks of the 'dominant culture' of an organization in much the same way, and notes that groups maintain their own power and the status quo by perpetuating beliefs about others that keep them subordinated (Meyerson 2001: 39). Moreno described the 'cultural conserve' as 'that category of things that has already been created – including intangibles such as customs or social rules that have already been created and accepted' (Blatner 2000: 75). While this conserve is not described as having the oppressing aspect of a 'dominant culture' it is considered the basis for good habits and much of what he calls 'civilization' and it is considered an ongoing social psychological construction, not something static (ibid.). The cultural conserve is also different to ideology since the conserve has a material aspect to it, all of the cultural artifacts that we have produced as well as the social patterns of interaction. This cultural conserve represents all that we have already created and relieves us of the burden of 'reinventing the wheel' as it were. However, for Moreno an over-reliance on the conserve was seen as a potential problem for an individual as it leads to repetitive behavior, which is unlikely to be appropriate to all situations in which it is used. This leads not to change but to stagnation. I imagine that the behavior of someone endlessly re-creating a particularly strict ideology would look the same. Thus Moreno saw that the healthy individual used an appropriate balance of both the accumulated history of the conserve and individual spontaneity. The interplay of the conserve and spontaneity means that we are both constrained by and create, or evolve, the cultural conserve in all our interactions (Blatner 2000: 82).

The key difference I perceive here is that both Meyerson and Moreno's descriptions appear to be placing this 'conserve' at a transcendent level, almost as if it were an entity in its own right, shaping our every move from 'outside'. I would suggest that there is no need for some mysterious and all-pervasive transcendent 'cultural conserve' if we hold the idea that this 'cultural conserve' of customs and rules is a patterning of our ongoing interaction that emerges in the form of self-organizing themes and is constantly re-created in our ongoing iterations of gesture and response (Stacey 2001: 144). The need for traditional methods and physical deliverables could be seen as a habit, a habit that is constantly re-created in our ongoing iterations of gesture and response and a habit that sustains certain power relations.

Ideology emerges from our interactions as a patterning of those interactions that we both shape while being shaped by them ourselves, showing both continuity and potential transformation. Some of this patterning is the ongoing themes of interaction in which we all collude to make the current environment seem natural, perpetuating the leadership of the leaders, shaping what is considered acceptable and what is not. Given that ideology is a patterning of our interaction emerging in the very act of interaction, it is very hard to 'see', and thus it becomes very difficult to challenge or ask questions that challenge it.

I have come to believe that this way of looking at ideology may be applied not only to a country where we all perpetuate the system that keeps the 'ruling classes' in control, or just to the top level of an organization. We see 'ruling classes' at many levels in our lives – monarchy, government, organizational leaders, family leaders and so on. I see glimpses of this process throughout my own organization in the way that most of us collude to keep in place 'methodologies' and the requirement to produce 'physical deliverables', even keeping in place the partnership structure of our firm.

For example, in a recent video conference call with our Belgian organization, I talked about some of the ideas I have been exploring. I asked them if they followed the methods that have been provided for us. Not one actually did, though some referred to them to validate what they were planning to do. I also asked them where the value is in what they do. Again, none saw the value of their work being in the report. Yet despite all of this we help create new methods, seemingly endless revisions to existing methods and write such material as a Change Readiness Assessment Report. Why? Because of the potential effect it would have on power relations within the organization if we did not and the implications that might have for our continued relationship.

While we constrain ourselves through re-creating habitual patterns of interaction, including those patterns we call ideology, part of what shapes those constraints is power. In any relationship where there is the potential for one to withhold the needs of the other, the withholder potentially has power over the other. This is relational – you cannot have power without relationship. In a relationship there is usually a complex set of these dynamics which make up the overall power balance in the relationship. This fits closely with ideology in that ideology is the ideas that keep the ruling classes (often those who have the ability to withhold the needs of others) in place and, as noted above, makes it all seem natural, thereby maintaining the power balance in their favor.

The power relations between people, and perhaps the ideology, are manifest in many mundane ways. I have begun to notice, and become very interested in, how they affect the way we configure ourselves spatially. I refer not only to the obvious manifestations such as who has what offices, but also to the more subtle. For example, take the story about Joan. While she was being deposed, people would avoid any real contact with her – they did not speak to her, they seemed to avoid whatever room she was in and, as I have said, they stayed away from the social event I tried to arrange for her.

A part of my practice seems to be to act into the patterning of the interactions of a group of people in such a way that it is often perceived as different and has the potential to create change, though it is impossible to tell in advance what might come out of a gesture such as this. My practice in general has many examples of this 'acting in': toys on the seats of the rather inhibited senior managers at a Dutch bank; telling a senior manager in a hierarchical, status-driven bank that 'in this situation, you are not important'; and attempting to change the way in which Joan's exit from the project was perceived. In each case, there is something about those interactions where I feel that I am taking a risk by saying or doing something unexpected or potentially even not acceptable, at the moment that the action is taken. I know when these moments come, because there is a bodily experience that is something like fright – a quickening of my heartbeat, a flush in my cheeks – because I know I am 'bending the rules', I am pushing against the constraints I have helped construct between us.

Meyerson's tempered radicals have to be pushing against such constraints or else they would not be noticed. They stand out because someone notices the difference in at least some of their relationships and what they attempt to do with that difference. This is not to say that these are the only people exploring difference in their relationship. These are just the ones that someone noticed. In order to start to understand this process I would like to move on to look at the concept of presence from Gestalt consulting, and role and spontaneity from psychodrama.

Business transformation (4)

I received a telephone call one day during the business transformation project. It was from one of my colleagues back in my consulting company.

'We're going to be presenting a "refresher" on our organization design approach at our next consulting away-day and since, as I understand it, you're doing organization design work with your client we thought it would be good if you could talk about the experience,' she said.

'This could be interesting,' I thought. I wondered what to do.

One idea I held for a fleeting moment to avoid any potential conflict was to hide behind the methodology by trying to construct a believable scenario about how we have done it by the book, inventing a few plausible stories about the experience that people would nod sagely to, and then promptly forget. It would have been perhaps the safest approach.

I felt that I wanted to be truthful. Everyone I work with is used to my taking a different position to that generally accepted in the company, but was I really going to be able to stand up in front of my colleagues and say, 'The methods you've just heard about are, I'm sure, very valuable and almost certainly well thought through. I have taken it upon myself to throw them away and make it up as I go along by simply talking a lot to many different people and see what comes out'? As I thought about how this might feel and role-played it in my mind, I felt the adrenaline and the excitement in large but manageable quantities. I decided that this was probably the right thing to do.

'It'll be interesting for them,' I thought, trying to justify and rationalize what had really become a decision based in my bodily feelings, a gut feel, 'and it will be interesting for me to reflect upon the repercussions.'

On the day, I sat through the presentation of the method. Then one colleague got up and talked about a very structured and controlled approach that led directly to a structure that the client had not thought of, but was delighted with. A second colleague talked about a much more messy process of evolving a design, but still through a structured process. Then it was my turn.

'Sometimes you can follow a logical predescribed method, detailing all the processes, analyzing activity requirements and deriving the job roles. On a major project it could take months to do – in one case I heard that it took nearly a year. Eventually you deliver a populated organization and in the short term your client is delighted until they realize that it is a perfect structure for how things were a year ago. Sometimes you just have to get on with it somehow and try to make sure you get a result that's "good enough"', I said.

I went on to describe 'conversational organization design' much as I did in the earlier narrative in this chapter. As I was talking I felt a mixture of nervousness and elation – the release of being able to talk free from at least a few of the usual constraints and to be true to myself. Interestingly, nobody said a word. There were one or two smiles out there but most people looked a little blank. I asked if there were any questions; still nobody said a word.

The final example of organization design was given by one of my peers, who talked about another, much more structured process based upon the implementation of Enterprise Resource Planning software. I found that I did not really listen much because I was rerunning my session over and over to myself in my mind, and wondering why there was so little reaction.

Since that day nobody has asked me about 'conversational organization design', so there are no good stories about the repercussions after all. Whether this is because it is not so deviant after all and everyone does this under the cover of our methodology, or it is too deviant and seen as subversive, is hard to tell. Either way, it is as if my 'deviant' message was too difficult to acknowledge, and so people colluded not to speak about it and thus to maintain the existing power relations.

Gestalt consulting and presence

When I engage with an organization, I am bringing my history, my patterns of interaction and my habitual behavior. As I interact with others, I come into contact with their history. In those interactions we are both potentially challenged by the differences we experience and the process we engage in to make sense of those differences and so evolve our identities. I believe that this is a better description of how differences drive change than the simplistic 'in the system' vs 'on the margins' explanation in Meyerson's book.

One way of looking at the consulting process that takes the idea of embodying 'difference' quite seriously is Nevis' Gestalt psychotherapy-based approach. To Nevis, a consultant is a disturber of organizational boundaries, particularly boundaries of knowledge, through teaching the client 'system' skills and providing a presence that is lacking (Nevis 2001: 52–53). By presence he means being the embodiment of the 'knowledge and values' that are believed to be essential by the consultant to bring about change (Nevis 2001: 69). He goes on to say that presence is the living embodiment of knowledge, not only standing for and expressing certain values, attitudes and skills, but modeling a way of approaching problems and stimulating the client to be that way too. Great teachers are those who have internalized what they teach and 'live' it (Nevis 2001: 69–70).

This resonates strongly for me with the quote from Gandhi that opened this chapter, 'being the change you wish to see in the world'. However, what Nevis is suggesting is that presence comes from our own embodied and lived beliefs and values, our history. It is possible to interpret the Gandhi quote in such a way as to try to superficially role-model a different way of being – to demonstrate how you wish others to behave by behaving that way yourself. The danger here is that the 'role-model' potentially does not understand the behavior he or she is modeling and that other people simply copy a set of perceived behaviors.

This for me is the difference between simply role-modeling a change and presence. Presence has to be 'real'; it cannot be 'worn' and discarded at convenient times like a raincoat because presence *is* the experience of relating to another, it is the bringing of a whole history of interaction into the encounter. Role-modeling is so often someone acting in a way in which he or she would like others to behave but that behavior is not based upon his or her own personal history. My experiences with organizations where someone is seen as a role-model would suggest that people can sense when the role-modeling is not based upon someone's history – is not 'real'. It is not spontaneous, and under pressure the role-modeling slips away and the individual's history takes over – some would say they revert to type. People seem to sense superficial or studied actions that aim to manipulate others, though they may not openly challenge such a role-model if that person is more senior. Another problem with the idea of a behavioral role model is that it is so often defined in advance of the context and issues within which someone will be operating. I have seen very detailed pictures painted in words of the behaviors expected of an individual in a role, often written by consultants or HR specialists from outside the operational organization, trying to second-guess what behavior will be appropriate and effective. I pity the poor manager who is instructed to behave in very specific ways that may well not come naturally, that may be outside their previous experience, but that they will be measured against.

Nevis avoids putting the consultant into a role where he or she is supposed to 'ensure' or 'guarantee' successful change. For Nevis, the goal of the Gestalt approach to organizational consulting is to raise the awareness of the client and enable the client to decide how to change, through contact with the embodied knowledge of the consultant. This avoids the common fantasy that the consultant can force change to happen in a complex network of interactions where the behavior is emergent. In the case of the organization design presentation, I stood up in front of the team and talked about what are for me some major drawbacks of the accepted ways of doing things and I also talked about an alternative. I have, I hope, engaged with my colleagues and we have made new meaning between us. I cannot mandate that they all behave in a particular way – all I can do is engage with them openly. We may perceive a difference between us and then begin the process of negotiating enough meaning so that we can go on together, and in that negotiation we both potentially change.

Nevis' understanding of presence and change does seem to be rooted in the idea of the autonomous individual, one of the issues I shared with Meyerson earlier. For example, the text states that 'the intervener becomes the embodiment of (their well conceived and assimilated) theory. The nature of this integration and how it is accomplished determines the quality of presence' (Nevis 2001: 78). So, once again, we have an individual making an autonomous choice about a theory, in this case a theory of change and interaction, and then embodying that theory. Again we have an approach to change that ignores the way in which the individual is constrained and also that knowledge (or theories) are developed and maintained 'between' people in interaction.

For me this raises questions about changes coming purely from the 'presence' of the individual. 'Presence' must be continually reconstructed in the relationship between people. A consultant with 'presence' in one relationship may find that it does not manifest the same way in another relationship. This is because 'presence' is continuously changing with each moment, with each new experience, with each new relationship. As mentioned at the beginning of this section, each relationship I engage in is influenced by my historic patterns of relating and the history of the other person. Presence is the experience of self in interaction with others and so is always shifting. If interaction constructs ongoing identity as continuity and change simultaneously, then spontaneity becomes important, since less repetitive responses are more likely to call forth less habitual responses in others.

Perhaps what has, in retrospect, been labeled a 'skilful practitioner' is simply a person in a relationship where both the client and the consultant are openly and spontaneously engaged with each other, where they are both a presence to each other or, in other words, evoking/provoking unique experiences of self with each other. Through that relationship, the difference between the two can be explored and something novel may emerge. To me this would suggest that the so-called 'skilful practitioner' is actually the 'skilful relationship'.

As I read Meyerson's descriptions of her tempered radicals, I think she is verging on seeing them almost as Nevis describes organizational consultants, as a presence for change. As Meyerson herself points out, it is in the exploration of the difference between people that change emerges. I am arguing that the tempered radical, just as with the concept of 'presence', is a quality of relationship that arises between people, which then may or may not ripple through other relationships in the organization. Thus Meyerson, in identifying her tempered radicals as autonomous individuals, is simply focusing on one side of what is actually a relationship out of which change arises and then only on the minority of relationships she can apparently identify as being the cause of a noticeable change.

Business transformation (5)

This project appears to have worked well. Not only have we achieved quite a robust solution to the client's problems, but there is a strong impression that we did it together and they played perhaps the major role. The design is theirs.

I feel that I have spoken much less and listened much more during the bigger meetings we have had about this project, like the progress meetings and senior team meetings, than I have in the past. I have sat in on some of the progress meetings and I have hardly felt the need to talk at all. Most of the talking and making sense of what we are doing has already happened by then in the myriad conversations I have had in people's offices, by coffee machines, or on the way to the sandwich shops at lunch-time. I have located myself in the open plan area just outside the client project manager's office among all of the administrators who are working on our project and near to the internal communications department. As a result I have a much richer experience of what is happening in that building than if I were working off-site or in some specially allocated project office.

Although I may be less vocal in some situations and do not play to the audience so much, I still find that my actions are clearly expressing a different way of being in the world to theirs. In addition to the above example about where I was sitting, only the other day I was with the client team preparing for a workshop where we would decide which of the 300 people (yes, it has now reached 300 from the original eighty) would stay and which would be leaving. I noticed how slowly this filing was being done – it was falling way behind our schedule. The people who had been hired to do it were temporary staff, together with one person whose role had been made redundant and was awaiting the announcement that there were no other roles available to offer her. As a result we had something of a 'motivation gap'. This client was a large organization with lots of people who perpetuate a hierarchical pattern to their interaction. People are very level-conscious – it is the sort of place where people really have said, 'I don't do that any more, if I helped with that career-wise I'd be regressing two years.' Granted, filing is usually dull, but I got up and started filing papers myself, showing how quickly it could be done and making a bit of a game of it where the others had to try and keep up with me. There were a few curious glances, and a few double-takes as people, including some of my consulting colleagues, noticed what I was doing. They looked over more often as we started to laugh about what we were doing and enjoy the good-natured competition, but there did not seem to be much overt reaction beyond the buzz in our little group. At first glance this is not very exciting, but I think there is more to it.

I had a vague idea that seeing a senior manager from an expensive consulting company getting up and filing was creating a bit of a stir and I was also aware that everyone who was witnessing that action was making sense of it and that the process would potentially contribute to some sort of change. As I became aware of this, I also considered whether it was causing too much of a stir or whether it would affect my credibility, and I decided to just get on with the filing. After the event I could create good stories to justify what I did and make it sound like a good logical decision where I was trying to break down the rigidity of the hierarchy and get more flexible working started, but that is not how it happened. I was simply and spontaneously being 'me'. My role as a consultant then is, to some extent, to be myself in relation to the changes I wish to bring about.

Role and spontaneity

The pattern of interactions that we would recognize as a role is continually reconstructed between us in the present with the potential for novelty that this implies. It is influenced by our history and the history of those with whom we interact. It is these patterns that we use ourselves when we 'trial run' internally what we are about to do and try to anticipate the reactions of others. At first I thought a 'role' was a pattern of interaction owned and exhibited by the individual that could be taken from one relationship or time to another. I have now come to believe that roles arise in particular relationships between people. We do not embody a role independently because it is created between us. We can see this in everyday life – people who perceive themselves as taking on the role of father do so in relation to a son or daughter and that role of father may be markedly different when in relationship with a different son or daughter. Our ability to be 'skillful' is therefore determined partly by our ability to recognize the patterns of interaction (roles) between us.

A pattern of interaction, or role, which I seem to participate in continually re-creating is that of 'useful subversive'. This is how I describe the pattern of interaction that is manifest through actions such as the presentation of 'conversational organization design', or when I start filing, or sit with the HR administrators.

Creativity and spontaneity are two closely related ideas. Blatner clarifies the difference between the two by suggesting that creativity is the activity of creating and spontaneity is the readiness to create (Blatner 2000: 80). Another definition of spontaneity is '[Spontaneity] propels the individual toward an adequate response to a new situation or a new response to an old situation' (Moreno 1953: 42) which is from Moreno himself, the father of psychodrama. This description is helpful, since it points to spontaneity being a style of response to a gesture. I think of spontaneity as being open to the potential and the movement of the present and having the confidence to respond and 'act into' the moment.

According to Blatner, developing spontaneity is, in part, closely related to developing receptivity to the non-rational, intuitive dimensions of mind (Blatner 2000: 84). This is not to say that spontaneity is more closely associated with emotion and action, which Moreno highlighted as a common error (Fox 1987: 43), since spontaneity appears just as often in thought as in action. As I am acting or thinking I sometimes find that my attention is attracted by something seemingly unrelated, possibly a thought or a bodily reaction. This often seems to be where I feel dissonance between the patterns of interaction that have made up my history and what is happening around me. This awareness offers the potential to do something differently. From my spontaneity, my preparedness to be creative, emerges an adequate response to the new situation.

While I think we all have the capacity to sense these dissonant moments, I think that through the experience of psychodrama individuals can become more aware of themselves and build confidence in acting into the 'difference'. Through the experience of improvisation, experimenting, talking and especially moving about (Blatner 2000: 86), we build our capacity to act this way. We develop our ability for spontaneity through practising. In the process of this 'acting in', the difference is made clearer and can be engaged with further, creating the potential for new meaning and insights. The experience of doing these things then becomes a part of our history of relating, part of the palette from which we paint our communicative interaction. Small changes in this interaction have the potential to be amplified though the complex process of human relating into significant change.

Some of the interactions described in this chapter, I feel, exhibit aspects of this creativity born out of spontaneity. While I am constrained by the ideologies that I help re-create moment to moment with my team, work colleagues, countrymen and so on, I am simultaneously spontaneous and creative. I am coming to realize that this is a key part of my practice.

Business transformation (6)

Gillian, one of my key clients, always struck me as being a nervous person. She would talk with a slightly thin voice but with 'queen's English' diction. Working with her could be incredibly frustrating, though, because she was perfectly capable of arguing for opposite positions in the course of a single conversation. In one conversation she talked to me about how her staff had not had any recent communication from us regarding the changes we were planning for the project management community – the 300 people who were likely to become about 200, with the other 100 being made redundant. I started to argue that we did not really have very much that we could tell them because, as she knew, we were still finalizing our plans of action. 'I don't think it's going to help to send a note saying "everything is as it was last week and, like we said last week, we will tell you just what is going to happen next week". Were I them, I would not feel any sense of comfort or progress in that', I said.

She was insistent, though, and so we started to talk about what had happened in the week to see whether there was something worth saying to show progress. I imagine that during the course of this exploration she forgot her opening position because her interactions started to change from encouraging some sort of communication to criticizing the suggested content of a communication we could send and then criticizing the idea of communicating at all at this time. In the end she told me that I was foolish for suggesting a communication with so little content. I felt my whole body tense with the injustice of it. It echoed some childhood experiences with a mother who regularly used to do the same thing to me and I felt the shame and incompetence I felt as a child being told I was stupid and not good enough. I had to put some physical space between Gillian and myself at that point, and it took me a while to get back to normal.

I did wonder what it was that created this rather odd interaction. As I talked to people around the organization I found several people questioning her role: 'What does she really do apart from sit in on meetings all over the place?' they asked. I started to try to imagine myself into her situation and experience how she might feel. I imagined that she was someone who was trying so hard to make a contribution of some sort, to warrant her position and salary, that logic was less important than survival. It would be an easy pattern to fall into – the organization was downsizing in all areas as the leaders of each function tried to meet the cost reduction challenge the CEO had issued. Nobody was particularly safe and a highly paid executive who was not sure of the value of his or her role was an obvious target.

Over time we had many meetings and discussions, several of which brought forth similar but less strong feelings in me each time. As Gillian became more and more engaged with our project, the pattern of contradicting herself and blaming others lessened, though she would seem to have little crises of confidence which raised both nervousness and irritation in me. I chose to keep quiet in these meetings and let her work through what she was thinking and feeling. I encouraged Gillian, despite her frustration, not to close down these conversations too quickly. Out of these emerged, as noted above, the new organization structure. Within this new structure was a role that Andy, the director in charge of the business transformation area, talked to Gillian about and suggested that she apply for.

Shortly after this point in time we were all surprised when Gillian was fired by the CEO for non-performance along with a number of other senior people, including some of Andy's top-level executive team.

Bodies of thought

Burkitt's (1999) attempt to locate the basis of all knowledge in bodily experience appeals in its simplicity and resonates with my own experience of 'knowing' through bodily sensation in a consulting engagement. I have had experiences in psychodrama where it would seem that I understood what was happening at a bodily level better than I knew what was happening consciously. For example, when enacting what appeared on the surface to be a simple, if slightly frustrating, conversation with someone, it was pointed out to me that I was pumping my hand into a fist. It was an action of which I had been completely unaware. Thus rather than continue with the dialogue we explored what was happening with the fist. By following what my body was suggesting, exploring the angry fist, I developed new insight. It has been suggested that this resembles the Cartesian split between mind and body, but that is not what I am saying. I believe that both the dialogue and the hand movements are aspects of a single thinking/feeling body. Both Stacey (2001) and Burkitt (1999) have made the concept of the thinking and feeling body central to their understanding of human interaction, our bodily experience being part and parcel of our ability to think and act spontaneously. I have described some of the feelings associated with my work and my experience in the final community meeting and in the meetings with Gillian. Those feelings were an integral part of the experience and the thoughts that emerged. Making sense of, and acting on, those feelings is an integral part of my practice. Each and every interaction is both shaped by and is shaping those feelings.

Drawing on Leontyev, Burkitt draws a picture of consciousness evolving out of bodily sensation, 'of body and mind united at the very point of origin' (Burkitt 1999: 38), where despite the subtlety enabled by language, all thought, all consciousness, is based in bodily sensation. For Burkitt we are 'not just located in the world symbolically; nor do we experience reality purely through the text: instead we are located in relations that transform the natural and social worlds in which we live' (Burkitt 1999: 2).

But where did this split between language and the sensuous body come from? Burkitt points to the development of the closed and rationalized Cartesian body, severed from, and in doubt of, its sensual experience, unable to be sure of any knowledge it may have of the world (Burkitt 1999: 49). This process changes our relations with others from being open and spontaneous, though without the nuances and differentiation we know today, to being closed and private with each interaction having many shades and subtleties to be considered and role-played in my mind before making a gesture into the world. This is not to say that I have a romanticized view of the past and wish for a return to the open spontaneity of the Middle Ages. It is simply that, as the rationalized post-Cartesian individual emerged through the Renaissance, we moved further and further away from sensate experience and relied upon language and rationality to explain the world. I suggest that this has impeded our understanding of human relations and communication and, of course, change in organizations. To get a clear picture of what is really happening we have to reintegrate the sensual experience of the body that the Enlightenment would equate to irrationality (Burkitt 1999: 149). This is a part of the practice I describe: an awareness of the integration of bodily sensation into the overall process of human interaction. Bodily sensations appear in many of the descriptions of practice in this chapter. It was a key element in my reaction to the sidelining of Joan, the presentation of 'conversational organization design', my actions at the last community meeting, dealing with Gillian and so on.

Like Burkitt, Stacey is insistent on talking about the interactions between bodies. He refers to the work of Damasio, who suggests that the body is continuously monitoring both internal (heartbeat, breathing) and external (the smell of coffee, someone's face) activity which is registered as feeling states (Stacey 2001: 82). When a person encounters similar situations he or she registers similar feeling states. Stacey picks up on this and suggests that this explains how we can call forth in ourselves a similar response to that of the other individual when making gestures towards each other. Given similar biology and similar body rhythms, he suggests that we have enough in common to anticipate how others would feel. We do this by role-playing our gestures, and evoking for ourselves a similar bodily response to that which may be experienced by the other person. Stacey also suggests that there is some kind of resonance between the body rhythms of the two interacting individuals (Stacey 2001: 83), and that people can attune to each other to some degree and experience similar rhythms to each other, which allows us to better anticipate the likely responses of others to our gestures (Stacey 2001: 91).

In the story about interacting with Gillian, I tried to imagine what it was like to be her – to put myself in her shoes. What enables this is, in part, a similar biology, but I think that what is more important is my history of relating with her and with others whose patterns of interaction I perceive as similar. I can then use these patterns to role-play conversations in my mind or imagine my way through situations imagining her reactions and gestures. This is the basis of psychodrama. It is the ability to take on the roles, the patterns of interactions of another, to play them out and gain insight from the action. In the case of Gillian I simply role-played the different roles in my mind and evoked in myself a range of bodily experience in so doing.

I think that the ability to do this is the explanation for how Meyerson's tempered radicals behave in ways that are not in line with the current ideology, yet not so far as to be rejected. We all constantly imagine our way into the future by internally role-playing our gestures against the experiences of past interactions with the people we know. Through this role-play we can anticipate whether our planned gesture will enable us to go on together or else find us isolated.

Away from the placebo prescriptions

In my day-to-day practice I find myself interacting with others in many contexts. There are two aspects to the flow of this interaction: one is patterned by a conversation about a formal methodology, the other is simply a conversation of trying to work out what to do next. I have come to think about the first aspect in terms of an ideological interaction about organizational change consulting whose relatively stable patterns enable and constrain how we (my colleagues and clients) talk about the rationale for our work in abstract, propositional terms which sustain current power relations. I liken this to a placebo, in the sense that the flow of these interactions may enable all concerned to feel engaged in change activity, even build a sense of being in control of the changes that they intend, despite the fact that little change is actually created. What comes out of this interaction is largely conservative and predictable.

Such interaction is interwoven with the second aspect, namely a pragmatic interaction in which our ongoing detailed activity is enabled and constrained by the patterning of the sense which we are continuously constructing among ourselves and which has the potential to shift power relations. Continuing the medical metaphor, I liken this to side effects which I suggest are stimulating real changes in the status quo. This interaction has the potential to be spontaneous, creative and unpredictable.

Within both of these aspects of the flow of interaction, I refer to the rich palette of communicative interaction open to us – not only vocal interaction, but bodily gestures, spatio–temporal relationships, even bodily feeling states. My own identity as a professional person is, not a stable 'thing', but a pattern in that ongoing rich process of interaction which emerges out of a history of interaction with others and the sense I have made of those interactions. That identity is unique to me, just as my personal history is unique to me, yet is constantly shifting with each new experience. Those shifts in identity are unknowable in advance, but recognizable in hindsight.

I continuously have to sustain connection to the sense-making of others in order to be recognized as a professional by colleagues and clients and to contribute to the evolution of my profession. I have come to see that my effectiveness resides in the creative tension of working in a way that calls into question existing patterns of 'making sense' of competent professional work. I see this not only in the way I verbally invite fresh sense-making with others but at least as significantly, in the way I participate as a moving, thinking, feeling, aware body shifting the play of spatio–temporal patterns among other such bodies and working with the fresh sense-making that this stimulates.

It is this particular appreciation of inviting fresh sense-making through bodily interaction that I believe others write about as 'working at the boundary', 'being marginal', being a 'tempered radical', 'challenging existing mind-sets' and so on, which constitutes the contribution I am making to professional practice. I am arguing that this subtle and detailed perspective is a missing element in much of the discussion about those promoting change and what they do; the traditional discussion focuses primarily on language-related sense-making. I suggest that my account of how and why bodily activity matters, including language, is theoretically consistent with a view of organizations as self-organizing patterns of relating.

The complexity of human relating in an organization means that we cannot know in advance of our interactions what the outcomes will be, but the patterning effect we find in most complex networks means that the outcome is likely to be recognizable as we come to live it because of the paradoxical nature of continuity and change occurring simultaneously. This recognizable outcome is both a problem and a benefit to us as participants in organizational change.

It is a problem because, in hindsight, it allows the appearance of control for our accounts of how organizations change; of plans coming to fruition through processes of control and so on. In this way the prescriptions of writers such as Kotter and Conner gain some measure of credibility and seduce us away from examining the detail of our experience of change as it is occurring.

It is a benefit because this capacity to recognize what seems to have led to the emergent outcome ensures our ability to continue, in the face of cascades of potentially disabling novelty. This recognizability is constructed not only in language but to a significant extent also in the shifting of our bodily gestures and spatio–temporal relations.

Bringing all of these threads together produces a picture that operates across a very wide range in terms of scale. It talks in terms of the grand scale of business transformation and grand methodologies, and yet also in terms of the detailed process of human interaction and sense-making. The stories I have offered here are small vignettes taken from a huge assignment, sometimes operating globally, affecting tens of thousands of people. How do I see this all fitting together?

Each and every consulting assignment is made up of a long succession of small vignettes; each and every methodology comprises a series of small steps that almost offer themselves as vignettes, scene by scene, in which the detail of significant dramatic action goes far beyond the verbal exchanges. As noted above, I do not wish to totally discredit methodologies, to banish them from the world of organizational consulting, never to darken our office doors again. I hope to vigorously encourage consultants to think again about what they are doing; to focus less on the delivery of reports or on pre-defined acts in a frozen script, but to pay close attention to the detail of the richness of ongoing human interaction as a form of organizational psychodrama and the sense-making going on there. For this is where real change happens.

Thus we achieve that which Conner and Kotter are trying to achieve, not through the prescriptions themselves, valuable though they may be, but through a side effect of those prescriptions – changes in the patterns of interaction throughout the organization. If you can engage with that sense-making, and take the risk that you will inevitably be changed in the process as well, you have the foundation for a new practice of change consulting.

References

Blatner, A. (2000) *Foundations of Psychodrama: History, Theory and Practice* (4th edn), New York: Springer.

Burkitt, I. (1999) *Bodies of Thought*, London: Sage.

Conner, D. (1992) *Managing at the Speed of Change*, New York: Villiard Books.

Dalal, F. (1998) *Taking the Group Seriously: Towards a Post-Foulkesian Group Analytic Theory*, London: Jessica Kingsley.

Fox, J. (ed.) (1987) *The Essential Moreno: Writing on Psychodrama, Group Method, and Spontaneity by J.L. Moreno MD*, New York: Springer.

Kotter, J. (1996) *Leading Change*, Boston, MA: Harvard Business School Press.

Meyerson, D. E. (2001) *Tempered Radicals: How People use Difference to Inspire Change at Work*, Boston, MA: Harvard Business School Press.

Moreno, J. L. (1953) *Who Shall Survive: Foundations of Sociometry, Group Psychotherapy and Sociodrama*, New York: Beacon House.

Nevis, E. C. (2001) *Organizational Consulting: A Gestalt Approach*, Cambridge, MA: Gestalt Press.

Stacey, R. (2001) *Complex Responsive Processes in Organizations: Learning and knowledge creation*, London: Routledge.

Editors' introduction to Chapter 7

Nicholas Sarra is employed by a National Health Service (NHS) Trust in the United Kingdom where his main concern is organizational development (OD). He describes the confusion people experience as they try to work out just what OD means in their context. As a way of doing OD, he suggests that, instead of trying to prepare a plan, those involved in the OD project should start by talking to those who are supposed to be changed by the OD project about what they are doing. He proposes a group visit to the Trust's forensic psychiatric hospital. As with other writers in this volume, he understands consulting and research to be the same reflective conversational practices. He makes sense of what he is doing by exploring how current patterns of power relations are sustained in processes of gossip, arguing that ways of talking (gossip) form what we do together and this can be changed only by entering into these ways of talking – this is the justification for seeing the visits to the psychiatric hospital as OD activities. For Sarra, change or development in an organization means change in the pattern of power relations.

Not surprisingly, Sarra encounters some skepticism and opposition to what he is doing. Many in the NHS place a great deal of emphasis on an evidence-based methodology, and so call upon Sarra to provide evidence of the success of the method he proposes in terms of testable outcomes. Sarra, however, points to the way in which this methodology is used as a rhetoric which conceals aspects of power relating, exerting control and defining what is valid meaning. The methodology amounts to an ideology that sustains current patterns of power relating. Sarra argues that the micro-diversity of human relating and the potential for the amplification of this micro-diversity renders any evidence-based methodology highly problematic with regard to OD. He argues that what he is doing amounts to OD because his activities focus on providing opportunities for the amplification of conversational diversity as the means of moving blocked communication and destructive human dynamics. He invites people to reflect on the pattern of power relations they are co-creating together and on the meaning of the routines they are following. In doing this he seeks to disrupt the stability of power relations and the conversational themes and routines that sustain them, thereby challenging what he sees as a totalitarian methodology.

Sarra places conversation at the center of his research-consulting methodology as he seeks to 'widen and deepen' communication through exploring potential meanings for amplification in discussion. This is how change happens, and without it people remain stuck in repetitive and destructive ways of talking and doing. He uses a narrative form of accounting for what is going on, pointing to how this reveals matters, such as power and gossip, which are usually covered over in the rational literature on organizational change. His method is highly participative in that he involves the entire hospital staff and the users of their services in the conversations. One of the users works with him as consultant. It is these people who are the organization, and change can only take place in them. Consulting research becomes collaborative sense-making, a kind of joint cultural enquiry. The methodology is highly subjective and involves paying attention to, and regularly discussing, felt experience. He describes his work as emotionally exhausting. The ideological and power dimensions of methodology are made explicit.

The result is a methodology of exploration in which outcomes cannot be known in advance but emerge in an unpredictable way. This is in strong contrast to the NHS methodologies of national strategies, targets, action plans and outcomes specified in advance. It is this, of course, that some find threatening but others find liberating.

7 Organizational development in the National Health Service

Nicholas Sarra

- Reflection
- Power
- An initial meeting
- Setting up
- Locks and keys
- The Mahler Clinic
- The canteen
- Open versus closed communication
- A request for outcomes
- The plenary process
- Conclusion

The question of how one undertakes organizational development is a priority for the National Health Service (NHS) Trust in the UK for which I do most of my work. I will describe a scenario which illustrates some of the dilemmas involved and then go on to explore how I am currently making sense of the presenting issues compared to other writers who are discussing similar topics. The Trust in question had recently completed a merger which united, within a single organization, a number of previously separate mental health services. A director of human resources and organizational development had been appointed. She decided to call a meeting of those who she felt could take the organizational development agenda forward. The meeting was tense and difficult. Not many people knew each other and the director voiced her dissatisfaction, saying that we were 'getting nowhere'. She wanted a direction and a plan of action. The meeting broke up in an acrimonious mood with people feeling confused and angry.

I went to see her afterwards and suggested to her that those at the meeting would be unable to fulfill her expectations and that, for the moment, people just needed to get to know each other and talk about their own respective experiences of the new organization. She suggested that I chair such a meeting and we agreed that it might come to represent an interesting microcosm of organizational experience from which we could get ideas. She asked me to send her a description of what the 'new meeting' would entail which she would then pass on to the other members of the group along with her authorization of myself taking the chair.

The time for the next meeting approached, and I was aware that she had not informed anyone about the change both in the format of the meeting and my role. In addition, there was no response to attempts to contact her in order to clarify the situation. I felt let down and concerned that the group might not accept my change in role unless prepared for it. I began to wonder if she might be less than enthusiastic about delegating authority to me.

The day arrived for the meeting and I met her by chance ten minutes beforehand in the corridor. She appeared flustered and said, 'Look, I really don't think I need to be at this meeting, just let me know how it goes.' I replied that she did need to be there in order to delegate her authority and that people would not know how to make sense of her absence. She then agreed to attend and to speak briefly about my role and the purpose of the group. The situation was further complicated since a number of mental health service users were due to join the meeting that day with the hope that they too would make an ongoing contribution to the process of organizational development.

The director arrived ten minutes late for the meeting and began to speak in a corporate style about the importance of organizational development. She spoke thus for some twenty-five minutes without once exploring how the group might engage with the issues or mentioning that I was to chair the meeting. Finally, and with a flourish of her arm (and something, I thought, of a sneer) she exclaimed, 'And now I pass you over to Nick's very capable hands.'

At this point one of the service users, who had just arrived, proceeded to engage her in a very long-winded monologue whose meaning was obscure. I remember thinking at the time that he was fixing her with his speech and gaze as one might fix a butterfly with a pin. She did indeed appear transfixed as her interlocutor droned on and on while the other ten participants seemed excluded and unable to intervene. However, the director had now given me some legitimacy to chair the meeting and so I interrupted and invited others to join the conversation. The director saw this as a means of exit and quit the room.

The next few meetings proved to be difficult. Some of the service users and the hospital chaplain were appalled at the idea that the task was initially nothing more than conversation, and seemed to experience that prospect as a profound threat. A theme began to dominate the meeting around the abuses of general psychiatry and consultant psychiatrists in particular, and I found myself rapidly entering a situation similar in many respects to that in which the director had found herself, namely that there was general confusion about what we were supposed to do coupled with a growing antagonism to the person in the leadership role. I realized that something had to change for the group to become useful and that I was being constrained in the direction I had hoped the group would take.

I then conceived a 'task' for the group. I thought it important at this stage that I provide a sense of direction and purpose for the group which could be more generally understood and accepted by the participants. This was my way of alleviating the anxiety within the meeting which I perceived as threatening to its continuity. I thought that by providing a task involving outsider groups, feelings of aggression and anxiety could be taken up and used more profitably while allowing the group to develop a sense of cohesiveness or a 'We' identity in the process of relating to other groups. We would thus go out into the organization as a group and experience how things were from our perspective. This would entail visiting institutions and departments, and entering into a variety of formal and informal conversations with the staff we would meet. The way we began to make sense of this new potential activity was something akin to portraying our felt experience of the institutions, wards or departments we might encounter. We were anxious that we should not be seen in any way as an inspectorate or an agency of audit or performance evaluation but wanted to provide something different which we felt was lacking, namely an unashamedly subjective impression of the places we might visit.

However, the group, although unanimously enthusiastic about this suggested task, reacted to and interpreted it in a number of ways, some of which I found alarming. Some of the service users and the chaplain started to speak as if they saw this as an opportunity for the shaming of poor practice. I felt I could sense an anticipatory delight over entering these places with an advantageous position in the power relations as if they were compensating for previous humiliating experiences.

Before I go on to describe how the group proceeded, I will endeavor to make sense of the above events.

Reflection

What I see happening in the above events is the ongoing movement of people finding ways forward through the ever shifting fluctuations of power relations. These fluctuations both enable and constrain simultaneously so that when one is constrained one is also potentially enabled and vice versa. It is this process (that is, one of power relating) which fundamentally constitutes human interaction. In the above story, I and those with whom I am relating are continually coming up against each other in the sense that none of us is able to move forward in the way we anticipate. We are thus constraining each other and, by doing so, are therefore enabled into a novel process which is largely unpredictable and possesses an emergent quality. I use the phrase 'novel process' to emphasize how the pattern of interaction changes in a way that the participants can neither control nor predict. Thus the expectations of the director in the first meeting proved unachievable, as did my own and others in the subsequent groups. Therefore the iterative interaction through the ongoing process of enabling constraining allowed for novelty to potentially arise in the sense that our journey together obliged us into patterns of relating which were new and unfamiliar, since they were co-created and thus outside any one individual's omnipotent control. Of course the unexpected directions which we find ourselves taking will not necessarily prove to be helpful ones.

I will now discuss a number of writers who I believe contribute to this way of thinking. Particularly relevant are those who conceive power in relational terms such as Elias (1998), Foucault (1975) and Stacey *et al.* (2000).

Power

The word 'power', generally defined as an ability or capacity to yield some outcome (*Cambridge Dictionary of Philosophy*), stems from the French verb *pouvoir*, to be able (*OED*). The debate over power as a concept was developed by Locke. In *An Essay Concerning Human Understanding* (1690), Locke differentiated active from passive powers so that, for example, a ball has the passive power to be kicked actively by a footballer. Within this concept there is the beginning of a sense of power being a relational concept; that is, one posited upon functional interdependency. The problem is generally viewed as being whether objects have intrinsic power in themselves or whether this property is contingent upon a reciprocal relationship. The view I will take is the latter, namely that it is not a property but a dynamic with qualities which drive both the movement of temporality in the natural world and the emergence of novelty in human relating. Difference and diversity are the intrinsic qualities inherent in the process of power relating which allow for the potential emergence of novelty.

Darwin suggests that novelty occurs through the process of chance variation subjected to competitive selection. Mead implies, through his understanding of Darwin, that the human vehicle for this adaptive process is the iterative movement of gesture and response between people. Mead does not use the word 'power' but refers instead to control which he sees as the business of adaptation and adjustment vital to human communication. I suggest that our adaptive and adjusting strategies, which are the processes of power relating, must change as we encounter difference and conflict. We then find ourselves other than where we intended.

Like many, Foucault sees power relations primarily as techniques of dominance and control, and in particular the control of discourse as seminal to the state's control of its subjects. He suggests that, over and above power relations being understood within the framework of an economic analysis (i.e. Marxism), there are two main discourses around power. One relates to repression which he argues for the sake of convenience is Reich's thesis. Foucault (1976) sees Reich like Freud, as interested in the mechanisms of repression which in Reich's case revolve around the internalization of social power relations. For example, the social repression of sexuality manifests itself in the individual as neurotic behavior and is somatically expressed as in Reich's concept of 'body armor' (Mairowitz 1986). The other discourse refers to the engagement of hostile forces which he sees as Nietzschean and which in its final analysis is concerned with war. However, he sees these two approaches as compatible since, for example, repression may be viewed as the outcome of war and both are political acts.

There remains the problem of how Foucault conceptualizes power which changes according to the time and context in which he is writing, so that power can be a 'materiality . . . operating on the very bodies of individuals' (Foucault 1975, p. 55) as well as something which 'is never localized here or there, never in anybody's hands, never appropriated as a commodity or piece of wealth' (Foucault 1976, p. 98). Thus, despite his occasional reifying of the concept, Foucault stresses the intangibility of the nature of power though not of its effects and that its effects manifest themselves only in action, for example, 'power is neither given, nor exchanged nor recovered, but rather exercised and . . . it only exists in action' (ibid., p. 88). He says that the effects of power relations are individualized or internalized as a historical process. This is similar to the thinking of Elias who specifically posits power as a multi-relational figuration which is nonetheless not in the possession of individuals: 'Power is not an amulet possessed by one person and not by another; it is a structural characteristic of human relationships – of all human relationships' (Elias 1998, p. 116).

Elias also sees power relations as concerned with dominance–submission and state formation taking the form of the acquisition by an elite of a set of monopolies, for example, a monopoly over the means to violence and a monopoly of taxation by monarch or state which, over considerable periods of time, becomes personalized so that there is a gradual shift of focus from an external to an internal locus of control. However, unlike Foucault, he places the emphasis on relational interdependencies, so that, for example, the monarch's construction of a bureaucracy in order to maintain the status quo of his or her power relations inevitably leads to an increasing dependency upon that bureaucracy and consequently an eventual shift in those power relations. For Elias, the process of group identity, the sense of 'I' and 'We', is formed through the interdependent power relating which occurs in an ongoing way between the activities and attitudes of different social groupings towards each other.

One of Elias' most original contributions is his exploration of gossip as a feature of interaction which fosters group cohesiveness and the articulation of insider/outsider identities. Gossip establishes a particular power ratio which favors the gossiper and his or her group at the expense of others. Furthermore, Elias suggests that outsiders with less 'chances' in power relations may identify with and begin to believe in the gossip directed towards them by established groups. Elias (1998, p. 251) writes:

> the collective disgrace attached to such groups by other more
> powerful groups and embodied in standard invectives and stereotyped

blame-gossip usually has a deep anchorage in the personality structure of their members as part of their individual identity and as such cannot be easily shaken off.

The implications of the above insights into the nature of gossip are significant for organizations, since gossip represents ever-present strata in the ongoing process of conversation between people at work. Especially in large, complex organizations such as the NHS, groups with various umbrella identities (e.g. nurses, doctors, managers, community teams and inpatient teams) are continually adjusting to each other in the ongoing interplay of power relating. Gossip is a key technique within the process of doing so. By gossiping, one may be covertly, perhaps even unconsciously, creating alliances and processes of alienation which bolster one's own or one's own group's power chances while attempting to diminish those of others. Thus, for example, in the above-mentioned tensions with the director, I found myself increasingly gossiping about her to trusted colleagues. In addition, my propensity to gossip increased in accordance with the tensions I was experiencing in our relationship. This achieved the aim of consolidating my own alliances while marking her as an outsider who was to be excluded so that my own power chances within our mutual circle of influence were enhanced, while hers were diminished, or at least that was my semi-conscious strategy. I refer to it as semi-conscious because at the time, these Machiavellian activities were masked behind a façade of rationalization which, only with some hindsight, I can make further sense of.

Thus the way we talk about each other at work influences our quality of communication and participation, and in turn, these ways of talking can only be influenced by further conversation. It is therefore only by entering into and participating within the organizational conversation in a way which encompasses difference that a shifting of rigid conversational patterning will occur. By 'encompassing difference', I mean to imply the open exchange of competing discourses or the construction of forums where sense-making may succeed in loosening itself from the shackles of both repression and the dominance/submission dynamic and hence the role for a style of organizational consultancy which can engage with the conversational patterning of the workplace. However, the dominance/submission dynamic can be a difficult one to shift and this was exemplified in the continuing problems I experienced in convening the organizational development group referred to above. In that case, the problems expressed between the group members and the director were transferred to myself when I took over as chairman and I had to participate very actively to bring about change.

Elias refers to power relations in their rawest form as the 'primal contest' (Elias 1998, p. 115) whereby people seek to annihilate each other with total ruthlessness. This also appears to be Rorty's (2000 view: 'the only real question is one of power, the question of which community is going to inherit the earth, mine or my opponent's.' While these are certainly important, even primary, aspects of power relating, they may negate the transformative nature of conflict and opposition whereby all parties are ultimately changed through the process of engagement. Therefore conflict is complex and as much about mutual transformation as it is about the desire to annihilate.

Foucault discusses how the above process of mutual transformation through conflict may be seen as a species of colonization (Foucault 1976, p. 86). He refers to how dominant discourses appropriate the domains of those whom they seek to subjugate by a spurious integration which masks control. Although this may be a means of domination, or, as Foucault terms it, a 'technique of power', it seems also an inevitability that the colonized will transform the colonizer. In their process of mutual engagement, the subjugated and the dominant will transform each other, rendering the quality of future 'power ratios' complex and indeterminate.

This, for example, is usually the case in long-standing cases of international conflict whereby, over time, the power relations frequently shift markedly to the problematic, for example, as to who is the aggressor and who the aggressed, or who is the oppressor and who the oppressed. This is so, even in extreme cases such as genocide where one might hypothesize total 'victory' because inevitably new discourses arise through the ongoing power relating between people which render single sense-making paradigms and homogeneity of discourse ultimately unsustainable.

This is not to suggest, however, that there is no point in doing anything or that we can excuse ourselves from the responsibility of participation on the grounds that we exist in a universe which 'self-organizes' socio-bio-diversity, making it pointless to attempt to control or plan anything. Quite the opposite is the case, since it is the quality of our interaction at a local level which determines the way we move forward together. In other words, self-organization is not something a manager can direct or control beyond his or her own participation. It is not a technique to be employed but rather a way of describing the patterning and (sometimes) disintegration which occur as the inevitable result of power relating, a key aspect of what Stacey terms 'complex responsive processes'. Self-organizing interactive processes mean that a single stakeholder could not subjugate or control such processes. A particular group or individual cannot control with certainty the shape of the future. In reality this is impossible due to the mutually transformative nature of engaging with others. However, this omnipotent idea of control remains a fantasy much beloved by many management consultants and, as we shall see, it informs the ideology of the NHS Modernisation Agency.

This is not to suggest any moral or constructive frame to these processes of mutual transformation since any change process may bring about disintegration and fragmentation or exacerbate conflictual tension as well as contribute to perceived constructive outcomes. In this light, the task which I set for the organizational development group endeavors to engage with a process of uncertainty as regards outcome. By deliberately avoiding features such as performance evaluation, we were hoping to engage more directly with the lived experience of the organization as opposed to the imposition of ideas of where we should be.

You will recall that we had decided upon a task for the organizational development group. That task was to visit institutions, departments and wards around the Trust for the purpose of conversing about the felt experience of entering into those situations. This would provide us with opportunities for getting to know the organization but also for developing reflective conversation in those areas we might visit. The purpose of such conversations would be to foster organizational development through direct participation and interaction. We also had the advantage of working alongside mental health service users who might bring to the process added weight and interest with their perceptions. I chose as our pilot project a regional forensic facility which I will refer to as Orchard Hospital.

There were a number of reasons for this choice. First, I knew the manager well and felt that she would be interested in such a project. This would enable relatively easy access to the institution and the authority required to do so. Second, and due to its forensic task, it was a relatively closed institution in terms of self-sufficiency and the impermeability of its boundaries. It is based on one site which we could manage to get around in a day or two without getting caught up in too many extraneous issues from the wider organization. Third, I knew that there were long-standing difficulties at the hospital which would be interesting and possibly helpful to explore, and that such an intervention, if we could manage it successfully, would establish our credibility for further projects.

An initial meeting

The first step, after getting the manager on board with the idea, was to meet up with the wider management team in order to secure their cooperation in the enterprise. And so on a rainy summer morning I sat down at the table of the 'boardroom' at Orchard Hospital with the manager and a group of ten or so senior clinicians who constituted the management team in order to persuade them of the viability of the project.

The group in general were very supportive but there was a great deal of aggressive questioning from the clinical director, a consultant psychiatrist, who I knew to have a reputation of being domineering and difficult to get along with. I began by outlining a proposed structure for the visit which initially comprised a day of informal and formal conversations with staff and patients from across the institution. This would be followed by a plenary where we would endeavor to make sense of our experiences with the help of the patients and staff. The clinical director objected to this on the grounds that we might open up a can of worms which would be difficult to contain. He then enquired as to the 'evidence' for this type of approach to organizational work and wanted to inspect the 'pedigree' of those whom I wished to bring along as colleagues on the project.

Now these requests, although perhaps reasonable in themselves, were issued with such vehemence and hostility that I immediately felt threatened and defensive. I wondered to myself whether he might also be feeling threatened and defensive about the project, and so endeavored to come alongside and reassure him about the potential benefits while acknowledging the dangers.

I could see, however, that the group were impatient of him and that he had no support. I often find the requests for evidence of one's practice, a ubiquitous feature of contemporary NHS culture, both oppressive and frequently spurious. Oppressive because evidence is frequently seen as validated by the outcomes of randomized control trials, which have limited value when applied to nonlinear feedback systems or, in Stacey's terms, complex responsive processes. This is because they are inevitably 'people-context-dependent' and therefore susceptible to the amplifications arising from the micro-diversity inherent in human interaction. This in effect may mean that clinical interventions which have proved efficacious in one area, perhaps in the USA, cannot be rolled out in a different context in the UK within the health service.

Now a randomized control may be appropriate with pharmaceutical drug trials, but is far more problematic when evaluating interventions in which human relating is the *modus operandus* and thus the interacting agencies are all operating, in analogy, as complex adaptive systems, and are therefore problematic in their ability to supply data with reliable constancy and predictability. The idealized concept of a deterministic and linear organizational process which is predictable and controllable in its outcomes and which helps form the tools of organizational strategy and planning is in reality purely a methodology to navigate the murkier waters of the emergent nonlinearity in human interaction. The pitfall is however that this linear methodology can be mistaken for or equated with the complexity of the nonlinear process itself.

There is also the problem of how novelty and creativity arise if one works solely within the parameters of evidence-based practice since inevitably one must work with formulae which exclude divergence or else one is not adhering to the evidence base. This then renders problematic how, in using an evidence-based paradigm, one is able to adapt a fixed methodology to changing circumstances with their differing agents, times and spaces.

The spurious quality which may sometimes hide beneath a call for evidence is the way in which rhetoric around research may conceal aspects of power relating since he or she who is able to define the parameters of valid meaning and discourse is then able to control what is discussable and what is not. I therefore felt, rightly or wrongly, that the clinical director was not genuinely interested in hearing about other interventions which had used the same methodology but was casting about for some means of asserting control by way of challenging both my intended procedure and the credibility of those who were to work alongside me. I surmised that he was probably feeling threatened by the project, since a process of open conversation might expose the nature of current power relating at Orchard Hospital and therefore potentially change the status quo which he embodied.

The rest of the team, however, were in favor of going ahead, and so we set dates for two days of conversation and plenary sessions with patients and staff at the hospital. I agreed that, following our visit, I would write a letter to everyone involved which would summarize our experiences and open up further possibilities for mutual sense-making and conversation about what it meant to live and work at Orchard Hospital.

Together with the manager I then set up the logistics for the proposed meetings and we awaited the appointed day.

Setting up

Orchard Hospital presents a bleak prospect. Its buildings, erected sometime in the middle of the twentieth century, forlornly straddle the grounds which are open and exposed to the weather. Everything appears somewhat run down and faded in appearance, and this impression is heightened by a number of disused buildings with boarded windows. The whole suggests that Orchard Hospital has seen more active and populous days. However, it remains home to about a hundred patients and several times that number of staff who work there.

Six of us arrived on the agreed day with little more than a sketchy agenda of people we might meet at various times to talk to. In fact the agenda developed itself during the day as people unexpectedly put themselves forward for conversation in ways we could not have predicted. For example, two of us went to the canteen for lunch and encountered there a team of occupational therapists who wished to talk. Similarly, as the day progressed, more and more people approached us and asked if it would be possible to meet with us, including a number who wanted to see us on our own.

The six of us, whom I shall refer to as the team, split up into pairs. Each pair consisted of a member of staff employed by the Trust and a mental health service user. Between us we tried, on that first day, to visit most of the major areas at the hospital. At various points we met up as a team to offer each other support and to find out about what the other pairs were experiencing. The following is my experience of that first day.

After meeting up with the team for a briefing, I paired up with Dilly, a likable and astute man who I found easy to work with. Dilly had had a series of psychiatric admissions over the years and was keen to involve himself with initiatives which promoted the development of mental health services. He was involved as a representative of service users in a number of initiatives of which this was one. He has a mild unassuming manner but can suddenly ask very sharp and pointed questions.

Locks and keys

Our first call was to meet with an information technology manager who wanted to complain about problems with 'communication'. He was struggling to make sense of why, with all the technology at his disposal, people consistently failed to operationalize their IT systems effectively, appearing sometimes to be subverting them. There was also clearly some kind of tension around his feelings of security or need to feel in control, for despite being in a non-clinical area, he chose to lock us in. These two issues, that of communication or the lack of it and that of locking in or out, arose repeatedly during the day and developed a thematic quality such that they appeared connected. For example, in a subsequent meeting with a member of the administrative staff, again in a non-clinical area, her first action was to turn the key in the door. This happened before she communicated to us her anxieties about her manager.

This 'locking behavior' seemed understandably resonant with the hospital's clinical environment where staff were legally required to keep under lock and key those whose illnesses represented a danger to society. Such locking behavior could therefore be understood to be so ingrained in the behavioral patterning of the institution that it permeated areas and interactions where it was, in fact, functionally unnecessary. It served as a vehicle (this is how we do things around here) for other situations which evoked anxieties concerning control in the process of power relating. In particular, it seemed, as behavior, to have become transferred to situations of a psychological nature where the perceived threat was located in the quality of relations with others so that in wanting to talk about her problems with her manager, her natural action was to turn the key.

The point I am trying to make here is that this locking behavior arose from a wider social and organizational context and psychological patterning in which lock and key represented a fundamental means of dealing with anxiety. This way of dealing with anxiety was thus experienced by individuals but could be understood to be symptomatic of organizing patterns at the hospital. Since these patterns were frequently enacted without apparent awareness of, or reflection on, their organizational context, one could say that the participants in these processes were unconscious of that which they were communicating about the wider institution. In other words they were unconscious of how their individual actions and thoughts, and by implication their sense of identity, were being created in an ongoing way through their organizational interaction.

Wherever Dilly and I went on that day, both staff and patients raised with us difficulties over something which was termed 'communication' behind which seemed to occur a complex form of power relating which might constrain, and even render impossible, the ability for all the concerned parties to make sense together of the situations in which they found themselves and thus to move forward in ways in which they could enable each other.

Orchard Hospital is composed of a number of distinct yet interdependent groupings, such as wards, professions and roles whose locations are often physically very clearly demarcated so that there is an amplified sense of who is an outsider and who an insider. Furthermore, in order to gain access to these various bastions, one has to usually negotiate one's way through a number of security or administrative hurdles.

The Mahler Clinic

Dilly and I had an appointment to visit the Mahler Clinic, a secure facility housing patients with mental illness who had committed serious and dangerous offences. We arrived at the expected time and after handing over our mobile phones and being checked for further items deemed a potential threat, we were told by the man at reception that 'more people were expected' and asked to wait in the reception area. As the minutes ticked by, I grew increasingly concerned. We were running a tight schedule and there was no sign of anyone coming to meet us. I could also not recall having seen the man at reception noticeably inform anyone of our arrival, so, after about fifteen minutes, I asked him what was happening and whether he had informed the charge nurse of our arrival. There was a tense pause followed by a flurry of activity, and within moments we were being ushered in through the inner door by an apologetic charge nurse who was as confused and irritated as we were as to why nobody had told her we had arrived. 'This sort of thing,' she told us in an exasperated tone, 'happens all the time.'

How is one to make sense of such an event? First, it seems important that potential meanings are explored and thus amplified for discussion. This is because accepting things at face value will, at best, not do justice to the complexity of human interaction in difficult circumstances and, at worst, collude with a repetitive and destructive dynamic. However, as I have suggested previously, the act of conversation of the type which might explore multiplicity of meaning threatens by its nature to change power relationships, and in particular to change the status quo inherent in those power relationships, or in other words to subjugate a dominant way of interpreting the world. Therefore one might expect the act of such exploratory conversation to potentially arouse hostility and non-compliance with fora set up for such purposes as perhaps I had experienced with the consultant psychiatrist. Some time later, having explored the geography of the Mahler Clinic, we again sought out the charge nurse and this time had to gain access to the administrative quarter of the clinic.

Although it was presumably apparent that we had legitimate business, we were asked to wait in the clinical area while a staff nurse disappeared behind a locked door to check whether it was 'all right' for us to enter the administrative area. When we finally sat down with the charge nurse in her office, we all wanted to discuss our experience of entering the Mahler Clinic and our impressions. My immediate thoughts were around the possible connection between 'communication problems' which everyone complained about and the issues of power and control which inevitably permeate forensic institutions and which seemed exemplified in our experience of the way in which people exercised control over the hospital doors. So it seemed that not only physical traffic was monitored and potentially prevented but conversational traffic as well. It seemed to me, with the heightened awareness and anxieties in the hospital over what should pass through and what be prevented, that endless possibilities presented themselves for difficulties in communication.

Furthermore, the individuals who found themselves in a position of control over the permeability of particular boundaries might deal with the situation in idiosyncratic ways so that the manner in which they allowed traffic to pass (conversational or otherwise) would vary according to how, as individuals, they were able to manage their anxiety. In order to maintain this sense of being in control in a potentially anxiety-provoking situation, one might find oneself not only delaying or preventing access by others, but also might evoke in others reciprocal themes of powerlessness and frustration.

Now clearly each individual would respond to these situations in different ways according to both their cumulative life experience and the organizing themes of the workplace. Such is the way in which I, together with Dilly and the charge nurse, began to make sense of events like our delayed entry into the Mahler Clinic. She, the charge nurse, was also concerned over the levels of sickness at the clinic. She had some thirteen members off sick at the time which to us seemed a disturbingly high ratio. She was thinking that this sickness was a way in which the staff could exert control. Their work was difficult and stressful, and they had to care for the patients in poor working conditions with poor pay and poor resources. This led to a general conversation in the workplace of feeling devalued. Many staff felt they would like to be engaged therapeutically with their patients but ended up 'feeling like jailers' due to staff shortages and lack of facilities.

There were, in addition, other aspects of meaning to the staff sickness issue. The unions had prevented, on the grounds of safety, the employment by the hospital of agency staff. With so many people off sick, this meant that staff had to work overtime in order to keep the place running. This, however, was also to their advantage since overtime rates of pay were considerably higher. So entrenched was this pattern of working at Orchard Hospital that staff had apparently come to rely on overtime as part of their pay-packet and (according to their managers) would decide whose turn it was to be off sick so that overtime would have to be offered.

However, the situation was extremely complex. Members of staff were required to work with very disturbed and disturbing patients at close quarters for protracted periods of time. If then, following Mead, our sense of who we are, and indeed our actions, are created in an ongoing way through our interactions with others, our sense of self is thus imbued with our social context just as we are imbuing that context with ourselves in an iterative cycle of co-creation. Now this raises a particular psychological tension for those working with disturbing patients, for how is one group to differentiate itself from the other? It also suggests that the issues of powerlessness, anger, guilt and confusion so prevalent with the patient group soon start to be experienced by the staff as their own.

At the Mahler Clinic there were a number of ways staff emphasized their difference, a number of what one might call 'group markers'. The most obvious one was the jingling bunch of keys worn with clear visibility at the hip so that it was immediately obvious who was a member of staff by the noise they made going down the corridor. Linked to this was the power to remove oneself from the situation of observation so that there existed in the clinic a process of mutual watchfulness in that both patients and staff regarded each other closely. The staff were more able to defend themselves by their ability to retreat into closed areas, leave the premises and go off sick.

Then there was the phenomenon of smoking used by patients to exclude staff by rendering a particular environment, the smoking room, so unpleasant as to make observation both unseeable and, for the observer, unbreathable. For the staff it was also a marker of who was who and with the advantage of maintaining a position of detachment in relation to the self-destructive capacities of others. So perhaps these subtle and not so subtle markers were, in some way, psychologically necessary for separating oneself out from perceived madness or from perceived agents of control.

While in the Mahler Clinic, we were invited to meet with the staff on Drake ward which was the usual point of entry for patients into the clinic and their assessment unit. Drake ward is a disturbing place which has the feel of a confined concrete bunker. Its decor is tattered and scuffed, and the walls and doors are done up in a shocking combination of lime green and magenta. The whole appearance and structure of the ward seems designed to encourage a psychotic episode. We were surprised on arrival at Drake that the staff's idea of meeting up with us was in terms of seeing us individually. We had expected to see them as a group. The reason given – and this seemed a ubiquitous rationalization at Orchard Hospital – was that they were 'short-staffed'. We wondered then as to whether their difficulties in meeting up as a group would also inevitably contribute to their problems with 'communication'. We gained the impression that their conversation was constrained within the confines of individual interaction or ritualized interaction with clear agendas such as a 'handover' or ward round.

A few weeks previously, however, an interesting series of events had occurred which we felt shed some light both on the nature of power relating at Orchard and subsequent meetings with the staff on Drake. There had been an uproar (at least from members of staff) when one of the patient's visitors to the clinic had been discovered in an act of fellatio with him in the 'library'. Sexual contact between patients and their visitors is forbidden. This event generated some kind of internal enquiry and increased observation of the patients while they were with their visitors. A short time after the above events one of the patients made an allegation that three members of staff were locking themselves in the toilet for the purposes of having sex together. An internal enquiry was launched and the members of staff in question were temporarily suspended. Managers were angry when they discovered that these members of staff had been in communication together while on suspension (I was surprised that they would have expected anything else). Eventually the members of staff were exonerated from the charge of having sex on duty but were reprimanded for locking themselves in the toilet. They had claimed that it was the only place where they could hold a private meeting.

The above events suggest to me that organizing themes around power and control are instrumental in creating particular situations which both mirror and amplify the dynamic tensions between groups at Orchard Hospital. Sexuality, that most private of human relations, becomes the vehicle for the struggle for control within power relations. Everyone shares the experience of sexuality and, in that sense, it represents all that may cross over from patients to staff and vice versa. This applies especially to those aspects of human relating to do with intimacy and being held or rejected, which evoke shameful feelings of dependency and exposure. There is, in this series of interactions, the sense of multiple condensed themes which revolve around the power to expose and control by the evocation of feelings of humiliation. This is achieved in both cases by raising anxieties of a breached taboo.

It was not surprising then that when we met up with a number of individuals on Drake ward we experienced 'stonewalling' in their responses. These staff had recently been through an internal enquiry and we wondered whether they were identifying us as another intervention out to expose misdemeanors. We encouraged them to talk about their experience of working at Orchard Hospital which they were only able to do in a very superficial way, telling us nothing other than that they were wary about talking to us.

The canteen

Of all the places mentioned by the staff in our conversations, the canteen was the one most regularly brought forward for discussion. It was a dreary institutional space, smelling of stale cooking oil. The tables had a regimented appearance, each one being laid out in exactly the same manner with identical cruet and vinegar bottles without tops on and filled to the same level. There were complaints about the quality of food, and staff working on shifts could not get a meal outside of the very restricted times structured around those working a nine to five day. The thing that excited the most conversation, however, was the existence of an adjacent 'consultants' dining-room'.

The way this separate dining-room for the consultants was rationalized was as follows: 'Staff may wish to speak confidentially to the consultants about the patients in their care and should have the opportunity to do so.' This raised a number of questions for us. Who were these confidences being protected from if the only other people in the canteen were staff? Were there not more appropriate forums for the discussion of patients than people's lunch-hours? If not, then why was that the case?

At lunch-time two of us had lunch with some patients on one of the wards, two of us had lunch with the consultants and myself, and Dilly joined an occupational therapy team in the main section of the canteen. On entering the canteen, I passed one of the consultants on his way to the 'dining-room' and asked him why there were two places for eating. He threw his hands into the air and in a jokey but rather loaded sort of way exclaimed, 'Don't ask!' However, his actions soon became clear in that many staff made sense of it in a way which suggested a view of the consultants as preserving a private and elite space, so that although the invitation was to join them for confidential clinical discussion, there seemed to be few who felt able to avail themselves of this facility.

The divided dining-room had come, for many, to physically express an aspect of power relating at Orchard Hospital. This concerns the legitimized authority of consultants to maintain their own hierarchical status and territory in such a way as to communicate clearly the superiority of their position. I felt also that the consultants had, in this arrangement, been able to remove themselves from the watchfulness of other professions in a way which seemed to mirror the dynamics between patients and staff. In this sense the canteen could be viewed as a microcosm of the hospital, a place where the prevalent organizing themes were made manifest. Thus the physical layout of the canteen, and the feelings and interactions it evoked, resonated with wider institutional themes around blocks to communication. All of this was exacerbated by the power relations between a variety of groupings which created a strong sense of 'us and them', of insiders and outsiders. These themes were further reinforced by the physical boundaries necessary for containing the patients but also permeating the staff groups of which the dining-room situation is an example. Here, the structure of the canteen with its different rooms emphasized hierarchical separation.

Open versus closed communication

During our time at Orchard Hospital, we were approached by a number of individuals who wanted to talk to us privately. They wanted to speak about all kinds of things, such as problems with regrading, difficulties with managers and other members of staff, and not being allowed to smoke on site. However, all of these issues had something in common: they were unable to speak about them openly.

There was a certain rigidity in the way in which power could be negotiated at Orchard Hospital that perhaps stemmed from the forensic environment and the anxieties around losing control which this seemed to generate. Policy and procedure had to be tightly adhered to and this was all underpinned by the requirements of the legislation. Therefore, when the inevitable differences arose they were especially difficult to work with, since they might threaten the status quo and thus, by implication, the whole institutional structure set up to contain society's anxieties around mentally ill offenders. Thus Orchard Hospital had become an extremely conservative institution, caught up in processes which undermined communication by means of maintaining the status quo of its power relations. Processes involving change at Orchard were always accompanied by warnings of clinical risk which masked more complex agendas around anxieties about these shifting power relations.

The above dynamics rendered open communication problematic, and with it the ability of staff to work creatively with the relational movement of the hospital. We experienced the result as staff finding open conversation between groups very difficult and opting instead for confining their experiences within small cliques which used gossip as a means of obtaining a sense of belonging by creating an inflated and projected sense of outsiders with whom difference was embodied. Thus the conversational patterning at Orchard Hospital was relatively stable in such a way that the hospital had an overwhelming ambience of a decaying institution sinking into turpitude. We were hoping that our intervention would disrupt the stability of the conversational patterning and enable novelty to arise. We would not be able to predict, however, whether or not the outcomes would be helpful.

A request for outcomes

At the end of the first day, we met up with a group of staff and patients to decide how to move forward. We knew that some staff were extremely worried about what we might say and whether or not we would expose them. We had not had sufficient time to make sense of our experiences as a team ourselves, and in particular how we would support and look after the patients and staff in the plenary process. So we talked to them about this, thanked them for their help with the project and agreed to meet up again in a fortnight's time. As we were finishing, one of the consultants said that this would be a useful process only if there was an 'action plan' leading to 'improvements' which could be 'evaluated' as 'outcomes'. Now this idea that there should be 'outcomes', improvements and an 'action plan' indicates a prevalent discourse within the NHS which is seductive in that it sounds so reasonable and achievable. Furthermore, there was the belief that by using such a methodology, one might be able to effectively steer a process and be accountable for its effectiveness.

The 'NHS Plan' includes a strategy known as the national service framework (nsf) which identifies specific areas for improvement and sets targets and criteria for those improvements against which 'performance' may be evaluated and judged. 'Performance' is held to as individual accountability so that chief executive officers and senior managers are to be replaced if targets, such as waiting lists, operations performed and financial balances, are not met. Again, this all sounds very reasonable, for who would not want services to improve and people who were doing a bad job to be removed from office? This agenda is driven centrally by the government, which also sets the targets and criteria for performance evaluation (the awarding of stars to NHS Trusts).

The current government has linked the fulfillment of its election manifesto very clearly to the achievement of particular targets in public sector services and so will lose political credibility and possibly re-election if these targets are not met. Furthermore, the government's private finance initiative (PFI) brings commercial interests (whose needs must be taken into account *vis-à-vis* the commercial viability of services) into direct relationship with the public sector without which the money will not be available to satisfy the conditions for easy entry into the single European currency (Euro).

In order to help this process along, a body known as the Modernisation Agency has been created to develop and convey the ideological backbone for the public service improvement agenda. This agency aims to 'ignite the hearts and minds of those in the health service with a passion for the continual improvement of services' (Helen Bevan, 2002). The Modernisation Agency sees itself as the instigator of a 'social movement', 'the greatest movement for organizational change which the world has ever known' (ibid.).

However, these 'improvements' are measured by centrally driven targets, the achievement of which are directly linked via job security with anxieties for senior managers such as whether or not they will be able to pay their mortgages. As one starts to explore the grandiose rhetoric employed by the Modernisation Agency and their political masters, there emerges a sense that the rationality it seeks to construct, and which we internalize over time as 'common sense', is based on a totalitarian ideology, that is, 'a polity which permits no rival loyalties or parties' (*OED*). I suggest the use of totalitarian in this context because the modernization discourse renders problematic other ways of seeing as anti-improvement, resistant to change, inadequate or clinically risky, making it difficult, and for some, dangerous, to speak differently.

This discourse is also linked with the domain of accountancy and its gradual rise as the major sense-making paradigm in public sector management over the past twenty years so that the language of accountancy and audit now seem entirely natural in, for example, a clinical environment. Shore and Wright (2000, p. 66) trace this to the advent of the Audit Commission in 1983:

> The birth of this agency marked the moment when the language associated with financial accounting shifted to embrace 'monitoring performance', identifying 'best practice', improving Value For Money (VFM). . . . Audit came to mean not just checking the books but the scrutiny of good government, and in the process, became instrumental in the formation of policy itself.

Further difficulties with the 'continual improvement' discourse are the ways in which many senior managers find themselves obliged to lie, cheat, 'massage' the figures, do anything to meet the targets, and are then scapegoated for doing so. The result is a great deal of focus upon the target area with the criteria being defined by people with little or no local knowledge, and all this to the detriment of interdependent systems which can be neglected or undermined.

There are some interesting precedents for totalitarian ideology in the public sector which in the past century were most visible under Stalin and

Mao Tse Tung with their 'Five Year Plans' and 'Great Leap Forward' respectively. Both exhorted the workers onward to ever greater productivity and believed in the feasibility of continual improvement being driven by a state-controlled ideology. Both were defeated in their aims of 'collectivization' by the mismatch between central directives and local condition and both made the error of neglecting biodiversity in favor of the survival of the fittest. However, the propensity for totalitarian ideology is not only the province of the former communist bloc but also emerges in the current control of the public sector in the guise of the 'new managerialism' promoted by the neo-liberal governments of the capitalist world where all intellectual production must be justified as compatible with the developmental needs of national and multinational business interests. Thus the apparent liberalism of the market economy may mask a species of power relating which renders all discourse invalid which does not have a clear commercial viability.

The plenary process

When we returned a fortnight later, we spent an hour and a half as a team deciding on how we were to approach the plenary process. We had a number of plenaries to convene in order to make the process available to staff and patients who would be unable to leave their locked wards. There would, however, be a main plenary and we decided to use a 'reflecting team' approach for the first part of it. This involves a technique whereby the team talks in front of, but not to, a group about how they experience them. We discussed amongst ourselves the kinds of issues we were going to raise and how we were going to refer to themes rather than to individuals in order to avoid betraying confidentiality or exposing people unnecessarily.

So that is what we did for the first half hour. The conversation between us developed very naturally and was unrehearsed. We spoke of our experiences at the hospital and the themes we had noticed. We also spoke of things that had possibly not been available for open conversation before, such as people not saying good morning to each other. This was something several people mentioned as a painful experience, and so we were able to introduce it without identifying individuals. My sense of what was happening in that situation resembled an attempt to maintain a particular quality of power relations so that, in not saying good morning, nothing would change and furthermore, one's non-interlocutor would feel the effect of one's power. About thirty people came to this plenary and they represented a broad cross-section of staff and patients. Having listened to us in silence for half an hour, we then talked as a whole group for a further hour. It seemed a very productive conversation with people helping each other to make sense of the themes around communication, power and control which we had brought up. We then divided again into pairs and went off to the wards, where again we sat with patients and staff so that together we could make sense of our experiences. It was a new situation for people at the hospital to sit together in this way across groupings with no agenda other than making sense of their experience of being together. Some were rather surprised at the quality of direct communication and what was able to be said so that, for example, patients on a particular ward were able to speak directly to staff about their feelings of rejection when staff were ill or on holiday and their jealousy regarding the staffs' home life. Staff were able to talk to patients about how they also felt watched by them and needed to have time away from them.

Finally we met up again as a team and debriefed. It was now my task to produce a draft letter which would, when finally agreed, be sent to everyone at the hospital. When the letter finally goes out, the manager of Orchard Hospital will ask people to form into groups to discuss it, and we hope it will provide a vehicle for further conversation. The letter expresses a theme of the hospital struggling in an everyday way with issues of power and control, and how these issues enter the everyday interactions of staff with other staff (for example, on two occasions we were locked into non-clinical areas), patients with staff and patients with other patients. The letter suggests that it is this that lies behind the 'communication' issues at the hospital, and indeed the perceived difficulty of people coming together to talk because this act in itself may threaten the status quo. The letter posed some questions and encouraged people to respond to them. Are issues of control linked with issues around what makes people/society anxious? In other words, what things make patients and staff anxious at Orchard Hospital and how do people find themselves coping with those anxieties? What places are there to come together to talk about and make sense of the anxieties to which one might be susceptible in a forensic environment?

The letter was sent to everyone, both patients and staff, and it was our intention that the hospital as a whole community would sit together in groups of their own making to make sense of the issues raised. By doing this we aimed to increase the conversational interaction at Orchard

Hospital which would inevitably bring a certain amount of emotional turbulence, since power relations would have to shift to accommodate new patterns of understanding. All of the issues mentioned in the letter related to points raised by either staff or patients but not previously made available as a discourse for the community to reflect upon. We then made ourselves available for further conversation should that need arise.

Conclusion

The methodology for the above project has not been planned in the orthodox sense but rather discovered as we went along together. It is influenced, however, by insights from complexity theory, for example, that increased interaction between agents will produce new patterns which, however, cannot be predicted or controlled. We as consultants also have a responsibility for, and an influence over, the 'outcomes', as everyone else does, through the quality and involvement of our participation. So what I am trying to do is to develop an approach towards organizational development/consultation which places a theory of complex responsive processes as central to the methodology employed.

This, in effect, means that our aim is to enter and participate with the ongoing interaction of the institution. Our gestures and responses as consultants then become integral to the flow of institutional life, being both effected by and having an effect upon the conversational patterning to be encountered. This means both taking conversation as a vehicle for self-organization seriously and also role-modeling a collaborative sense-making activity. By this, I mean an active participation in the interaction while encouraging the amplification of meanings and discourses available within the conversation and fostering an attitude of cultural enquiry. Now through this role-modeling of collaborative sense-making which is both a public and private activity, one enters in a very active way into the processes by which people at work make sense of who they are in relation to one another and the various tasks in which they are engaged. Furthermore, the public role-modeling by the consultants of collaborative sense-making constitutes a kind of cultural enquiry. This may resonate with the private role-playing of people at work (that is, their mental activities), so that the ongoing role-play conversation which people experience as a 'mind' potentially finds a reciprocal discourse in the public arena. In this interaction it may both modify and become modified in the same movement.

Thus the central organizing vehicle of the institution is its ongoing conversational interaction within the frame of what Stacey (2000, p. 195) describes as 'Biological organisms . . . resonating bodily with each other' and in which the consultants participate along with everyone else in discovering 'how we go on from here'.

For the consultancy team in the above project, an important element in this process of discovering 'how we go on together' has been regular discussion of our own felt experience which we used to make sense of the situations we encountered in much the same way as one might make use of counter-transference if working psychoanalytically. In other words, we discussed with each other, in between our meetings with staff and patients, the meaning of our emotional experience in the light of the institutional context in which we were working. Thus in talking about my feelings of anxiety at being locked into a non-clinical area, I was able eventually to make sense of an organizing theme influencing the behaviors of those within the hospital, namely that an institutional response to anxiety was to attempt to lock it out.

During the consultation process, I experienced an exhausting intensity of emotional experience that left me feeling thoroughly drained at the end of each day's work and which often seemed to resonate powerfully with the institutional issues. For example, the initial meeting with the management team where I had faced a hostile response from a consultant psychiatrist played on my mind for days and left me feeling vulnerable, powerless and with the urge to humiliate him. Interestingly these feelings turned out to be institutionally thematic in the staff interaction, as in the occurrences of people not saying good morning to each other and the accompanying feelings experienced in consequence.

I feel proud of the work we developed at Orchard Hospital and of sustaining with my colleagues a process of interaction which for myself has sometimes been fraught with uncertainty and complex anxieties. In my leadership role I have tried to encourage people to stay in relationship with one another in the presence of negotiating sometimes irreconcilable differences or, in other words, not to resort to patterns of fight or flight as the only method of response.

I have also attempted to place power relating as central to my way of understanding organizational process. This then draws attention to the mutual creation of interactive patterns rather than emphasizing the defenses which individuals might employ as coping strategies; the latter representing a Tavistock style of organizational intervention. In placing participation through interaction as key to the process of organizational development, I am also differentiating myself from programs adopting a systems approach which rely on a template. These may include, for example, programs such as 'Total Quality Management' and 'Pursuing Perfection', both of which have been influential in the Health Service. I suggest that such programs are ultimately futile precisely because local conditions and the emergent power relations which create them inevitably transform these projects beyond recognition. In other words, the effects of local interaction will differ over time from those expected from a strategic template. The future, as such, cannot be determined. However, I suggest that we can and indeed do influence the emergent organizational process through our interactions with others and that these interactions are synonymous with power relating. Our methodologies for consultancy should therefore take the above into consideration.

References

Elias, N. (1998) *On Civilization, Power, and Knowledge*, ed. S. Mennell and J. Goudsblom, Chicago, IL: University of Chicago Press.

Foucault, M. (1975) 'Body Power', in *Power/Knowledge: Selected Interviews and Other Writings by Michel Foucault 1972–1977*, ed. Colin Gordon (1980), London: Harvester Press.

Foucault, M. (1976) 'Two Lectures', in *Power/Knowledge: Selected Interviews and Other Writings by Michel Foucault 1972–1977*, ed. Colin Gordon (1980), London: Harvester Press.

Mairowitz, D. Z. (1986) *Reich for Beginners*, London: Unwin Paperbacks.

Mead, G. H. (1934) *Mind, Self and Society*, Chicago, IL: University of Chicago Press.

Miller, E. (1993) *From Dependency to Autonomy: Studies in Organization and Change*, London: Free Association Books.

Nietzsche, F. (1886) 'Beyond Good and Evil', in *A Nietzsche Reader, Selected and Translated with an Introduction by R.J. Hollingdale* (1977), Penguin classics, London: Penguin Books.

Nietzsche, F. (1887) 'On the Genealogy of Morals', in *A Nietzsche Reader, Selected and Translated with an Introduction by R.J. Hollingdale* (1977), Penguin classics, London: Penguin Books.

Rorty, R. (2000) *Rorty and his Critics*, ed. R. Brandom, Oxford: Blackwell.

Shaw, P. (2002) *Changing Conversations in Organizations: A complexity approach to change*, London: Routledge.

Shore, C. and Wright, S. (2000) 'Coercive Accountability', in *Audit Cultures*, ed. Marilyn Strathern, London: Routledge.

Shotter, J. (1993) *Conversational Realities: Constructing Life through Language*, London: Sage.

Stacey, R. (2000) *Strategic Management and Organizational Dynamics, The Challenge of Complexity*, London: Pearson Education.

Stacey, R., Griffin, D. and Shaw, P. (2000) *Complexity and Management: Fad or radical challenge to systems thinking?*, London: Routledge.

Index